Transforming Cybersecurity Audit Practices with Agility and Artificial Intelligence (AI)

In an era where cyber threats evolve faster than traditional defenses can adapt, the need for a paradigm shift in cybersecurity auditing has never been more urgent. *Transforming Cybersecurity Audit Practices with Agility and Artificial Intelligence (AI)* presents a groundbreaking approach to modernizing audit methodologies by integrating agile principles and artificial intelligence (AI). This book explores how conventional audit frameworks – often rigid, reactive, and siloed – can be reimagined into dynamic, proactive, and intelligent systems that align with the pace of digital transformation.

Drawing from real-world case studies, industry standards, and emerging technologies, this book provides a comprehensive roadmap for cybersecurity audit, cybersecurity, and information technology professionals seeking to enhance audit and risk management effectiveness and resilience. It delves into the application of agile methodologies to audit planning, execution, and reporting, enabling continuous assurance and iterative risk assessment. Simultaneously, the book examines the transformative role of AI in automating control testing, anomaly detection, and predictive analytics, thereby reducing human error and increasing audit precision.

Key themes include the cultural and organizational shifts required to embrace agility, the ethical and governance considerations of AI in auditing, and the development of hybrid audit models that balance automation with human oversight. This book also offers practical tools, frameworks, and metrics to guide implementation and measure success.

Whether you're modernizing an internal cybersecurity audit function or building a next-generation cybersecurity assurance program, this book equips you with the insights and strategies to lead with confidence in a rapidly changing threat landscape. It is both a call to action and a practical guide for transforming cybersecurity audits into agile, intelligent, and future-ready practices.

Keywords: Cybersecurity Audit, Cybersecurity Risk Management, Cyber Threat Intelligence, Data Privacy, Artificial Intelligence, Adversarial AI, AI Ethics, AI Governance, Responsible AI, Machine Learning, Large Language Models, Natural Language Processing, Robotic Process Automation, Recommender, Predictive Analytics, AI and Human Element, Agile, Agility, Partnerships, Culture, Continuous Learning.

Security, Audit and Leadership Series

Series Editor: Dan Swanson, Dan Swanson and Associates, Ltd., Winnipeg, Manitoba, Canada.

The scope and mandate for internal audit continues to evolve each year, as does the complexity of the business environment and speed of the changing risk landscape in which it must operate. The fundamental goal of this exciting series is to produce leading-edge books on critical subjects facing security and audit executives and practitioners. Key topics addressed include Leadership, Cybersecurity, Security Leadership, Privacy, Strategic Risk Management, Auditing IT, Audit Management and Leadership, and Operational Auditing.

Guardians of the Digital Age: *Securing the Future*
By **Elçin Biren**

Ironwill 360° Leadership: *A Blueprint for Level 5 Unicorn Leadership*
By Douglas P. Pflug

Behavioral Insights in Cybersecurity: *A Guide to Digital Human Factors*
By Dustin S. Sachs

Integrated Assurance: *Unified Risk Strategy*
By Patrick Hayes

Preparing for Sustainability Audits: *A Practical Guide for IT Sector*
By Mahsa Fidanboy

Scaling Pyramids: *Leadership Lessons from a Mid-Level Bureaucrat*
By Christopher Stitt

Program Architecture: *Fight the Good Fight*
By Gideon T. Rasmussen

Operation Carder Kaos: *How One Agent Penetrated the Underground Community*
By Richard K. LaTulip

Digitalization and Women's Rights: *Women and Sustainability: Volume 2*
By Muharrem Kılıç and Sezer Bozkus Kahyaoglu

Governance, Risk and Compliance: *Demystifying the Risk and Data Privacy Landscape*
By Dr Michael Brass

It's Not in the Manual: *Real-World Leadership for Security and Risk Professionals*
By Michael Gips

Transforming Cybersecurity Audit Practices with Agility and Artificial Intelligence (AI)
By Dr. Linda Kostic

Transforming Cybersecurity Audit Practices with Agility and Artificial Intelligence (AI)

Dr. Linda Kostic
CISSP, CISA, CIMP, CSCU, CPA

CRC Press
Taylor & Francis Group
Boca Raton London New York

CRC Press is an imprint of the
Taylor & Francis Group, an **informa** business

Designed cover image: Shutterstock ID: 2596868389

First edition published 2026
by CRC Press
2385 NW Executive Center Drive, Suite 320, Boca Raton FL 33431

and by CRC Press
4 Park Square, Milton Park, Abingdon, Oxon, OX14 4RN

CRC Press is an imprint of Taylor & Francis Group, LLC

ISBN: 9781041070436 (hbk)
ISBN: 9781041073987 (pbk)
ISBN: 9781003640301 (ebk)

DOI: 10.1201/9781003640301

Typeset in Sabon
by KnowledgeWorks Global Ltd.

Dedication

I dedicate this book to my many colleagues and family members. To the colleagues who collaborated with me through various business and professional organization initiatives – your commitment to improving culture and cybersecurity auditing processes was both inspiring and transformative. The diversity within our group sparked creative and exciting changes that made auditing not only more effective but also genuinely enjoyable.

A heartfelt thank you goes out to my husband, sons, daughters-in-law, and granddaughter for cheering me up when I was stuck or procrastinating on developing material for the book, and for their patience and understanding when I had to miss cherished family time – especially our annual fourth of July week at our vacation home. Your love, encouragement, and unwavering support made this journey possible.

I am also deeply grateful to my grandparents, whose wisdom I was fortunate to absorb well into adulthood. My maternal grandparents taught me the value of financial literacy and lifelong learning, encouraging me to embrace opportunities even when I didn't meet every qualification. My paternal grandparents nurtured my curiosity and resilience, instilling in me the importance of exercising my mind every day. I also honor my aunt, who showed me how the art of salesmanship could be applied to auditing – proof that skills from one domain can thrive in another.

To my students and fellow educators: your passion, curiosity, and drive to grow have continually inspired me. This book reflects our shared values – bridging theory with practice, building strong partnerships, and integrating agility and artificial intelligence into the evolving cybersecurity audit landscape.

Thank you for being part of this journey.

Contents

List of figures and tables

Figures

Tables

Forewords

In today's rapidly evolving digital and artificial intelligence (AI)-driven world, the demands on cybersecurity auditors have never been higher or more urgent. What once relied on static, compliance-based methods now require agility, insight, and innovation to remain effective. *Transforming Audit Practices with Agility and AI* meets this challenge head-on.

Over the past three decades, I have had the opportunity to lead IT audits and complex technology transformation initiatives across some of the world's largest organizations and complex global environments such as the United Nations and the Financial Services industry. If there is one truth that holds across all these environments, it is this: Cybersecurity risk evolves faster than our traditional audit methods can keep up. That is why *Transforming Cybersecurity Audit Practices with Agility and Artificial Intelligence (AI)* by Dr. Linda Kostic is such a timely and essential contribution. This is not just another technical book or audit framework. It is a well-rounded, strategic, and deeply practical guide for professionals seeking to modernize how we think about, plan, and execute cybersecurity audits in the digital age, with a focus on agility and AI.

Dr. Kostic brings a rare combination of practitioner's depth, an educator's clarity, and a strategist's vision to the topic of modernizing cybersecurity auditing. She expertly blends three elements often siloed in our field: audit standards, agile methodologies, and AI. She doesn't just explore them theoretically, she brings them to life with real-world relevance. From foundational audit objectives to nuanced AI use cases like chatbot assessments, recommender systems, and predictive analytics, this book provides both context and detailed concrete guidance.

One of the standout features of this work is how it addresses culture, collaboration, and communication, areas that are often overlooked in technical audit literature. By tying in the three lines of defense, change management principles, and strategies for influencing audit culture, Dr. Kostic positions auditors not just as reviewers, but as change agents and partners in organizational resilience.

As someone who has conducted cybersecurity audits, managed global data privacy reviews, and assessed resilience frameworks under the lens of evolving and strict regulatory regimes, I found this book to be both authentic and actionable. I know the challenges firsthand: siloed communication, outdated methodologies, and a growing gap between innovation and oversight. This book responds to those challenges with clarity and confidence. It reflects the real pressures audit teams face (tight deadlines, fragmented systems, compliance and regulatory burdens) and offers realistic, forward-thinking solutions that practitioners can begin applying immediately.

This book is also incredibly valuable for audit clients, compliance leaders, and executives. It clarifies the "why" behind agile and AI-enabled audit approaches, fosters mutual understanding, and sets the stage for more effective partnerships between internal audit and the broader organization. The result? Better outcomes, reduced friction, and audits that deliver more meaningful insights faster.

Transforming Cybersecurity Audit Practices with Agility and Artificial Intelligence (AI) is a must-read for anyone ready to lead their organization through the next evolution of audit excellence. I was completely riveted and thoroughly enjoyed reading this book. I wholeheartedly recommend it, and I expect it will remain a go-to reference for years to come.

Anita Sulcer, ***Information Technology Consultant and Cybersecurity audit professional***

Dr. Linda Kostic was (and continues to be) my first mentor in the world of auditing, cyber and information security. She graciously took me under her wing and taught me the ropes at my first job at a U.S. "Big Four" bank. Her enthusiasm for learning more about the industry, auditing principles and best practices, and emerging cyber risks made her outshine in her key senior management role. Although living halfway across the country from me, Linda has proven to be a meaningful connection and someone I'm proud to call a good friend. She has shown me the value of building relationships with those around me, how to keep a thirst for knowledge, and to stay curious by not following the status quo just because "that's how it's always been done." Her sage guidance, utilizing her expansive knowledge and experiences in the field, has helped me in turn to grow and thrive in my own internal audit career, and as a person.

In conjunction with her Doctorate in Information Assurance & Cybersecurity, Linda has decades of experience in the fields of operational risk and cyber auditing. Continuing with her credentials, she holds a number of globally-recognized certifications (CPA, CISA, CSCU, CISSP, and CIMP) and is an adjunct professor at the University of Maryland Global Campus. She is an avid contributor to ISACA's framework development, publications, and an active Board and committee service member of its Greater Washington, District of Columbia (GWDC) chapter. During her leisure time, Linda runs marathons, participates in classes to pursue her passion for continuous learning and loves to spend time with her family.

Notwithstanding her retirement, Linda is once again keenly demonstrating her ardent teaching and mentoring essence by producing this excellent publication about the ever-changing and progressing world of auditing and cyber security. This work includes popular industry topics such as the implementation of agility in audit practices and the exciting changes A.I. brings. Through her writing, she helps guide the auditors of today and tomorrow to follow best practices, industry frameworks/standards, and emerging trends. There are real-world use cases from her experience, as well as helpful external sources for reference in the development and implementation of key audit principles. This work will prove to be a valuable source for new and experienced auditors alike to introduce and/or reinforce their understanding of the nature of auditing and cyber and information security.

Pauleen Speegle Chong, ***Cyber Internal Audit Manager, CISA***

Preface

In an age of rapid technological advancement, the intersection of artificial intelligence (AI) and cybersecurity has emerged as a critical focal point for professionals, educators, and policymakers alike. This book was written to provide a practical and accessible guide for understanding how AI is transforming the cybersecurity landscape – introducing new capabilities, amplifying existing threats, and challenging conventional approaches to risk management. It is designed for readers who want to develop a foundational understanding of AI in cybersecurity contexts, as well as those who are preparing to navigate the increasingly complex decisions that come with securing digital systems in an AI-driven world.

Throughout my career in cybersecurity, risk management, and internal audit leadership, I've seen firsthand how static, checklist-driven audit practices can fail to capture the complexity and velocity of modern digital ecosystems. While working with major institutions and teaching future cybersecurity leaders, I observed the power of agile frameworks, collaborative partnerships, and intelligent automation to elevate both the impact and the perception of the audit function. This book distills those observations into a practical guide, blending traditional audit requirements with modern tools and mindsets to bring cybersecurity auditing into innovative and creative approaches. This book – *Transforming Cybersecurity Audit Practices with Agility and Artificial Intelligence (AI)* – is both a response to that need and a reflection of my journey across industry, academia, and professional service.

Thank you for joining me on this journey toward a smarter, more agile future for cybersecurity auditing.

Dr. Linda Kostic, ***CISA, CISSP, CSCU, CIMP, CPA***
July 2025

About the author

Dr. Linda Kostic is a dynamic and accomplished technology, cybersecurity, and risk professional with over three decades of industry experience and a strong passion for education and professional development. She currently serves as an adjunct professor at the University of Maryland Global Campus (UMGC), where she teaches undergraduate and graduate courses in cybersecurity governance, cybersecurity engineering, leadership, and information assurance. Her teaching approach emphasizes practical, real-world application and integrates AI-powered tools like ChatGPT to foster engagement and accessibility in online and hybrid classrooms.

Dr. Kostic holds a Doctorate in Information Assurance & Cybersecurity, a Master of Science in Telecommunications, and a Bachelor of Science in Accounting. She brings a unique blend of academic depth and corporate leadership, having held senior roles at Citi, T. Rowe Price, Transamerica, and E*TRADE Financial (now Morgan Stanley). Her expertise spans cybersecurity strategy, information technology and cybersecurity risk management, artificial intelligence, internal audit, threat intelligence, incident response, threat intelligence, and governance frameworks including National Institute of Standards and Technology (NIST) and International Organization for Standardization (ISO) 31000.

She is also a published author and curriculum innovator. The Transforming Cybersecurity Audit Practices with Agility and AI is a book that merges her technical acumen with her vision for the future of cybersecurity auditing. Certified as a CPA, CISA, CISSP, CSCU, and CIMP, Dr. Kostic is an active contributor to ISACA's professional community, holding leadership positions and contributing to publications and framework development.

Through her work, Dr. Kostic continues to empower learners and professionals to adapt to evolving challenges in cybersecurity by blending rigor, innovation, and lifelong learning. Her LinkedIn profile reflects her commitment to professional growth, diversity, and mentorship across the technology and cybersecurity audit communities.

Acknowledgements

I would like to extend my sincere gratitude to my colleagues who graciously took the time to review my book proposal and chapter drafts. Your thoughtful feedback, encouragement, and attention to detail were instrumental in refining the structure, content, and clarity of my work. Each of you brought unique perspectives that enriched the overall quality of the manuscript, and I am deeply appreciative of your willingness to support this project. Your contributions have not only strengthened the final product but also affirmed the collaborative spirit that underpins our shared professional goals.

A heartfelt thank you goes out to Rundeep Mondair, Yehuda Schmidt, Pauleen Speegle, Anita Sulcer, and Tom Zolezzi for contributing to this milestone with such care and professionalism, offering thoughtful critiques, constructive suggestions, and steady encouragement that helped shape the book's direction and sharpen its message. I would also like to thank Jim Wiggins and Dennis Salguero for their invaluable insights into the book proposal. That guidance provided thoughtful technical detail and professional development perspectives to enhance all the chapters.

And a heartfelt thank you goes out to Julie Kostic for designing the creative book cover. I truly appreciate her taking time from her busy schedule to craft a design that beautifully aligns with the book's overall objective.

List of abbreviations

1LoD (First Line of Defense) is responsible for owning and managing risks directly within business operations, ensuring that internal controls are properly designed and executed.

2LoD (Second Line of Defense) provides independent oversight and guidance by developing risk management policies, monitoring compliance, and supporting the first line in implementing effective controls.

3LoD (Third Line of Defense) refers to the internal audit function, which provides independent assurance to senior management and the board on the effectiveness of governance, risk management, and internal controls implemented by the first and second lines.

3PAO (Third Party Assessment Organization) is an independent entity accredited to assess and validate the security and compliance of cloud service providers, particularly under frameworks like FedRAMP.

ACL (Audit Control Language) is a data analytics software used by auditors to access, analyze, and test large volumes of data for patterns, anomalies, and control effectiveness.

AI (Artificial Intelligence) is the simulation of human intelligence by machines, enabling them to perform tasks such as learning, reasoning, problem-solving, and decision-making.

AI RMF (Artificial Intelligence Risk Management Framework) is a structured approach developed by National Institute of Standards and Technology (NIST) to help organizations manage risks associated with the design, development, deployment, and use of AI systems in a trustworthy and responsible manner.

AISC (Artificial Intelligence Security Center) is an initiative established to advance the secure, responsible, and ethical development and deployment of AI technologies across defense operations.

ANN (Artificial Neural Network) is a computational model inspired by the human brain that processes information through interconnected nodes (neurons) to recognize patterns, learn from data, and perform tasks such as classification, prediction, and decision-making.

ATT&CK (Adversarial Tactics, Techniques & Common Knowledge (MITRE)) is a globally accessible knowledge base that documents adversary behaviors based on real-world observations, helping organizations understand and defend against cyber threats.

AUC (Area Under the Curve) is a performance metric for classification models that represents the degree of separability between classes, with higher values indicating better model accuracy in distinguishing between positive and negative outcomes.

AWS (Amazon Web Services) is a comprehensive cloud computing platform that provides scalable infrastructure, storage, analytics, and machine learning services to individuals, businesses, and governments worldwide.

BERT. (Bidirectional Encoder Representations from Transformers) is a natural language processing model developed by Google that understands the context of words in a sentence by analyzing them in both directions, enabling more accurate language understanding and tasks such as question answering and sentiment analysis.

BYOD (Bring Your Own Device) is a policy that allows employees to use their personal devices, such as smartphones and laptops, for work-related activities, raising both productivity and security considerations.

C4IR (Centre for the Fourth Industrial Revolution) is a World Economic Forum initiative that collaborates globally to shape the development and deployment of emerging technologies in a human-centered and ethical manner.

CAB (Change Advisory Board) is a group of stakeholders responsible for evaluating, approving, and prioritizing changes to IT systems to ensure minimal risk and disruption.

CAE (Chief Audit Executive) is the senior-most leader responsible for overseeing the internal audit function and reporting on risk management, controls, and governance to executive leadership and the board.

CCM (Continuous Control Monitoring) refers to the automated, ongoing monitoring of internal controls to detect and respond to risks in real-time.

CCPA (California Consumer Privacy Act) is a state law that grants California residents rights over their personal data, including access, deletion, and opting out of data sales.

CCTV (Closed-Circuit Television) is a video surveillance system used to monitor and record activities for security and safety purposes within a defined area.

Certified Authorization Professional (CAP) is a credential offered by $(ISC)^2$ that validates expertise in risk management and authorizing information systems under frameworks such as the RMF.

CET (Certified in Emerging Technology) is an ISACA certification that demonstrates proficiency in foundational and advanced concepts related to blockchain, AI, cloud, and IoT technologies.

CIS (Center for Internet Security) is a nonprofit organization that provides cybersecurity best practices, including the CIS Controls and benchmarks, to help organizations improve their cyber defense posture.

CISA (Certified Information Systems Auditor) is a globally recognized certification from ISACA that validates expertise in auditing, controlling, and assuring information systems.

CISSP (Certified Information Systems Security Professional) is a certification from (International Information System Security Certification Consortium $(ISC)^2$) that demonstrates deep knowledge in designing and managing a cybersecurity program.

CEO (Chief Executive Officer) is the highest-ranking executive responsible for the overall strategy, direction, and performance of an organization.

ChatGPT (Chat Generative Pre-Trained Transformer) is an AI language model developed by OpenAI that generates human-like text responses based on input prompts.

CI/CD (Continuous Integration/Continuous Deployment) refers to software development practices that automate the building, testing, and deployment of applications to improve code quality and delivery speed.

CIO (Chief Information Officer) is the executive responsible for overseeing an organization's IT strategy, infrastructure, and technology implementation.

CISO (Chief Information Security Officer) leads the organization's information security strategy, ensuring protection of digital assets and compliance with cybersecurity regulations.

CMMC (Cybersecurity Maturity Model Certification) is a U.S. Department of Defense framework that ensures contractors meet required cybersecurity standards to protect sensitive information.

CNN (Convolutional Neural Network) is a type of deep learning model primarily used for image recognition and processing by mimicking how the human visual cortex works.

COBIT (Control Objectives for Information and Related Technologies) is an ISACA framework for IT governance and management that aligns business goals with IT processes.

COSO (Committee of Sponsoring Organizations of the Treadway Commission) provides a widely used framework for internal control, enterprise risk management, and fraud deterrence.

CPE (Continuing Professional Education) consists of ongoing learning activities required to maintain professional certifications and stay current in one's field.

CPU (Central Processing Unit) is the primary component of a computer that performs instructions and processes data for all computing tasks.

CRO (Chief Risk Officer) is the executive responsible for identifying, managing, and mitigating an organization's strategic, operational, and compliance risks.

CSAM (Cybersecurity Asset Management) is the process of identifying, tracking, and securing all digital assets in an organization's IT environment.

CSP (Cloud Service Provider) offers cloud-based computing services such as storage, servers, databases, and networking over the internet.

CTR (Click-Through Rate) is a digital marketing metric that measures the percentage of users who click on a specific link or advertisement.

CVSS (Common Vulnerability Scoring System) is a standardized method for rating the severity of software vulnerabilities to help prioritize remediation.

DAG (Directed Acyclic Graph) is a data structure used in computing and blockchain that represents a set of activities where each edge has a direction and no cycles exist.

DevSecOps (Development Security Operations) integrates security practices into the DevOps process to ensure secure and compliant software delivery.

DIY (Do It Yourself) refers to the practice of creating or repairing things independently without the direct aid of professionals.

DLP (Data Loss Prevention) is a security strategy and technology used to prevent unauthorized access, transfer, or loss of sensitive data.

DQN (Deep Q-Network) is a reinforcement learning algorithm that uses deep learning to optimize decision-making in complex environments.

EDA (Exploratory Data Analysis) involves summarizing and visualizing data sets to uncover patterns, detect anomalies, and guide further analysis.

EDR (Endpoint Detection and Response) is a cybersecurity solution that continuously monitors endpoints to detect, investigate, and respond to threats.

eMASS (Enterprise Mission Assurance Support Service) is a United States (U.S.) Department of Defense (DoD) tool used for managing cybersecurity compliance and risk documentation in RMF workflows.

ERM (Enterprise Risk Management) is a holistic approach to identifying, assessing, and mitigating risks across an entire organization.

ESG (Environmental, Social, and Governance) is a framework for evaluating an organization's sustainability, social responsibility, and ethical governance practices.

ETL (Extract, Transform, Load) is a data integration process that extracts data from sources, transforms it for analysis, and loads it into a data warehouse.

EU (European Union) is a political and economic union of 27 European countries that operates under shared laws, policies, and a common market.

F1 Score is a metric that combines precision and recall to evaluate the accuracy of a classification model, particularly when data is imbalanced.

FDIC (Federal Deposit Insurance Corporation) is a U.S. government agency that insures bank deposits and promotes stability in the financial system.

FPR (False Positive Rate) is the proportion of incorrect positive predictions among all actual negatives, often used in evaluating model performance.

FedRAMP (Federal Risk and Authorization Management Program) is a U.S. government program that standardizes security assessments for cloud products and services.

FFIEC (Federal Financial Institutions Examination Council) is a U.S. interagency body that develops uniform standards for the examination and supervision of financial institutions.

FISMA (Federal Information Security Modernization Act) mandates federal agencies to implement comprehensive information security programs to protect government information and operations.

GAGAS (Generally Accepted Government Auditing Standards), also known as the Yellow Book, provides guidelines for audits of government organizations and programs.

GAN (Generative Adversarial Network) is a type of AI model composed of two neural networks – a generator and a discriminator – that compete to produce increasingly realistic data outputs.

GAO (Government Accountability Office) is a U.S. congressional watchdog agency that audits and evaluates government operations to ensure accountability and transparency.

GDPR (General Data Protection Regulation) is a European Union (EU) regulation that governs data protection and privacy for individuals within the EU and European Economic Area (EEA).

GenAI (Generative Artificial Intelligence) refers to AI technologies that can generate new content, such as text, images, audio, or code, based on training data.

GLBA (Gramm-Leach-Bliley Act) is a U.S. federal law that requires financial institutions to protect consumers' private data.

GPAI (Global Partnership on Artificial Intelligence) is an international initiative that promotes the responsible development and use of AI grounded in human rights, inclusion, and innovation.

GPT (Generative Pre-Trained Transformer) is a family of AI language models trained to generate human-like text using transformer-based neural network architecture.

GPU (Graphics Processing Unit) is a specialized processor designed for parallel processing, essential for rendering graphics and accelerating AI model training.

GRC (Governance, Risk, and Compliance) is a coordinated strategy for managing an organization's overall governance, risk management, and compliance with regulations.

HER (Health Record) refers to digital or electronic documentation of a patient's medical history, treatments, and health data.

HVAC (Heating, Ventilation, and Air Conditioning) systems are responsible for regulating indoor environmental comfort in buildings.

HIPAA (Health Insurance Portability and Accountability Act) is a U.S. law that sets national standards for the protection of sensitive patient health information.

IA (Internal Audit) is an independent, objective assurance activity that evaluates and improves the effectiveness of risk management, control, and governance.

IAM (Identity Access Management) is a framework for managing digital identities and controlling access to resources within an organization.

IAPP (International Association of Privacy Professionals) is a global organization dedicated to privacy education, certification, and policy development.

IDEA (Interactive Data Extraction and Analysis) is a data analytics tool used by auditors for data extraction, transformation, and analysis.

IDS/IPS (Intrusion Detection/Prevention System) are security technologies that monitor network traffic for malicious activity and can alert or block suspicious behavior.

IEEE (Institute of Electrical and Electronics Engineers) is a professional association dedicated to advancing technology for the benefit of humanity, especially in electrical and electronic engineering.

IIA (Institute of Internal Auditors) is a global professional association that provides standards, guidance, and certifications for internal auditors.

IOC (Indicators of Compromise) are forensic data artifacts that indicate a potential intrusion or malicious activity on a system or network.

IPPF (International Professional Practices Framework) is the global framework issued by the IIA that outlines the standards and guidance for internal audit practice.

IR (Incident Reporting) is the process of formally notifying relevant parties about a security incident, including its nature, scope, and remediation steps.

ISCM (Information Security Continuous Monitoring) is the process of maintaining ongoing awareness of information security, vulnerabilities, and threats to support risk management decisions.

ISMS (Information Security Management System) is a systematic approach to managing sensitive company information to ensure its confidentiality, integrity, and availability.

ISO/IEC 27001 is an international standard for managing information security through the implementation of an ISMS.

ISSM (Information Systems Security Manager) is responsible for implementing and managing cybersecurity programs and ensuring system compliance with security policies.

ISSO (Information System Security Officer) ensures that information systems are operated, maintained, and disposed of in accordance with security policies and procedures.

IT (Information Technology) encompasses the use of computers, storage, networking, and other infrastructure to create, process, and manage information.

JTC (Joint Technical Committee) is a collaborative body formed by ISO and IEC to develop international IT standards, including those for cybersecurity and AI.

KPI (Key Performance Indicator) is a measurable value used to assess the success of an organization or individual in achieving key objectives.

KRI (Key Risk Indicator) is a metric used to signal the potential for future risk events and help organizations monitor emerging threats.

LIME (Local Interpretable Model-agnostic Explanations) is a technique used to explain predictions made by machine learning models by approximating them locally with interpretable models.

LLaMA (Large Language Model Meta AI) is a family of large language models developed by Meta that are designed for advanced natural language understanding and generation tasks.

LLM (Large Language Model) is a type of AI model trained on vast amounts of text data to perform complex language tasks such as translation, summarization, and dialogue.

MFA (Multi-Factor Authentication) enhances account security by requiring users to provide multiple forms of verification to gain access.

MIT (Massachusetts Institute of Technology) is a world-renowned university known for its research and innovation in science, engineering, and technology.

ML (Machine Learning) is a subset of AI that enables systems to learn from data and improve performance without being explicitly programmed.

MTTD (Mean Time to Detect) is the average time it takes for an organization to detect a security incident after it has occurred.

MTTR (Mean Time to Respond) is the average time it takes to contain, mitigate, and resolve a security incident after detection.

NAIC-ISAO (National Artificial Intelligence and Cybersecurity Information Sharing and Analysis Organization) facilitates information sharing and collaboration to enhance AI and cybersecurity resilience across sectors.

NAIRR (National AI Research Resource) is a U.S. initiative aimed at providing researchers and educators access to computational resources, datasets, and tools to advance AI innovation.

NDCG (Normalized Discounted Cumulative Gain) is a ranking quality metric used to evaluate the relevance of search engine results or recommendation systems.

NGO (Nongovernmental Organization) is a non-profit group independent of government that operates to address social, environmental, or humanitarian issues.

NIST (National Institute of Standards and Technology) is a U.S. federal agency that develops technology, standards, and guidelines to promote innovation and cybersecurity.

NIST Cybersecurity Framework provides voluntary guidance, based on existing standards, for organizations to better manage and reduce cybersecurity risk.

NIST RMF (Risk Management Framework) is a structured process developed by NIST to integrate security and risk management activities into the system development life cycle.

NLP (Natural Language Processing) is a field of AI focused on enabling machines to understand, interpret, and generate human language.

NSA (National Security Agency) is a U.S. government agency responsible for global monitoring and cybersecurity operations in support of national defense.

OCC (Office of the Comptroller of the Currency) regulates and supervises national banks and federal savings associations in the United States.

OECD (Organization for Economic Co-operation and Development) is an international organization that promotes policies to improve global economic and social well-being.

OIG (Office of Inspector General) conducts audits and investigations to prevent fraud, waste, and abuse within government agencies and programs.

OWASP (Open Web Application Security Project) is a nonprofit foundation that works to improve the security of software through open-source projects and community-led resources.

PAI (Partnership on AI) is a multi-stakeholder organization that promotes responsible AI development and practices through collaboration among academia, industry, and civil society.

PaLM (Pathways Language Model) is a large-scale AI model developed by Google using the Pathways system to perform complex reasoning and language tasks.

PCI-DSS (Payment Card Industry Data Security Standard) is a set of security standards designed to protect cardholder data and ensure secure handling of credit card transactions.

PentestGPT (Penetration Testing Generative Pre-Trained Transformer) is an AI-driven assistant designed to support ethical hacking by simulating penetration testing activities.

PII (Personally Identifiable Information) refers to any data that can be used to identify a specific individual, such as name, address, or social security number.

POA&M (Plan of Action & Milestones) is a management tool used to document planned remediation actions for identified security vulnerabilities.

PoC (Proof of Concept) is a demonstration used to validate the feasibility of an idea, solution, or technology in a practical scenario.

Power BI (Power Business Intelligence) is a Microsoft analytics tool that enables users to visualize data and share insights across an organization.

RACI (Responsible, Accountable, Consulted, Informed) is a responsibility assignment matrix that clarifies roles and responsibilities in projects or processes.

RBAC (Role-Based Access Control) is a method of regulating access to resources based on users' roles within an organization.

RLHF (Reinforcement Learning from Human Feedback) is an AI training method where models learn desired behavior by incorporating human preferences during reinforcement learning.

RNN (Recurrent Neural Network) is a type of neural network designed to process sequential data, commonly used in time-series analysis and language modeling.

ROC (Receiver Operating Characteristic) is a graphical plot used to assess the performance of a binary classification model.

ROC-AUC (Receiver Operating Characteristic Area Under the Curve) quantifies the overall ability of a binary classifier to discriminate between classes.

ROI (Return on Investment) is a financial metric used to evaluate the profitability or efficiency of an investment.

RPA (Robotic Process Automation) is a technology that automates repetitive, rule-based tasks by mimicking human interactions with digital systems.

RSA (Rivest-Shamir-Adleman) is a widely used public-key cryptosystem for secure data transmission.

SANS (SysAdmin, Audit, Network and Security) is a cybersecurity training and research organization known for its professional certifications and security resources.

SAR (Security Assessment Report) documents the findings, vulnerabilities, and recommendations resulting from a system's security assessment.

SCA (Security Control Assessment) is the process of evaluating the effectiveness of security controls implemented in an information system.

SDK (Software Development Kit) is a set of tools, libraries, and documentation that developers use to create software applications.

SDLC (System Development Life Cycle) is a structured process for planning, developing, testing, deploying, and maintaining information systems.

SGD (Stochastic Gradient Descent) is an optimization algorithm used to train machine learning models by updating parameters iteratively based on random data samples.

SHAP (SHapley Additive exPlanations) is a model-agnostic method for explaining the output of machine learning models by assigning feature importance.

SIEM (Security Information and Event Management) is a system that aggregates and analyzes security event data in real time for threat detection and incident response.

SLA (Service Level Agreement) is a formal contract that defines the expected performance and service standards between a provider and a customer.

SME (Subject Matter Expert) is an individual with deep expertise in a specific area or discipline who contributes knowledge to support decision-making or project success.

SOC (Security Operations Center) is a centralized team that monitors, detects, investigates, and responds to cybersecurity threats and incidents.

SOC 2 (System and Organization Controls 2) is an auditing framework that evaluates a service provider's controls related to security, availability, processing integrity, confidentiality, and privacy.

SOX (Sarbanes-Oxley Act) is a U.S. law that establishes regulations for financial reporting and internal controls to prevent corporate fraud.

SP (Special Publication) refers to NIST's formal guidance documents on standards and best practices across various domains, including cybersecurity.

SQL (Structured Query Language) is a standard programming language used to manage and manipulate relational databases.

SSP (System Security Plan) outlines the security requirements and controls in place for an information system, as part of RMF documentation.

TCO (Total Cost of Ownership) calculates the comprehensive cost of acquiring, operating, and maintaining a product or system over its entire lifecycle.

TPR (True Positive Rate) is the ratio of correctly identified positive cases out of all actual positive cases, also known as sensitivity.

TPU (Tensor Processing Unit) is a custom AI accelerator chip developed by Google for efficient training and inference of machine learning models.

TTP (Tactics, Techniques, and Procedures) describe the behavior and methods used by threat actors to conduct cyberattacks.

UBA (User Behavior Analytics) uses machine learning to analyze user behavior patterns and detect anomalies that may indicate insider threats or compromised accounts.

UI/UX (User Interface/User Experience) focuses on designing intuitive and satisfying interactions between users and digital products.

UPS (Uninterruptable Power Supply) provides backup power to devices during electrical outages to prevent data loss and system disruptions.

USB (Universal Serial Bus) is a standard interface used for connecting and transferring data between computers and peripheral devices.

VAE (Variational Autoencoders) are a type of generative model used in unsupervised learning to generate new data similar to training inputs.

ViT (Vision Transformer) is an AI model architecture that applies transformer principles to image recognition tasks for improved accuracy.

XAI (Explainable Artificial Intelligence) refers to methods and techniques that make AI model decisions transparent, understandable, and interpretable to humans.

XML (Extensible Markup Language) is a markup language used to structure, store, and transport data in a readable and platform-independent format.

AI usage statement

This book integrates multiple Generative Artificial Intelligence (AI) tools to enrich its content and support scholarly development through prompt engineering and source exploration.

OpenAI ChatGPT 4o (2024): The Study and Learn model was utilized to brainstorm topic ideas throughout the book. Additionally, the Scholar GPT variant was employed to identify authoritative reference sources for Chapters 4, 5, and 6. Last, Chapter 3 includes a dedicated prompt engineering conversation conducted with ChatGPT, illustrating its use in academic exploration.

Google Gemini 2.0 Flash (2025): This model was similarly used for topic brainstorming and for sourcing authoritative references for Chapters 4, 5, and 6. Furthermore, it was employed to cross-validate and compare information generated by OpenAI ChatGPT 4o.

Microsoft 365 Copilot Enterprise (2024): This tool was used to review and refine grammar, readability, and accessibility across all chapters, ensuring clarity and consistency in professional writing.

An introduction

Charting a new course for cybersecurity audit professionals

0.1 OPENING INSIGHTS

The objective of this introduction is to present the purpose and scope of this book. It offers an overview of each chapter and highlights the relationships among them. At a high level, the book demonstrates how agility and artificial intelligence (AI) can align with auditing standards, foster collaboration across organizational teams, and influence behavior and cultural change. These techniques and approaches are integrated into the cybersecurity audit process to enhance efficiency, improve accuracy, and support value-added recommendations. Additionally, these enhancements are conveyed through a foundation–concept–relationship framework designed to guide the reader through the evolving landscape of cybersecurity auditing.

0.2 WHY THIS BOOK, WHY NOW

Let's Talk Cybersecurity Auditing – And Why It's More Exciting Than Ever! Cybersecurity auditing doesn't have to be dull. In fact, it can be fun, especially with the transformative power of AI. AI is reshaping how cybersecurity auditors perform their work, reducing manual tasks and unlocking opportunities to be more creative, analytical, and innovative. Why should individuals think of cybersecurity auditing as fun? Because AI is changing how cybersecurity auditors execute audit tasks. AI is instrumental in making the cybersecurity audit function exciting with so many opportunities to be creative, innovative, and analytical. One of my previous employers exhibited leadership and culture traits that allowed cybersecurity auditors to create unique audit programs, build partnerships, and use technology to automate the audit activities. Turnover at the firm was low due to strong opportunities for growth and learning. As a result, professionals from this organization were highly sought after for other cybersecurity roles.

DOI: 10.1201/9781003640301-1

0.2.1 Addressing measurable cybersecurity audit deficiencies

Recent articles and industry assessments have highlighted persistent deficiencies in cybersecurity audit practices, including outdated methodologies, insufficient technical expertise, fragmented stakeholder communication, and a lack of agility in responding to evolving threats. Many audits fail to provide timely, actionable insights due to rigid, checklist-driven approaches and limited integration of emerging technologies. Additionally, the growing complexity of digital ecosystems has outpaced traditional audit techniques, leading to blind spots in risk identification and control validation.

This book is designed to directly confront these challenges by introducing modern, agile cybersecurity audit strategies grounded in real-world practices. Through a focus on building cross-functional partnerships, influencing cultural change, adopting iterative audit methods, and leveraging AI tools, readers will gain practical guidance for transforming audit functions. The goal is to move beyond compliance and toward proactive, value-driven cybersecurity assurance – empowering audit professionals to deliver timely insights, improve risk resilience, and align more effectively with organizational priorities. Here's what several cybersecurity audit experts had to say:

- While cybersecurity remains a critical priority for organizations, the Jefferson Wells 2023 Survey revealed a notable gap in audit coverage. Only 70 percent of large companies' internal audit departments assessed cyber risks, and this figure drops to just 40 percent when considering all companies. Several factors contributed to this shortfall, including a lack of technical expertise within audit teams and a nationwide shortage of qualified cybersecurity auditors (Zaki, 2023).
- As reliance on AI technology continues to grow exponentially, the demand for comprehensive cybersecurity auditors is expected to surge. These auditors will need to possess a hybrid skill set, combining traditional audit expertise with deep knowledge of AI systems, data privacy, and model governance. Organizations that fail to invest in upskilling their audit teams risk falling behind in identifying and mitigating emerging AI-driven cyber threats (Kulkarni, 2024).
- The growth of the cybersecurity talent pool has not kept pace with the rapid advancement of AI technology. This gap has contributed to an increased risk of data breaches, as organizations struggle to effectively identify and mitigate AI-related cybersecurity threats. To address this challenge, it is recommended that organizations map the necessary AI skillsets to existing cybersecurity roles, including those of cybersecurity auditors (Lyon et al., 2024).
- An ISC2 (2024) research study noted a 4.8 million cybersecurity workforce shortage, which was an increase of 19 percent from the previous year (ISC2, 2024).

Important Note: To entice cybersecurity professionals into the cybersecurity audit profession, audit leadership should take a strategic and value-driven approach that highlights the unique benefits, career growth opportunities, and meaningful impact of audit work. Here are key methods to achieve that goal:

1. **Emphasize Mission and Impact**
   - **Show Purpose:** Communicate how cybersecurity audit contributes to protecting critical infrastructure, data, and trust; appealing to professionals who want to make a tangible difference.
   - **Highlight Risk Influence:** Illustrate how auditors directly influence enterprise risk posture and cybersecurity resilience.
2. **Offer Skill Development and Career Growth**
   - **Upskill in AI, Cloud, and Zero Trust:** Position audit as a pathway to gain emerging skills, such as AI model governance, cloud security assessments, and Zero Trust validation.
   - **Certifications and Training:** Provide support for certifications that include non-audit specific certifications to show long-term professional value.
3. **Promote Audit as a Strategic and Technical Role**
   - **Break Stereotypes:** Reframe audit not as a check-the-box activity, but as a strategic function with hands-on access to diverse technologies and systems.
   - **Technology Exposure:** Emphasize exposure to a wide range of tools, platforms, and enterprise environments, more varied than many operational security roles.
4. **Bridging Security and Audit through Experiential Learning**
   - **Partnerships:** Allow cybersecurity personnel to temporarily join the cybersecurity audit team for a defined period – typically 6–12 months – providing firsthand exposure to audit processes, risk assessments, and governance practices. Allow cybersecurity audit professionals to temporarily join the first or second line of defense cybersecurity roles, preferably on AI teams.
   - **Rotational Roles:** Conversely, allow cybersecurity audit professionals to temporarily rotate into first or second line of defense cybersecurity roles, ideally within teams focused on AI and emerging technologies. This cross-functional experience enhances their technical understanding, fosters collaboration, and strengthens the audit function's ability to assess and advise on advanced cybersecurity initiatives.
   - **Benefit:** Cybersecurity professionals gain a broader understanding of organizational risk and compliance frameworks, while audit leaders benefit from fresh technical perspectives and stronger cross-functional collaboration. This experiential learning helps demystify the audit role, highlights its strategic impact, and often leads participants to pursue permanent positions within audit.

5. **Foster a Culture of Innovation**
    - **Agile Audit Concepts:** Introduce agile auditing concepts that encourage continuous improvement, innovation, and collaboration.
    - **Tool Integration:** Highlight how cybersecurity audit is embracing AI, automation, and advanced analytics to modernize the profession.

📩 Messaging examples for cybersecurity audit recruitment

In a competitive talent market, your job posting is only as strong as its first impression. Crafting a compelling, attention-grabbing header can be the difference between attracting top cybersecurity talent or getting lost in the noise. Below are some examples using a Chatbot to generate additional ideas.

- "*Join a cybersecurity audit team that doesn't just assess, they innovate and protect.*"
- "*Become a trusted advisor to leadership while expanding your technical skillset in AI, cloud, and emerging threats.*"
- "*Cybersecurity audit is where security meets strategy – are you ready to lead the future?*"
- "*Join the Front Lines of Cyber Defense – We're Hiring Elite Audit Professionals to Safeguard the Digital World!*"
- "*Ready to Elevate Your Cybersecurity Career? Explore Growth-Driven Roles in High-Impact Audit Teams!*"

💡**Critical Thinking Moment:** As you read through this book, consider the techniques presented that can enhance cybersecurity auditor job satisfaction. Reflect on how these approaches can be used to effectively communicate value, foster engagement, and support retention. Also, identify networking opportunities where you can showcase successes, both to attract new talent and to inspire existing cybersecurity professionals to explore roles within the audit function.

0.2.2 Future-ready auditing: Embracing agility and AI

Let's transition away from hiring cybersecurity audit professionals and talk about enhancing the skills of existing cybersecurity audit professionals to retain those professionals. Did you know that nearly two-thirds of audit hours are devoted to administrative tasks? Imagine the possibilities when AI takes that burden, freeing auditors to focus on what truly matters: analyzing risks, identifying threats, and delivering real-time insights. According to PwC's 2023 survey, internal audit departments can improve their return on investment by adopting technologies like AI.

Why do so many individuals shy away from a cybersecurity audit career? First, as noted in recent research, audit functions continue to spend a significant amount of time on administrative tasks that reduce analytical time. This is most often because many audit tests are manually executed against a significant amount of data. The use of emerging technology in partnership with agile methodology is not consistently applied, potentially because the requisite skillsets are not available or the culture is not supportive of change. This could also be prevalent because of the insufficient availability of actionable published materials. Existing reference materials consist of separate Agile Auditing and AI capabilities for audit activities, but no reference materials with actionable information using the combined concepts and tools. As an example, Jaleel (2023) published an ISACA article on how to obtain and use Chat Generative Pre-Trained Transformer (ChatGPT) along with the benefits, but no specific ChatGPT command/phrase examples provided. As another example, the Internal Audit, Risk and Compliance Private Sector Kenya LinkedIn Group (2024) published a brief article titled "Enhancing Audit Agility with AI and Analytics" from a theoretical perspective without providing actionable use cases. This gap in existing reference materials demonstrates the need to communicate and encourage use of agile concepts and AI tools that will benefit the audit community.

Second, there are publications that articulate the extensive administrative hours audit functions spend in lieu of value-added activities. As an example, Norman Marks (2023) published an article claiming that audit departments need to remove non-value-added activities. As another example, Kim (2016) claims that for every six hours an auditor spends testing, four hours are spent on administrative activities. What is also interesting is that PWC (2017) claimed that surveyed managers believed only 44 percent of audit functions add value in 2017, which was down from 54 percent the previous year. What is important to note is that the 2017 report date encouraging the reader to implement Agile Auditing has not been realized in my previous employer's internal audit functions, resulting in significant inefficiencies. As a final data point, PWC's 2023 report indicated that 52 percent of executives say the internal audit function has no plans to invest in AI in the next three years.

Third, many cybersecurity subject matter experts preferred roles in the first or second line of defense in lieu of audit because there was less administrative work. Conversely, many auditors with extensive AI, machine learning, and data analysis left audit for first and second line of defense roles. It is important to reduce the current administrative requirements to attract and retain the requisite subject matter experts, and provide value-added opinion on the cybersecurity control environment communicated to process and control owner management teams.

Let's switch the topic from why agility and AI will make a difference in cybersecurity roles and focus on careers. Cybersecurity auditors have the benefit of focusing on a broad field divided into multiple domains, each focusing on different aspects of security. These cybersecurity fields range from strategy, governance, operations, incident response, data classification, risk management, identity and access management (IAM), penetration and other proactive testing, security software development, and many more.

While this book is intended for cybersecurity audits, many of the concepts can be applied to other audit domains, such as finance. The objective of this book was to focus on one domain for purposes of providing examples (refer Chapter 5 – Harnessing Artificial Intelligence: Enhancing Cybersecurity Audits through Automation and Insight). Another objective is to inspire cybersecurity professionals to become cybersecurity auditors, allowing those individuals to be creative and innovative, and learn more cybersecurity domains. The goal is to make cybersecurity auditing fun, learn about risks and controls, partner with other firm or agency personnel, and not be dreaded as audit activities are assigned.

Still wondering if cybersecurity auditing is for you? Consider this: cybersecurity auditors master a powerful blend of technical acumen, sharp analytical thinking, and deep regulatory insight. They come from all walks of life: information technology (IT), compliance, risk, even non-technical fields, and thrive in the ever-evolving cybersecurity landscape. With countless domains to explore, from cloud security to threat intelligence, there's a niche waiting for every curious, driven professional. Your skills *will* translate. The only question is: where will you make your impact? Here are the key skills cybersecurity professionals typically possess:

1. **Technical Proficiency**
    - **Networking and Infrastructure Security:** Understanding firewalls, Intrusion Detection/Intrusion Prevention Systems (IDS/IPS), Virtual Private Networks (VPNs), and network protocols.
    - **Operating Systems Security:** Familiarity with securing Windows, Linux, and cloud-based environments.
    - **Application Security:** Ability to assess vulnerabilities in software, web applications, and APIs.
    - **Cloud Security:** Knowledge of Amazon Web Services (AWS), Azure, and Google Cloud security frameworks and controls.
    - **Cryptography:** Understanding encryption methods, public key infrastructure (PKI), and data protection strategies.
2. **Security Frameworks and Compliance Knowledge**
    - **National Institute of Standards and Technology (NIST) 800-53/ Risk Management Framework (RMF):** Essential for federal cybersecurity audits.
    - **NIST Cybersecurity Framework (CSF):** Used widely across industries.
    - **International Organization for Standardization (ISO) 27001:** International standard for information security management.
    - **Federal Information Security Management Act/Federal Risk and Authorization Management Program (FISMA/FedRAMP):** Compliance requirements for federal agencies and cloud service providers.

- **Payment Card Industry Data Security Standard (PCI DSS), Health Insurance Portability and Accountability Act (HIPAA), General Data Protection Regulation (GDPR):** Depending on the industry being audited.

3. **Risk Management and Assessment**
   - **Threat Modeling:** Identifying potential threats and vulnerabilities.
   - **Risk Assessment Methodologies:** Factor Analysis of Information Risk (FAIR), Operationally Critical Threat, Asset, and Vulnerability Evaluation (OCTAVE), and qualitative/quantitative risk analysis.
   - **Security Controls Evaluation:** Assessing effectiveness of controls and recommending improvements.
4. **Audit and Assessment Skills**
   - **Penetration Testing and Vulnerability Management:** Even if not conducting tests, auditors should understand them.
   - **Log Analysis and Forensics:** Reviewing security logs for anomalies.
   - **Third-Party Risk Assessment:** Evaluating vendor security practices.
   - **Audit Reporting and Documentation:** Writing clear and actionable audit reports.
5. **Soft Skills and Professionalism**
   - **Attention to Detail:** Small misconfigurations can create big vulnerabilities.
   - **Critical Thinking:** Evaluating security from an attacker's perspective.
   - **Communication Skills:** Explaining findings to technical and non-technical stakeholders.
   - **Ethical Judgment and Confidentiality:** Handling sensitive security information responsibly.
   - **Project Management:** Coordinating audits and following up on remediation efforts.
6. **Continuous Learning and Certifications**
   - **Certified Information Systems Auditor (CISA):** Gold standard for cybersecurity auditors.
   - **CISSP Certified Information Systems Security Professional (CISSP):** Broad security expertise.
   - **Certified in Risk and Information Systems Control (CRISC):** Risk management-focused.
   - **Certified Ethical Hacker (CEH):** Understanding attacker tactics.
   - **Certified Cloud Security Professional (CCSP):** Important for cloud audits.

🛠 **Important Note:** Be aware that each of the chapters will contain use of AI, proving that AI is versatile and can be used for multiple audit and non-audit activities. I consider non-audit activities to be researching emerging threats, as one example. Cybersecurity auditors must remain current on cybersecurity threats, mirroring management and risk management professionals' activities. This provides an independent view that complements those who conduct similar activities.

0.3 FOUNDATIONS FOR INNOVATION AND INSIGHT

This book is designed as a practical resource for both current cybersecurity auditors and professionals seeking to transition into the cybersecurity auditing field. Also, this book is relevant for cybersecurity risk professionals. In addition to providing guidance, it aims to inspire critical, innovative, and creative thinking. While audit standards outline what is expected, this book focuses on how to effectively execute cybersecurity audit activities.

As a strategy for reading this book, readers with extensive cybersecurity auditing experience may choose to skip Chapter 1 – Understanding Audit Objectives, Expectations, Concepts, and Opportunities, as it reviews widely recognized auditing standards. Likewise, professionals already working in collaborative and innovative environments may wish to bypass Chapter 2 – Building Partnerships for Success. Instead, readers are encouraged to explore the chapter's most relevant to their development goals, particularly those offering foundational knowledge and those designed to challenge conventional thinking and inspire approaches that drive exceptional audit outcomes.

0.3.1 Chapter 1 – Understanding audit objectives, expectations, concepts, and opportunities

This chapter provides a comprehensive overview of audit objectives, and the expectations placed on modern audit functions, including cybersecurity audit functions. It introduces key concepts that guide effective auditing, including risk assessment, compliance alignment, and performance evaluation. Readers will also explore emerging opportunities to enhance audit value, such as integrating technology, adopting agile practices, and fostering continuous improvement. By understanding these elements, auditors can better meet stakeholder expectations and contribute to organizational success.

0.3.2 Chapter 2 – Building partnerships for success

This chapter emphasizes that strong partnerships are essential for achieving sustainable success in today's interconnected business and cybersecurity environments. This chapter examines the strategies for cultivating effective collaborations between internal teams, external stakeholders, and cross-functional partners. Readers will learn how to align goals, foster trust, and leverage diverse expertise to drive innovation and overcome complex challenges. By building resilient partnerships, organizations can enhance agility, improve decision-making, and achieve shared objectives.

0.3.3 Chapter 3 – How to influence behaviors and culture

This chapter explores how audit leaders and cybersecurity professionals can influence mindsets, behaviors, and organizational norms to create a foundation that supports the successful integration of AI applications and agile methodologies. Culture often dictates the pace at which innovation is accepted and operationalized. Resistance to change, fear of automation, and legacy thinking can hinder progress, even when the technological capabilities are sound. To overcome these barriers, this chapter will examine strategies to build trust in AI systems, foster collaboration across traditional silos, and encourage continuous learning and experimentation. By aligning behavior with agile values, such as transparency, adaptability, and incremental improvement, organizations can unlock the full potential of AI-driven tools while maintaining audit integrity, accountability, and resilience.

0.3.4 Chapter 4 – Agility in action: Rethinking cybersecurity audit

This chapter explores objectives and expectations through the lens of cybersecurity auditing, emphasizing the application of agile concepts in a rapidly evolving threat landscape. It introduces key concepts that distinguish agile practices, such as iterative planning, continuous feedback, and cross-functional collaboration – from traditional, rigid audit approaches and counterproductive behaviors like excessive multitasking. The chapter also highlights the relationship between Agile and Lean Management concepts, showcasing how both support value-driven, efficient, and responsive audit processes. Readers will gain insight into how agile cybersecurity audit teams operate, adapt to emerging risks, and deliver continuous assurance while aligning with organizational priorities. By the end of this chapter, you'll be prepared to implement agile concepts that drive efficiency, innovation, and continuous improvement.

0.3.5 Chapter 5 – Harnessing artificial intelligence: Enhancing cybersecurity audits through automation and insight

This chapter supports the idea that we stand at a turning point in the evolution of cybersecurity auditing. The age of manual reviews, fragmented data, and retrospective insights is giving way to a new paradigm, one where AI empowers auditors to work faster, think deeper, and anticipate risks before they materialize. AI is not simply a tool; it's an enabler of a profound shift. As cyber threats grow more sophisticated and data volumes soar, traditional auditing methods, no matter how refined, can no longer keep pace. Forward-thinking auditors now harness AI to analyze complex data sets, detect subtle patterns of risk, and automate routine tasks, freeing human talent to focus on strategy, judgment, and innovation.

But the real promise of AI lies beyond automation. It offers the potential to reshape how audits are conceived, executed, and evolved. Imagine audits that adapt in real time, that learn from past findings, and that provide predictive insights to secure the future, not just evaluating the past. This chapter challenges cybersecurity auditors to move beyond compliance checklists and embrace a mindset of continuous learning, creative problem-solving, and technological curiosity. By integrating AI thoughtfully and ethically, cybersecurity auditors can not only enhance their effectiveness but also help lead the profession into a more agile, insightful, and resilient future.

The journey begins here.

0.3.6 Chapter 6 – Unlocking artificial intelligence: Knowledge, context, and curated resources

This chapter explores additional concepts and best practices that cybersecurity auditors should consider, enhancing their effectiveness and adapting to the evolving landscape. As cybersecurity auditors embrace agility, AI, and cultural change, defining and evaluating success becomes essential. Success should be measured not only by compliance but also by value delivered, such as improved risk mitigation, audit efficiency, and insights that drive better decision-making. Establishing clear metrics and conducting periodic self-assessments will help teams gauge progress and adapt to evolving challenges. In addition, internal and external information sharing fosters a learning culture, promotes innovation, and strengthens partnerships across the cybersecurity and audit communities. Looking ahead, staying informed on emerging AI trends and continually evaluating their impact will ensure that auditors remain not only relevant but also leaders in shaping the future of the profession.

0.4 CHAPTER RELATIONSHIPS

The chapters in this book are organized using a **foundation–concept–relationship** framework to guide the reader through the evolving landscape of cybersecurity auditing. Chapter 1 lays the foundation by detailing the essential professional standards and practices that govern internal auditing and Offices of Inspector General (OIG), with a specific emphasis on cybersecurity auditing.

Chapters 2 through 4 introduce and explore core concepts that help auditors achieve cybersecurity audit objectives more efficiently and effectively. These chapters build on the foundation by presenting practical strategies, tools, and methodologies.

Chapter 5 then connects the foundational practices and key concepts by demonstrating how **AI** can enhance both the *what* and the *how* of cybersecurity auditing, showcasing real-world applications and opportunities for innovation.

Finally, Chapter 6 offers concluding insights that synthesize the book's main lessons, reflect on current trends, and encourage readers to consider future developments and potential advancements in the field.

Figure 0.1 illustrates the relationship between the chapters and how they build upon one another. It provides a visual representation of the book's structure, highlighting the progression from foundational practices to conceptual understanding and ultimately to the integration of AI in cybersecurity auditing.

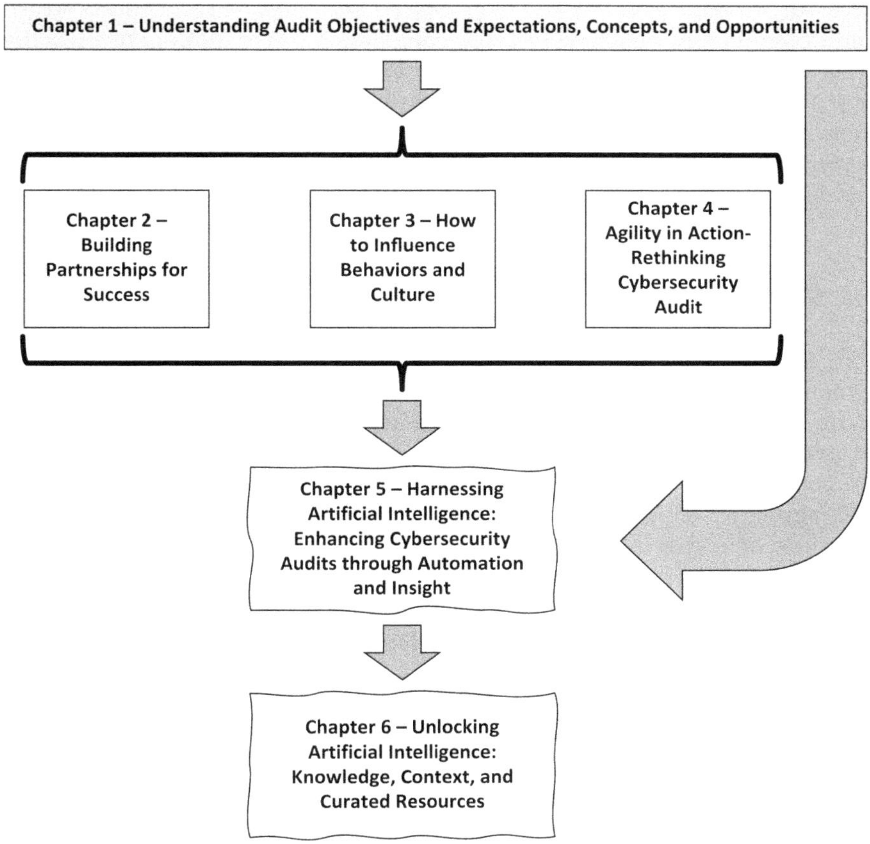

Figure 0.1 Chapter structure and thematic relationships across the book.

0.5 BE THE DIFFERENCE: INSPIRE AGILITY, TRUST, AND INNOVATION

This book is designed to be both a guide and a catalyst, equipping you with the insights, strategies, and tools needed to transform the way cybersecurity audits are conducted. Whether you're a seasoned auditor, a cybersecurity professional transitioning into audit, or a leader shaping audit strategy, you'll find practical value in each chapter. The content is organized to align with four foundational pillars: building partnerships, influencing behavior and culture, achieving audit objectives, and embracing agility. Each chapter includes key takeaways, real-world examples, and optional prompts to encourage reflection and application in your unique environment.

You don't need to read this book cover to cover in one sitting. Instead, treat it as a modular resource: focus on sections that align with your immediate needs or strategic goals. If you're grappling with how to incorporate AI into audit planning, jump ahead to those chapters. If you're looking to shift your audit team's mindset from traditional to agile, start with the chapters on culture and behavior. Use the checklists, prompts, and frameworks as working tools, not just theory, and revisit them as your cybersecurity audit program maturity grows. The goal isn't just to inform, but to inspire you to act, lead, and influence the future of cybersecurity auditing.

0.6 SUMMARY

This introduction provided a high-level overview of this book's chapters. Cybersecurity auditing plays a critical role in evaluating the effectiveness of an organization's security controls, compliance posture, and risk management strategies. At its core, the audit function is responsible for ensuring objectivity, confidentiality, and competency while aligning with organizational goals and regulatory requirements. Clear audit objectives help define the scope and priorities of engagements, enabling cybersecurity auditors to assess technical safeguards, detect vulnerabilities, and recommend actionable improvements. These objectives are best achieved when auditors operate within a well-defined framework that fosters collaboration, continuous learning, and alignment with leadership expectations.

Furthering the collaboration discussion, building strong partnerships is essential for audit success, particularly in cybersecurity where collaboration across IT, security, legal, and operational teams is critical. Effective auditors influence behaviors and culture by modeling ethical conduct, promoting transparency, and engaging stakeholders in open dialogue. An agile audit mindset, one that embraces adaptability, incremental value delivery, and responsiveness to change, further enhances audit effectiveness. When combined with Lean Management principles, agility helps audit teams reduce waste, prioritize critical risks, and improve overall efficiency. Last, the integration of AI into audit processes brings additional opportunities, such as automated control testing, anomaly detection, and predictive risk analysis. By leveraging AI alongside agile practices, cybersecurity auditors can scale their capabilities, enhance decision-making, and deliver deeper insights with greater speed and precision.

Let's begin transforming the cybersecurity audit practices.

Chapter 1

Understanding audit objectives, expectations, concepts, and opportunities

1.1 LEARNING OBJECTIVES

By the end of this chapter, readers will be able to:

1. **Define the primary objectives and expectations** of annual audit planning, individual audits, continuous audits, and internal consulting engagements, ensuring compliance, security, and operational efficiency.
2. **Identify key expectations** from auditors, auditees, and stakeholders throughout the audit life cycle.
3. **Explain fundamental audit concepts**, including independence, evidence-based audit, and professional skepticism.
4. **Identify the key roles** involved in the audit process, including auditors, system owners, cybersecurity officers, and senior leadership.
5. **Identify and leverage opportunities for improvement** that will be applied to Chapter 4 –Agility in Action: Rethinking Cybersecurity Audit and Chapter 5 – Harnessing Artificial Intelligence: Enhancing Cybersecurity Audits through Automation and Insight.

1.2 OPENING INSIGHTS

This chapter outlines the fundamental audit requirements that apply across all audit domains, including cybersecurity, forming the essential framework upon which effective audit practices are built. These requirements establish the baseline expectations for auditors, ensuring consistency, accountability, and compliance with established standards and regulations. By introducing these core principles early in the book, this chapter provides the necessary foundation for understanding how audit activities are structured and governed across diverse contexts. The concepts presented here will serve as a reference point for the discussions in Chapters 3, 4, and 5, which build upon this framework to demonstrate how building partnerships, agile methodologies, artificial intelligence applications, and advanced analytics can be integrated while maintaining alignment with these foundational audit requirements.

DOI: 10.1201/9781003640301-2

Pro Tip: Consider creating a checklist of points specific to your organization to enhance your approach to Chapter 4 – Agility in Action: Rethinking Cybersecurity Audit and Chapter 5 – Harnessing Artificial Intelligence: Enhancing Cybersecurity Audits through Automation and Insight. This checklist can aid in aligning audit practices with organizational goals. In addition, this checklist should be revisited periodically to incorporate evolving risks and technologies after you implement practices from this book.

1.3 AUDIT OBJECTIVES AND EXPECTATIONS

Internal Audit (IA) Departments and Offices of Inspector General (OIG) are considered IA functions for purposes of this book. Many of the concepts discussed in this book may also be applicable to external auditors and contractors, depending on the nature of the engagement. This conclusion reflects the broad applicability of industry standards across audit groups, industries, and government entities.

1.3.1 Audit standard application

Now, let us shift from theory to practical application by exploring how these standards can be applied to real-world audit scenarios. Table 1.1 summarizes the three primary audit standard elements. It is important to note that while these standards are owned by different organizations and touch upon unique information, the standard content is the same. Keep in mind that the key concepts and expectations from these standards have been summarized in Table 1.1 for discussion purposes. For direct standard section references and further reading, consult the references in the end matter of this book.

Table 1.1 Relationship between major audit standards

Standard content	*Institute of Internal Auditors (2024a)*	*ISACA (2020)*	*GAO Yellow Book (U.S. GAO 2024)*
Ethics and Professionalism • ***Integrity*** • ***Objectivity*** • ***Competency*** • ***Due Professional Care*** • ***Confidentiality***	✓	✓	✓
Governance • ***Board oversight*** • ***Independence*** • ***Charter and Standards***	✓	✓	✓
Audit Function • ***Strategy*** • ***Resources*** • ***Communication*** • ***Quality***	✓	✓	✓

(Continued)

Table 1.1 Relationship between major audit standards (*Continued*)

Standard content	*Institute of Internal Auditors (2024a)*	*ISACA (2020)*	*GAO Yellow Book (U.S. GAO 2024)*
Audit Engagement • ***Risk Assessment*** • ***Objectives and Scope*** • ***Subject Matter Expertise*** • ***Analysis*** • ***Action Plans*** • ***Ongoing Monitoring***	✓	✓	✓
Continuing Professional Education (CPE)/Ongoing Professional Development • ***Maintain Competence and Relevance*** • ***Full Professional and Ethical Considerations*** • ***Enhance Audit Quality and Innovation***	✓	✓	✓

These standards are rooted in fundamental principles that guide the process of examining and evaluating an organization's cybersecurity processes, systems, and controls to ensure compliance with established requirements. Let's break down the key concepts that shape this process:

- **Independence and Objectivity:** Auditors must remain unbiased and free from conflicts of interest to ensure their findings are impartial and reliable.
- **Documentation and Evidence:** Collecting sufficient, appropriate evidence to support audit findings is crucial. Documentation serves as a record of work performed and conclusions reached and must stand on its own without verbal explanations.
- **Materiality:** This concept helps auditors focus on significant issues that could impact decision-making. It defines the threshold at which an issue is considered important enough to affect the audit outcome.
- **Risk-Based Approach:** Auditors prioritize areas with higher-risk levels, focusing on processes or systems more likely to have deficiencies or vulnerabilities.
- **Compliance and Conformance:** Auditors assess whether an organization complies with relevant laws, regulations, policies, and standards. For example, in federal cybersecurity, this might include validating compliance with National Institute of Standards and Technology (NIST) Special Publication (SP) 800-53 (NIST, 2020.a.) and NIST Cybersecurity Framework (CSF) (NIST, 2025.a.).
- **Internal Controls:** Evaluating the design and effectiveness of an organization's internal controls helps ensure resources are used effectively, risks are managed, and objectives are met.

- **Audit Trail:** A clear, documented history of transactions and changes that auditors use to trace actions back to their source, ensuring accountability and transparency.
- **Reporting and Findings:** The final output of an audit is typically a report detailing observations, findings, and recommendations for remediation or improvement.
- **Continuous Monitoring and Follow-Up:** Audit activities should not always be one-off events. Continuous monitoring assists in identifying new high-risk scenarios, and periodic follow-ups help ensure that corrective actions are implemented and sustained.

🎯 **Pro Tip:** Conduct a roundtable discussion to continue building on the above. The roundtable should include individuals from various subject matter expert groups and could include external subject matter experts.

1.3.2 Cybersecurity audit profession

The cybersecurity audit profession has evolved over the decades because of new technologies, expanded cybersecurity standards, and emerging cybersecurity threats. It now focuses on evaluating an organization's information security practices, systems, and controls to ensure they protect sensitive data, comply with relevant regulations, and effectively manage cyber risks. Let us break it down:

- **Role and Responsibilities:** Cybersecurity auditors assess an organization's security posture by examining technical controls, policies, and procedures. They verify compliance with frameworks like NIST SP 800-53, International Organization for Standardization/International Electrotechnical Commission (ISO/IEC) 27001, and Federal Information Security Modernization Act (FISMA), identify vulnerabilities, and recommend improvements.
- **Key Skills and Knowledge Areas:** Auditors need a strong grasp of cybersecurity principles, risk management, and regulatory requirements. They must understand network security, encryption, access controls, incident response, and cloud security, along with auditing methodologies and tools.
- **Frameworks and Standards:** Auditors rely on established guidelines to assess security controls, such as NIST, Center for Internet (CIS) Critical Security Controls, System and Organization Controls (SOC) 2, and Payment Card Industry Data Security Standard (PCI-DSS). For federal systems, adherence to NIST Risk Management Framework (RMF) and continuous monitoring requirements are critical.
- **Tools and Techniques:** Cybersecurity auditors use vulnerability scanners, log analysis tools, and configuration management utilities. They

also conduct interviews, review documentation, and perform hands-on testing to validate security measures.

- **Reporting and Recommendations**: After conducting audits, auditors compile detailed reports outlining findings, risk levels, and remediation recommendations. Clear communication is essential to help organizations prioritize and address vulnerabilities.
- **Certifications and Qualifications**: Many auditors hold credentials like Certified Information Systems Auditor (CISA), Certified Information Systems Security Professional (CISSP), or Certified Authorization Professional (CAP), which demonstrate expertise in security and audit practices.
- **Collaboration and Ongoing Monitoring**: Cybersecurity auditors work closely with system owners, security teams, and executives to foster a culture of continuous improvement. They may participate in ongoing assessments, penetration testing, and incident reviews to adapt to evolving threats.
- **CPE/Ongoing Professional Development**: Auditing standards (e.g., IIA, GAO) require internal auditors to engage in continuous learning to stay current with evolving risks, technologies, and regulatory expectations. Standards such as the IIA's Global Internal Audit Standards and GAO's Yellow Book mandate a minimum number of CPE hours annually to uphold professional competence and ethical performance. Ongoing development ensures auditors can apply emerging tools (e.g., data analytics, AI) and methodologies, thereby improving audit effectiveness, efficiency, and value delivery.

🛠 **Important Note:** Understanding these key concepts not only enhances audit effectiveness but also helps identify gaps and opportunities for strengthening cybersecurity controls.

1.4 THE VALUE OF INTERNAL AUDIT (IA) AND OFFICE OF INSPECTOR GENERAL (OIG)

Let us move beyond the "what" and focus on "how" those objectives are achieved. One could argue that IA/OIG must continually demonstrate its value to the organization. In addition to the standards previously mentioned, banking regulations and federal government requirements outline supplementary "what" activities that IA/OIG must address. It is up to the IA/OIG department to determine "how" to execute these objectives effectively, leveraging soft skills, such as building relationships, fostering collaboration and trust with stakeholders.

This section explores the concept of adding value, while Chapter 4 – Agility in Action: Rethinking Cybersecurity Audit and Chapter 5 – Harnessing Artificial Intelligence: Enhancing Cybersecurity Audits through Automation and Insight will provide actionable strategies to help IA/OIG effectively demonstrate its "value add" to stakeholders. For clarity, stakeholders in this context do not include external auditors or regulatory examiners, as an example.

🛠 **Important Note:** By mastering both technical and interpersonal aspects of auditing, IA/OIG offers organizations independent assurance, advice, and insight to improve operations and safeguard value, and enable transformation from a compliance function to a trusted advisor.

1.4.1 Value-added communication approach

IA/OIG provides significant value to an organization by offering independent and objective assurance, insights, and recommendations to improve operations, manage risks, and enhance governance. Here are some key benefits:

- **Defining IA/OIG:** Explain the role of IA/OIG within an organization, its purpose, and its responsibilities. Stress the skillsets and how those skillsets can complement the work management executes, providing another pair of eyes.
- **Risk Management and Assurance:** Show how IA/OIGs help manage risks by providing independent assurance on processes, controls, and governance. Independently identifying, assessing, and providing mitigation strategies for cybersecurity risks that could impact organizational objectives.
- **Cost Efficiency:** Discuss how IA/OIGs can help organizations save costs by identifying inefficiencies, fraud, and potential areas of improvement that could also reduce operational losses. Identifies weaknesses that could be exploited for fraud and recommends controls to prevent or reduce those risks.
- **Value beyond Compliance:** Highlight how IA/OIGs provide insights into strategic goals, operational effectiveness, and overall organizational health. Ensures adherence to laws, regulations, and internal policies to avoid legal and financial penalties.
- **IA/OIG's Role in Decision-Making:** Demonstrate how IA/OIG findings influence executive decisions and organizational strategies.
- **Operational Efficiency:** Evaluates and improves business processes, ensuring resources are used effectively.
- **Governance Enhancement:** Strengthens oversight by providing insights to executive leadership and boards on risk and control effectiveness.
- **Financial Integrity:** Verifies the accuracy of financial reporting and internal controls, boosting stakeholder confidence.
- **Continuous Improvement:** Promotes a culture of accountability and improvement through regular assessments and feedback.

🎯 **Pro Tip:** Conduct periodic meetings with stakeholders to provide real-world examples that align with the categories above.

1.4.2 Value-added examples

Let us explore specific examples where IA/OIG can add value beyond formal audits. These examples illustrate how IA/OIG can maintain independence while offering valuable insights on risk and control practices. This information can be stored in an audit repository to inform future audits, enhance risk assessments, and support continuous improvement – without requiring a formal audit report for these activities (Somani, 2024).

1. **Risk Management and Mitigation**
   - Review the firm's/government entity's cybersecurity risk appetite statement.
   - Share best practices on cybersecurity key risk and performance indicators. Consider initiating a roundtable discussion to evaluate how these metrics align with the organization's risk tolerances and strategic objectives.
   - Evaluate the cybersecurity risk management framework against best practices.
2. **Strategic Insight and Advisory Role**
   - Evaluate the potential cybersecurity risks associated with strategic objectives.
   - Share emerging cybersecurity threats/risks, including those identified through networking forums or industry collaborations.
3. **Process Improvement and Efficiency**
   - Share process flows developed during an audit or internal consulting engagement, highlighting risks, controls, and potential gaps. These insights can identify process inefficiencies and drive continuous improvement across the organization.
   - Participate in new system implementations or process redesign efforts to provide risk and control insights during the development phase.
4. **Cost and Risk Reduction**
   - Identify inefficiencies and weaknesses in processes and controls, can help organizations reduce costs, operational losses, and mitigate risks.
5. **Proactive Approach**
   - Proactive approach to identifying and addressing potential issues before they escalate.

🛠 **Important Note:** By engaging in these activities, IA/OIG can establish itself as a trusted advisor, contributing to the organization's resilience and strategic success.

1.5 AUDIT ROLE EXPLAINED

This section begins by exploring the history of auditing, providing brief context on how audit practices have evolved – and should continue to evolve with the integration of AI tools. When I accepted my first auditing role, I was reminded of the bank examiner in "It's a Wonderful Life." That examiner was initially portrayed as cold and focused solely on finding problems, but the examiner eventually exhibited empathy when it became clear the bank would not fail (Lam & White, 2016). This analogy reminds us that auditors should not be seen as individuals solely focused on finding problems but as trusted business partners who contribute to organizational success. As the audit profession evolves, incorporating AI tools can further enhance this partnership.

Levy (2020) highlights that partnership concept, in the early days of auditing, auditors independently determined the scope of their reviews, as formal standards did not yet exist to ensure consistency and quality. Over time, frameworks and standards were developed by reputable organizations such as the Institute of Internal Auditors (IIA), to guide auditors and safeguard shareholder interests (Levy, 2020). This evolution mirrors the goals of the Securities and Exchange Commission and IA/OIG departments – to protect stakeholders through consistent, high-quality audit practices. Today, the introduction of AI tools presents a similar opportunity to enhance audit efficiency and effectiveness.

As audit practices continue to evolve, AI tools offer transformative potential in enhancing audit effectiveness. In this book, we will explore four critical audit role areas where AI can provide valuable support:

- **Audit Planning and Risk Assessment**
- **Audit Program Development**
- **Continuous Monitoring and Improvement**
- **Internal Consulting Engagements**

> **Note:** This chapter is just the beginning, Chapter 4 – Agility in Action: Rethinking Cybersecurity Audit and Chapter 5 – Harnessing Artificial Intelligence: Enhancing Cybersecurity Audits through Automation and Insight will delve deeper into how AI can bring agility and innovation to these audit activities.

1.5.1 Audit planning and risk assessment

The **annual audit process** is a structured, systematic approach used by internal and external auditors to evaluate an organization's controls, processes, and compliance with applicable standards, laws, and policies. This process helps identify risks, ensure operational effectiveness, and provide insights for improvement.

Here is a breakdown of the typical **annual audit process:**

> **Objective:** Establish the audit scope, objectives, and timeline while identifying high-risk areas.

Key Activities

- **Understand the Organization:** Gain a deep understanding of business operations, objectives, and processes.

- **Perform Risk Assessment:** Identify and assess potential risks that could impact the organization's financial statements, cybersecurity, or compliance posture.
- **Review Prior Year's Findings:** Analyze previous audit reports to identify recurring issues or emerging risks.
- **Define the Scope and Objectives:** Determine audit boundaries, focus areas, and high-risk processes that require detailed examination.
- **Develop an Audit Plan:** Create a formalized audit plan that outlines the audit strategy, resources, and timelines.
- **Team Composition:** Assign the engagement team and scheduling of resources to ensure the level of experience, use of experts, and scheduling team members.

📄 **Output:** Audit plan approved by senior management and the audit committee or Inspector General with a communication to Congress.

Figure 1.1 provides an overview of the annual audit process. Note that this process is repeated when new information is identified through the continuous monitoring process, applying the agile concepts. The annual designation is intended to be the minimal frequency.

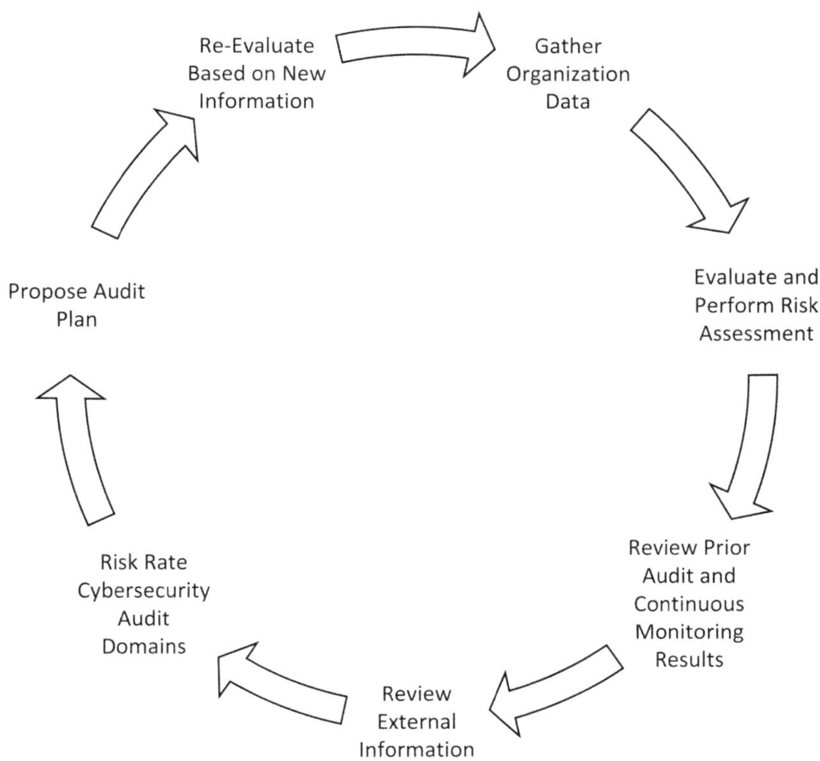

Figure 1.1 Annual audit plan process.

1.5.2 Audit program development

1. Audit Program

📝 **Objective:** Create a detailed audit program that defines the procedures and tests to be performed.

🔑 ***Key Activities***

- **Design Audit Procedures:** Develop specific steps to test controls, processes, and compliance with policies or regulations.
- **Select Sampling Methodology:** Determine sampling approaches to ensure statistically valid and representative audit results.
- **Set Testing Criteria:** Define benchmarks and thresholds to evaluate audit results effectively.
- **Audit Execution:** Begin fieldwork, analysis and evaluation of findings, reporting and communication, remediation, and follow-up with details in the sections below.

📄 **Output:** Audit program ready for execution.

2. Fieldwork and Audit Execution

📝 **Objective:** Execute the audit plan and gather evidence to evaluate controls and compliance.

🔑 ***Key Activities***

- **Conduct Interviews and Walkthroughs:** Engage with process owners to understand workflows and identify key controls.
- **Test Controls and Processes:** Perform detailed testing of transactions, data, and procedures to identify control gaps.
- **Evaluate Supporting Documentation:** Review policies, procedures, and records to ensure compliance.
- **Identify Exceptions and Issues:** Document any control deficiencies, process gaps, or regulatory non-compliance.

📄 **Output:** Preliminary findings and audit documentation.

3. Analysis and Evaluation of Findings

📝 **Objective:** Analyze the audit results and assess the impact of identified issues.

Key Activities

- **Classify Findings by Risk Severity:** Categorize issues as high, medium, or low based on their potential impact.
- **Perform Root Cause Analysis:** Identify the underlying reasons for control deficiencies or gaps.
- **Quantify Impact:** Estimate the financial, operational, and reputational risks associated with the findings.

Output: Draft of audit observations with supporting evidence.

4. **Reporting and Communication**

Objective: Communicate audit results clearly and effectively to stakeholders.

Key Activities

- **Draft the Audit Report:** Summarize findings, observations, and recommendations.
- **Review with Management:** Discuss findings with management to validate accuracy and gather feedback.
- **Issue Final Report:** Deliver the final report to senior management and the audit committee.

Output: Final audit report with actionable recommendations.

5. **Remediation and Follow-Up**

Objective: Ensure identified issues are addressed and corrective actions are implemented.

Key Activities

- **Develop Action Plans:** Collaborate with management to create remediation plans for each identified issue.
- **Monitor Progress:** Track the implementation of corrective actions to mitigate risks.
- **Conduct Follow-Up Audits:** Verify that previously identified deficiencies have been resolved.

Output: Updated status reports on corrective actions and issue closure.

Figure 1.2 provides an overview of the individual audit program process. Note that this process is repeated when new information is identified, applying the agile concepts. The annual designation is the minimal frequency.

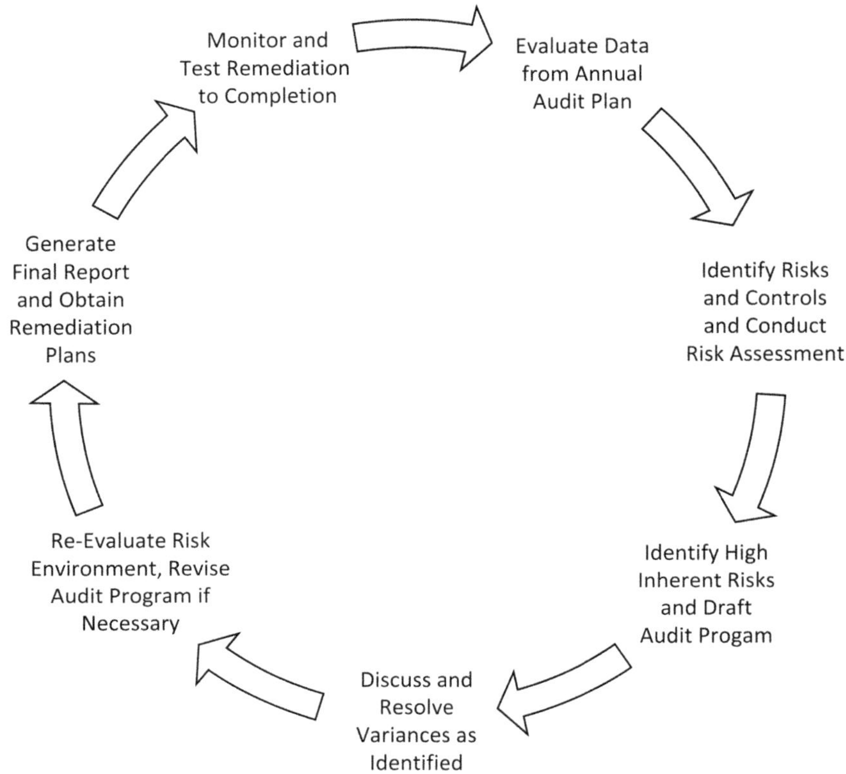

Figure 1.2 Audit program process.

1.5.3 Continuous monitoring and improvement

Continuous cybersecurity monitoring is a **proactive** approach to evaluating and analyzing both **internal systems and processes** and **external emerging threats**, such as zero-day vulnerabilities and third-party service provider risks. This continuous monitoring involves leveraging tools such as **Security Information and Event Management** (SIEM) platforms, threat intelligence feeds, and vulnerability management systems to refresh risk assessments as new information emerges. The results of these refreshed risk assessments may influence changes to the overall audit plan or adjustments to individual audit program testing, ensuring that audit procedures remain aligned with the evolving cybersecurity landscape.

1. **Continuous Monitoring and Improvement**

📝 **Objective:** Leverage audit insights to drive ongoing improvements and identify emerging risks.

🔑 *Key Activities*

- **Establish Continuous Monitoring Processes:** Use data analytics and AI tools to monitor high-risk areas.
- **Review and Update Audit Programs:** Modify audit plans and procedures based on lessons learned and evolving risks.
- **Provide Ongoing Training:** Educate the audit team on emerging risks, technologies, and regulatory changes.

📋 **Output:** Enhanced audit processes and proactive risk management.

Figure 1.3 provides an overview of the entire continuous monitoring and improvement process. Note that there are multiple steps that support the key activities.

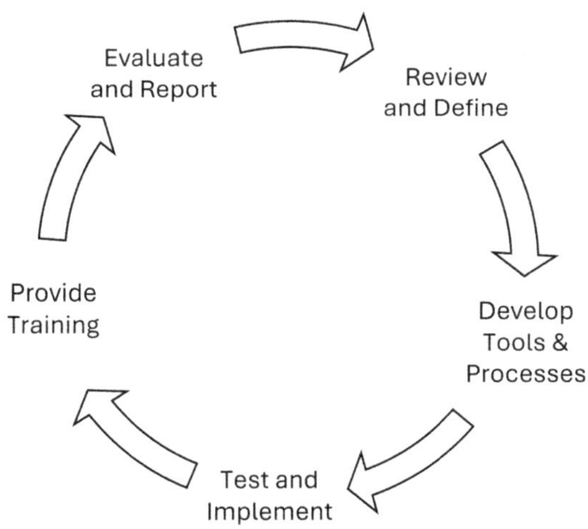

Figure 1.3 Continuous monitoring and improvement process.

🎯 Pro Tips

- Leverage from industry recognized standards and best practices, such as the Information Security Continuous Monitoring (ISCM) for Federal Information Systems and Organizations (NIST, 2011).
- Leverage agile concepts and AI tools for risk assessment, continuous monitoring, and audit execution to significantly enhance efficiency, accuracy, and value. These concepts are explored in depth in Chapter 4 – Agility in Action: Rethinking Cybersecurity Audit and Chapter 5 – Harnessing Artificial Intelligence: Enhancing Cybersecurity Audits through Automation and Insight.

1.5.4 Internal consulting engagements

Internal consulting engagements provide an opportunity for internal auditors to leverage their expertise beyond traditional assurance roles by offering **advisory services** that enhance risk management, internal controls, and governance processes. These engagements focus on **proactive collaboration** with management to identify potential risks, improve operational efficiency, and strengthen cybersecurity measures without compromising audit independence. Unlike assurance audits, which evaluate compliance with established standards, internal consulting engagements emphasize **value-added insights** and recommendations that help organizations achieve strategic objectives. By aligning their knowledge of controls, processes, and emerging technologies with business goals, auditors can offer meaningful guidance to support informed decision-making and strengthen the overall control environment.

> ⚠ **Caution:** Cybersecurity audit professionals involved in internal consulting engagements should not perform an audit in the same area. This practice will ensure meeting the independence audit standard.

Below is a structured breakdown of cybersecurity internal consulting engagements, grouped by **Objective, Key Activities**, and **Output** to ensure a clear understanding of each phase.

1. **Define Scope and Engagement Parameters**

> **Objective:** Defining the audit scope and engagement parameters ensures a clear understanding of what will be reviewed, aligning the audit's focus with organizational risks, priorities, and objectives. It also establishes boundaries, expectations, and resource needs, promoting efficiency, accountability, and compliance with professional standards.

Key Activities

- Identify business goals and cybersecurity objectives.
- Determine the scope of the internal consulting engagement, focusing on high-risk areas (e.g., network security, identity management, cloud security).
- Engage key stakeholders Chief Information Officer (CIO), Chief Information Security Officer (CISO), and Information Technology (IT) teams to define expectations.
- Establish timelines and resource requirements.

Output

- Scope definition document outlining cybersecurity focus areas.
- Agreed-upon timeline, resources, and deliverables.

2. Assess Current Cybersecurity Posture

Objective: Defining the audit scope and engagement parameters ensures a clear understanding of what will be reviewed, aligning the audit's focus with organizational risks, priorities, and objectives. It also establishes boundaries, expectations, and resource needs, promoting efficiency, accountability, and compliance with professional standards.

Key Activities

- Conduct a cybersecurity maturity assessment using established frameworks (e.g., NIST CSF, ISO 27001, CIS Controls).
- Perform gap analysis to identify weaknesses in security controls.
- Evaluate incident response plans, security monitoring processes, and data protection practices.
- Assess compliance with relevant regulations and industry standards (e.g., General Data Protection Regulation (GDPR), Cybersecurity Maturity Model Certification (CMMC), PCI DSS).

Output

- Cybersecurity assessment report identifying gaps, risks, and areas for improvement.
- Maturity level scoring aligned with the chosen framework.

3. Analyze Risks and Identify Control Enhancements

Objective: The objective of analyzing risk and identifying control enhancements is to understand potential threats and vulnerabilities that could impact organizational objectives. This process enables the development of targeted improvements to strengthen controls, reduce risk exposure, and enhance operational resilience.

Key Activities

- Map identified risks to cybersecurity domains and business processes.
- Prioritize risks based on likelihood, impact, and organization's risk appetite.
- Recommend technical and procedural controls to mitigate high-risk vulnerabilities.
- Collaborate with business units to align security controls with business goals.

Output

- Risk analysis matrix with prioritized risks and suggested control enhancements.
- Recommended security controls aligned with industry best practices.

4. Develop and Communicate Actionable Recommendations

Objective: The objective of developing and communicating actionable recommendations is to provide clear, practical steps that address identified risks and control deficiencies. This ensures that stakeholders can implement meaningful improvements that enhance compliance, strengthen operations, and support organizational goals.

Key Activities

- Develop detailed remediation plans with timelines and resource estimates.
- Provide guidance on security control implementation and optimization.
- Share emerging cybersecurity trends and innovative technologies for future consideration.
- Conduct knowledge transfer sessions to enhance cybersecurity awareness.

Output

- Actionable recommendations and roadmap for control improvements.
- Knowledge transfer materials and cybersecurity awareness documentation.

5. Monitor Progress and Provide Ongoing Advisory

Objective: Monitoring progress ensures that audit recommendations are implemented effectively, and corrective actions are tracked to closure. Providing ongoing advisory support helps organizations adapt to emerging risks, strengthen internal controls, and continuously improve their risk management practices.

Key Activities

- Establish mechanisms to track implementation progress.
- Conduct periodic follow-ups to assess remediation effectiveness.
- Provide advisory on emerging threats, changes in regulations, and evolving cybersecurity technologies.
- Refine cybersecurity strategy based on continuous monitoring outcomes.

Output

- Progress reports with status updates on control implementation.
- Ongoing advisory and updated cybersecurity strategy recommendations.

6. Evaluate Internal Consulting Engagement Effectiveness

Objective: Evaluating internal consulting engagement effectiveness is to determine whether the engagement met its intended goals, delivered value, and supported decision-making within the organization. This evaluation also helps identify lessons learned and opportunities to enhance the quality and impact of future internal consulting activities.

Key Activities

- Obtain feedback from stakeholders on the effectiveness of the engagement.
- Assess whether recommended controls have reduced identified risks.
- Identify lessons learned to enhance future internal consulting engagements.

Output

- Post-engagement review report with performance metrics.
- Lessons-learned documents to refine future internal consulting processes.

This structured approach ensures that cybersecurity internal consulting engagements deliver **actionable insights, risk reduction, and value-added recommendations** while maintaining alignment with organizational objectives.

Tips for a successful internal cybersecurity consulting engagement

Here are some tips to help ensure that your cybersecurity internal consulting engagements are effective, valuable, and aligned with organizational goals:

1. **Understand the Business Context**
   Tip: Before diving into technical details, take the time to understand the business objectives and strategic goals. This ensures that your cybersecurity recommendations are aligned with the organization's needs.
   Action: Ask questions like: "What are the company's key priorities?" or "How does cybersecurity support the broader business strategy?"

2. **Engage Stakeholders Early and Often**
   Tip: Building strong relationships with key stakeholders (e.g., CISO, IT leadership, business unit heads) from the start is critical for success.
   Action: Schedule initial discovery meetings, maintain open communication, and ask for feedback throughout the engagement to ensure alignment and buy-in.

3. **Tailor Recommendations to the Organization's Risk Appetite**
   💡 **Tip:** Cybersecurity solutions should be customized to fit the organization's risk tolerance, size, and industry-specific requirements.
   👉 **Action:** Use a risk assessment to guide your recommendations, focusing on controls that are both practical and effective within the organization's environment.

4. **Be Proactive, Not Just Reactive**
   💡 **Tip:** Cybersecurity is ever evolving, so it's important to provide solutions that are forward-thinking and adaptable to emerging threats.
   👉 **Action:** Incorporate emerging technologies (like AI, machine learning (ML), and threat intelligence platforms) into your recommendations to prepare the organization for future threats.

5. **Focus on Actionable, Measurable Outcomes**
   💡 **Tip:** Avoid theoretical advice. Instead, provide practical, measurable recommendations that can be tracked for progress.
   👉 **Action:** Use clear metrics (e.g., risk reduction percentage, number of vulnerabilities mitigated) to measure the effectiveness of your recommendations.

6. **Ensure Effective Communication**
   💡 **Tip:** Tailor your communication style based on your audience (technical teams vs. executive leadership). Focus on translating technical jargon into language that aligns with the business's priorities.
   👉 **Action:** Use visual aids, such as risk matrices, dashboards, and charts, to help convey complex information in a simple and impactful way.

7. **Promote a Collaborative, Team-Oriented Approach**
   💡 **Tip:** Cybersecurity is a team effort that requires input from various departments. Work closely with IT, legal, compliance, and HR teams to ensure that the cybersecurity strategy is holistic and well integrated across the organization.
   👉 **Action:** Encourage brainstorming sessions, cross-departmental workshops, and knowledge-sharing to foster collaboration.

8. **Document, Document, Document**
   💡 **Tip:** Thorough documentation not only helps in keeping track of the engagement but also provides clarity on the recommendations, implementation steps, and progress.
   👉 **Action:** Ensure that all deliverables (reports, frameworks, risk matrices) are clearly documented and accessible to stakeholders for future reference.

9. **Emphasize the Importance of Cybersecurity Culture**
   💡 **Tip:** Cybersecurity is not just about technology; it's also about **culture and tone at the top**. Helping the organization cultivate a culture of cybersecurity can have a long-term impact on its security posture.
   👉 **Action:** Recommend employee training, awareness programs, and leadership involvement to promote a proactive cybersecurity mindset across the organization.

10. **Be Prepared to Provide Post-Engagement Support**
    💡 **Tip:** The end of the internal consulting engagement does not mean the end of your involvement. Be ready to offer continued support and monitor progress after implementation.
    ☝ **Action:** Propose ongoing advisory services or periodic check-ins to track how well your recommendations have been implemented and to adjust the approach as necessary.

🛠 **Important Note:** By following the above, you will increase the likelihood of your cybersecurity internal consulting engagements adding significant value to the organization, while helping them stay secure and resilient against evolving threats.

1.6 REAL-WORLD LESSONS

This section describes case studies from independent research and analysis, sharing the background on how certain audit practices inspired this book. One observation is a direct correlation between a firm's size and culture, which often influences the complexity of audit processes. A second observation was that some complexity appeared to stem from overly prescriptive audit department requirements. And a third observation was if a firm was in business for several decades resulting in a hesitancy to change.

AI tools, such as OpenAI Chat Generative Pre-Trained Transformer (ChatGPT), were not available or encouraged at any of the firms discussed. Had these tools been available, the auditors would have been more creative and innovative, enhancing audit practices. Chapter 4 – Agility in Action: Rethinking Cybersecurity Audit and Chapter 5 – Harnessing Artificial Intelligence: Enhancing Cybersecurity Audits through Automation and Insight will explore how AI and ML can automate tasks, detect anomalies, and enhance audit efficiency and quality. This, in turn, will transform the cybersecurity audit function into a more proactive, data-driven, and value-focused discipline.

As previously mentioned, the following real-world examples were selected based on personal research, with an emphasis on diversity in organizational culture and size. Each example presents key positive and negative insights designed to inspire critical thinking about how these firms may compare to your own organization. Additionally, a few Generative AI prompt examples are included for each firm to encourage further exploration and analysis, continuing a critical thinking approach.

1.6.1 Firm A

These learnings begin with a firm that was ahead of their time in innovation, noting that this observation occurred prior to 2005. Without realizing it, the firm naturally embraced auditing with agility by fostering a collaborative and innovative culture. The firm's culture mirrored that of innovative technology companies like Google, likely due to its employee population being under the age of 35. With approximately six thousand (6,000) employees across multiple international locations, the culture was deemed similar to Google because of:

- A game room with pool and ping pong tables.
- Informal gatherings where employees discussed innovative ideas for the firm's website functionality.
- A fire pole connecting the second and first floors at the main headquarters.
- The President and Chief Executive Officer (CEO), who did not have offices. Instead they worked from cubicles like all employees, mingled frequently, and participated in brainstorming sessions.
- The IA team, viewed as trusted business partners, actively participated in brainstorming and strategy meetings, often offering insights on risks and controls.
- A centralized audit function of about 15 individuals, each assigned as business partners to specific work areas. The audit methodology was distilled into a concise five-page document, covering key requirements while allowing for creative and agile audit approaches.
- The firm-maintained compliance with audit standards while allowing flexibility, an advantage often found in smaller audit departments.
- Notably, all audits passed regulatory examinations conducted by banking authorities.

Key Positive Insights

- Encouraged transparency and open communication with the IA team.
- Allowed internal auditors to be creative and innovative, resulting in value-added work, reduced turnover, and increased internal transfers.
- Simplified audit methodology, leading to quicker audit execution.
- Maintained independence while partnering effectively with business associates.
- Brainstorming sessions ensured diverse perspectives and deeper understanding of business processes.

! *Key Negative Takeaways*

- Prioritization of management requests was required due to insufficient audit staffing, limiting the capacity to meet all special project requests. Prioritization was achieved by first-come-first-serve in addition to focusing on higher-risk activities.

Generative AI Examples

These Generative AI examples offer valuable inspiration for crafting prompts that help identify cybersecurity audit priorities. While the AI-generated output can surface new insights, it's essential for cybersecurity professionals to critically evaluate the results. The primary objective is to uncover novel information that can inform and enhance audit activities.

⚠ **Caution:** Confirm that the Generative AI tool is secure and approved by audit management before executing prompts.

- Prompt: "*Describe the best mechanism to prioritize management requests. Include risk-based approach.*"
- Prompt: "*Describe how to determine if an open audit should be postponed based on a management request that is high risk.*"

1.6.2 Firm B

This next firm was much smaller, with only 250 employees and five audit staff members. There was a lack of in-depth audit experience, which encouraged the audit team to research and take the lead in shaping audit practices. While this autonomy allowed for greater innovation, it also required the team to ensure adherence to audit standards without the benefit of internal expertise. External networking was required to identify best practices, which provided a diversity of approaches and provided a benchmarking mechanism.

One memorable experience involved participating in system testing during the firm's migration from a mainframe to AS400 systems, evaluating the process from a risk and control perspective. Another advantage of working in a smaller firm was the ability to generate queries directly from the AS400 system. For those unfamiliar with IBM's AS400, the operating system contains hundreds of useful commands, including "DSP" (display) commands that provide flexible output and data selection options (Integrative Systems, 2025). This functionality allowed for targeted reviews, such as identifying mortgage loans with interest rates outside a specified range, which enhanced the efficiency of control testing.

Key Positive Insights: AS400 queries used for cybersecurity audit control testing were often requested by management to be included in their reporting queue, providing value-added information.

- Encouraging internal auditors to be creative and innovative resulted in value-added work, reduced turnover, and increased internal position transfers.
- IA maintained independence while effectively partnering with business associates.

- Brainstorming sessions with business associates ensured diverse perspectives and a full understanding of business areas.

! Key Negative Takeaways

- Due to the firm's small size, audit work became repetitive, prompting a need for continuous learning and external networking.

Generative AI Examples

These Generative AI examples offer valuable inspiration for crafting prompts that help identify cybersecurity audit priorities. While the AI-generated output can surface new insights, it's essential for cybersecurity professionals to critically evaluate the results. The primary objective is to uncover novel information that can inform and enhance audit activities.

⚠ **Caution:** Confirm that the Generative AI tool is secure and approved by audit management before executing prompts.

- Prompt: "*The current audit approach is to repeat the same audit steps from the previous audit. Describe an approach to encourage audit leadership to revise audit scopes.*"
- Prompt: "*Describe the best cybersecurity audit networking opportunities.*"
- Prompt: "*Describe the best approach to encourage brainstorming sessions in a professional networking environment.*"

1.6.3 Firm C

This final firm is an international financial services firm with over 100 years of history. The culture was highly structured and conservative, vastly different from Firm A. Unlike Firm A, audit teams were spread across multiple international locations, and cybersecurity domains were assigned to individuals with minimal change year-over-year. While this structure provided stability, it also limited opportunities for cross-domain collaboration and knowledge-sharing. Moreover, the audit methodology document was over 100 pages and often left to interpretation.

Key Positive Takeaways

- The firm's large size provided many opportunities to gain experience in several cybersecurity domains.
- The diversity of cybersecurity exposure enabled auditors to develop deep cybersecurity technical expertise in assigned domains.

! *Key Negative Takeaways*

- The audit methodology was highly complex, often emphasizing form over substance, leading to quality assurance and regulatory concerns.
- Time pressures prevented effective information sharing across cybersecurity and other audit groups, limiting collaboration.
- The structured environment left little room for creativity or innovation, contributing to low morale and high turnover.
- Access to data was limited to a centralized audit query tool, preventing individual auditors from generating unique queries and creatively exploring data.
- Fixed audit timelines and significant administrative requirements restricted the number of controls tested, reducing the potential for providing value-added insights. Employees were evaluated primarily on meeting deadlines, with criticism for even minor delays.

Generative AI Examples

These Generative AI examples offer valuable inspiration for crafting prompts that help identify cybersecurity audit priorities. While the AI-generated output can surface new insights, it's essential for cybersecurity professionals to critically evaluate the results. The primary objective is to uncover novel information that can inform and enhance audit activities.

⚠ **Caution:** Confirm that the Generative AI tool is secure and approved by audit management before executing prompts.

- Prompt: "*Describe techniques to encourage audit leaders to simplify the audit methodology.*"
- Prompt: "*Considering audit time is restrictive, describe techniques for encouraging information sharing.*"
- Prompt: "*Provide suggestions on how to convince audit leadership to extend an audit timeline. Consider the risk environment and relationship with audit testing.*"
- Prompt: "*Provide ideas on how to convince management that data can be secured when using Generative AI.*"

1.6.4 Inspiration for future innovation

Firm C's audit culture inspired me to think more deeply about auditing with agility and incorporating AI tools to enhance audit effectiveness. The reliance on manual processes not only slowed down audit execution but also reduced agility, limiting the team's ability to quickly adapt to emerging threats and regulatory changes. These experiences highlighted how automated solutions and AI-driven insights could improve audit quality by enabling auditors to focus on high-value tasks.

In addition, as cybersecurity threats continue to evolve, it became clear that cybersecurity auditors must leverage the same AI tools employed by both cybersecurity professionals and cybercriminals. Incorporating AI into audit practices can enhance the ability to predict, detect, and respond to threats, ensuring that audit methodologies remain adaptive and resilient. These reflections reinforced my belief that transforming audit methodologies using AI and agile approaches is essential to maintaining relevance and effectiveness in today's dynamic cybersecurity environment.

> 🛠 **Important Note:** These inspiration for future innovation ideas will be further explored in Chapter 4 –Agility in Action: Rethinking Cybersecurity Audit and Chapter 5 – Harnessing Artificial Intelligence: Enhancing Cybersecurity Audits through Automation and Insight.

1.7 AUDIT COMPLEXITY AND CHALLENGES (OPPORTUNITIES) EXPLAINED

The audit processes can be complex due to numerous factors that influence design, execution, and reporting, including degrees of difficulty and intricacy. In your role as a cybersecurity control assessor, you encounter many of these complexities. Several factors contribute to this complexity, influencing the effort, expertise, and time required to conduct a thorough and accurate assessment. You may identify other complexities and challenges, consider writing those down and thinking about those ideas when you read Chapter 4 –Agility in Action: Rethinking Cybersecurity Audit and Chapter 5 – Harnessing Artificial Intelligence: Enhancing Cybersecurity Audits through Automation and Insight. Let us break down complexities into key elements.

1. **Audit Methodology:** The audit methodology is long with a significant amount of data for all audit process requirements. There can also be multiple changes occurring throughout the year without considering work in progress. This can result in increased administrative hours.
2. **Audit Management:** Audit team members may be working on more than one audit activity in a single day. While multi-tasking is a common practice, it diverts an individual's attention, reducing efficiencies, decreased productivity, increased stress, and higher risk of errors and can "tax the brain" (Davis, 2023)
3. **Time Constraints:** Tight deadlines or limited resources can heighten complexity, forcing auditors to prioritize certain areas or streamline procedures while still ensuring accuracy and thoroughness.

4. **Organizational Size and Structure:** Larger organizations with complex hierarchies, multiple locations, and diverse operations tend to have more intricate audit requirements. Understanding and assessing numerous business units or subsidiaries adds layers of complexity.
5. **Regulatory and Compliance Requirements:** Audits involving strict regulatory frameworks (like NIST, FISMA, or Health Insurance Portability and Accountability Act (HIPAA)) require deep knowledge of applicable laws and standards. Frequent updates to these regulations add another layer of difficulty.
6. **Technology and System Architecture:** In modern audits, especially security and IT audits, complex system architectures, cloud environments, and hybrid infrastructures demand specialized expertise to properly assess security controls, configurations, and data flows.
7. **Control Environment:** The number and nature of internal controls, their interdependencies, and how well they are documented and implemented affect complexity. Weak or poorly defined controls can make the audit more challenging.
8. **Data Volume and Quality:** Auditors need to sift through large datasets, logs, or records to validate compliance. If data is inconsistent, incomplete, or poorly organized, the audit becomes more time intensive.
9. **Diversity of Audit Types:** There are multiple audit types: financial, operational, IT/cybersecurity, and compliance. The complexity also arises from the need for specialized knowledge in each audit type, integration of findings across diverse audit areas, balancing multiple objectives across various audit disciplines, lack of communication across all groups resulting in duplicating or missing significant risk areas.
10. **Scope of Different Audit Frameworks:** Different audit frameworks (e.g., Committee of Sponsoring Organizations of the Treadway Commission (COSO), Control Objectives for Information and Related Technologies (COBIT), ISO 27001, GAO Yellow Book) provide unique standards and guidelines for different types of audits and a unique focus. Understanding how these frameworks interrelate, and applying them correctly across different contexts, can be challenging. In addition, audit frameworks are often influenced by evolving regulatory requirements. Keeping up with changes in industry standards, government regulations, and legal requirements can add complexity, especially when different audits must adhere to different sets of guidelines.
11. **Global and Cross-Functional Considerations:** In multinational organizations, audits may need to account for regional regulatory variations, diverse cultural expectations, and differing legal standards. Coordinating audits across multiple regions or jurisdictions adds a layer of complexity, particularly when audit frameworks need to be applied in varying regulatory environments. Audit teams are often composed of diverse individuals, including financial auditors, IT specialists, and compliance experts. Managing such a multi-disciplinary team requires

balancing different skill sets, backgrounds, and perspectives to ensure the audit is comprehensive and effective.

12. **Involvement of Multiple Stakeholders**
    - **Diverse Interests:** Audits often involve multiple stakeholders, including senior management, business unit leaders, auditors, regulatory bodies, and sometimes external auditors. Each stakeholder may have different objectives and expectations from the audit, which can create challenges in aligning the scope and focus of the audit.
    - **Communication Challenges:** Keeping all stakeholders informed and managing their input effectively requires strong communication and coordination. Differing priorities can lead to conflicts or delays if expectations are not well-managed.
    - **Impact of Findings:** Audit findings can have significant consequences for various departments, affecting operations, strategy, and regulatory compliance. Balancing these interests can add complexity, especially when audit recommendations require changes in business processes or systems.

Navigating these complexities requires strong coordination, effective communication, and a deep understanding of both organizational objectives and technical standards. The successful execution of audits, especially in highly regulated or multifaceted environments like cybersecurity, relies on integrating diverse expertise while managing expectations and aligning with the organization's broader strategic goals.

🛠 **Important Note:** As observed in the real-world lessons section, culture can play a role in complexity, but that topic is excluded from this chapter because it is explored in Chapter 3 – How to Influence Behaviors and Culture.

🎯 **Pro Tips**

- Develop a list of all manual tasks related to audit data collection, risk assessment, control testing, and reporting that could be turned into AI opportunities. By automating these tasks, audit teams can reduce errors, increase efficiency, and focus on delivering higher-value insights. Regularly update this list as AI technologies and audit requirements evolve.
- Develop a list of and prioritize the complexities and challenges, focusing on those that will yield higher-quality automation.

1.8 RELEVANCE TO CYBERSECURITY AUDITING

Cybersecurity auditing is a specialized subset of internal auditing that focuses on evaluating an organization's information security posture, identifying vulnerabilities, and ensuring compliance with applicable security laws, regulations, and standards. While cybersecurity auditing has unique technical requirements, it aligns closely with established **audit standards** that provide a framework for ensuring consistent, high-quality audit practices.

Below is an overview of how key **audit standards** align with cybersecurity auditing:

1. **The IIA Global Internal Audit Standards**
   The **IIA Standards** (formerly the International Professional Practices Framework (IPPF)) provide a globally recognized framework that guides internal auditors on best practices, principles, and ethical standards (IIA, 2024b).
   Alignment with Cybersecurity Auditing
   - **Standard 2100 – Nature of Work:** IA/OIG should evaluate and contribute to the improvement of governance, risk management, and control processes. Cybersecurity audits align with this standard by assessing how well an organization's security controls mitigate cyber risks.
   - **Standard 2200 – Engagement Planning:** Cybersecurity audits require a risk-based approach to define scope, identify high-risk systems, and evaluate critical assets, aligning with IIA's emphasis on risk-based auditing.
   - **Standard 2410 – Criteria for Communicating Results:** Cybersecurity audit findings must be communicated with clarity and precision, including identifying high-risk vulnerabilities, which mirrors the IIA's emphasis on clear, actionable reporting.

   Cybersecurity Use Case
   - Assessing the effectiveness of an organization's **incident response** and **vulnerability management** processes ensures compliance with Standard 2100.
   - Risk-based scoping in cybersecurity audits (penetration testing or vulnerability assessments) aligns with Standard 2200.

2. **ISACA COBIT Framework**
   The **COBIT** framework, developed by ISACA, provides best practices for IT governance, management, and control (ISACA, 2018).
   Alignment with Cybersecurity Auditing
   - **Domain APO12 – Manage Risk:** Evaluates IT-related risk, including cybersecurity threats, ensuring alignment with an organization's risk tolerance.
   - **Domain DSS05 – Manage Security Services:** Covers cybersecurity practices such as access management, threat detection, and incident response, which align with cybersecurity audit objectives.
   - **Domain MEA03 – Monitor, Evaluate, and Assess Compliance:** Ensures that cybersecurity controls align with compliance requirements and organizational policies.

Cybersecurity Use Case

- Performing a cybersecurity gap assessment to evaluate whether an organization's cybersecurity controls align with COBIT domains.
- Reviewing IT governance processes to ensure cybersecurity risks are managed effectively and align with APO12.

3. **Government Auditing Standards (GAO Yellow Book)**
   The **Yellow Book** (Generally Accepted Government Auditing Standards (GAGAS)) issued by the U. S. Government Accountability Office (GAO) sets standards for government audits, including performance, financial, and IT audits (U. S. GAO, 2024).

   Alignment with Cybersecurity Auditing

   - **Standard 6.06 – Risk Assessment and Planning:** Cybersecurity audits assess risks associated with data confidentiality, integrity, and availability, aligning with the Yellow Book's emphasis on risk-based planning.
   - **Standard 8.27 – Criteria for Evidence:** Cybersecurity audits generate evidence through testing, system logs, and penetration testing results, aligning with the requirement for sufficient, appropriate evidence.
   - **Standard 9.30 – Reporting Findings:** Reporting cybersecurity vulnerabilities, control weaknesses, and compliance gaps align with Yellow Book reporting requirements.

   Cybersecurity Use Case

   - Conducting an audit of a federal agency's compliance with **FISMA** regulations while adhering to GAGAS standards.
   - Evaluating the effectiveness of **continuous monitoring programs** to ensure alignment with Yellow Book's performance audit criteria.

4. **NIST CSF**
   Though not a formal audit standard, the **NIST CSF** is widely used as a benchmark for evaluating cybersecurity practices (NIST, 2025.b.).

   Alignment with Cybersecurity Auditing

   - **Identify (ID):** Evaluates asset management, risk management, and third-party service provider security.
   - **Protect (PR):** Assesses access controls, awareness training, and data security measures.
   - Detect (DE): Reviews continuous monitoring and incident detection capabilities.
   - **Respond (RS):** Evaluates incident response planning and communication protocols.
   - **Recover (RC):** Examines resilience and recovery processes after a cybersecurity event.

   Cybersecurity Use Case

   - Mapping cybersecurity audit procedures to the NIST CSF to ensure an organization's security posture meets industry standards.

- Performing a gap analysis against the NIST CSF to assess the maturity of security controls and identify improvement areas.

5. **ISO/IEC 27001 – Information Security Management System (ISMS)**
The **ISO 27001** standard specifies requirements for establishing, implementing, maintaining, and continually improving an ISMS (ISO, 2022).
🔄 **Alignment with Cybersecurity Auditing**
    - **Clause 6 – Planning:** Cybersecurity audits align with risk assessment and treatment plans defined in ISO 27001.
    - **Clause 9 – Performance Evaluation:** Audits assess ongoing security performance and evaluate key metrics.
    - **Clause 10 – Improvement:** Cybersecurity audit findings can drive continuous improvement in ISMS controls.

    🔐 **Cybersecurity Use Case**
    - Conducting an ISO 27001 compliance audit to evaluate the effectiveness of an organization's information security program.
    - Assessing the implementation of corrective actions after a cybersecurity breach in alignment with ISO 27001 Clause 10.

Table 1.2 describes the auditing standard elements relevant to cybersecurity auditing, which complements the other auditing standards previously mentioned in this chapter. As shown in the table, while each standard varies in presentation and terminology, there are common cybersecurity auditing activities.

Table 1.2 How audit standards align with cybersecurity auditing

Audit standard	*Key alignment with cybersecurity auditing*
IIA Global Standards (Institute of Internal Auditors, 2024a)	Governance, risk management, control testing, and communication
ISACA COBIT (ISACA, 2020)	IT governance, risk management, and security services
GAO Yellow Book (GAGAS) (U. S. GAO, 2024)	Risk assessment, evidence gathering, and reporting
NIST CSF (NIST, 2025.b.)	Cybersecurity posture assessment and continuous monitoring
ISO/IEC 27001 (ISO/IEC, 2022)	ISMS compliance, performance evaluation, and continuous improvement

🛠 **Important Note:** Integrating AI-driven tools into cybersecurity audits enhances efficiency by automating control testing, expediently identifying anomalies, and enabling continuous monitoring – further aligning with audit standards and promoting agile audit practices.

1.9 FUTURE OF CYBERSECURITY AUDITING

As AI continues to revolutionize the auditing landscape, it brings both **unprecedented opportunities** and **emerging risks**. AI-driven tools can enhance audit efficiency, automate repetitive tasks, and improve risk detection through advanced analytics. However, these advancements also introduce challenges, such as **data privacy concerns, model bias, intellectual property, unclear legal regulation, and a lack of transparency in decision-making processes**. Auditors must balance the potential of AI with a vigilant approach to identifying and mitigating associated risks. Looking ahead, the future of AI in auditing promises continuous innovation, but success will depend on establishing governance frameworks that ensure AI solutions align with regulatory standards and ethical principles. This section explores the critical risks of AI adoption in audits while providing insights into how future advancements may shape the audit profession.

> 🛠 **Important Note:** Humans will continue to be an important element of creating and employing AI tools. AI is not yet mature and learning as individuals use these tools and refresh the ML training dataset. Subject matter experts will be required to apply critical thinking. Critical thinking is defined as analyzing data or problems to arrive at the best solution. It can also be defined as synthesizing and paraphrasing information from multiple sources (Johnston & Pollock, 2023). The AI output requires analysis and evaluation to ensure integrity. As one example, I created a prompt to create a CISSP certificate image, and the word "certificate" was misspelled. Minor grammatical errors have also been identified.

Below are key trends and opportunities as identified by various authoritative sources.

1. **Enhanced Risk Assessment and Predictive Analytics**
   Future Impact
   - AI models will shift from traditional, reactive risk assessments to **proactive, predictive analysis** that identifies emerging threats before they materialize.
   - Advanced algorithms will analyze historical data, identify anomalies, and predict high-risk areas for auditors to focus on during audit activities.

   💼 **Opportunities for Auditors (Dennis, 2024)**
   - Use AI to develop **continuous risk monitoring frameworks.**
   - Leverage ML models to assess evolving cybersecurity threats and financial risks.
2. **Automated Audit Planning and Scoping**
   Future Impact
   - AI will automate **audit planning and scoping** by analyzing large datasets to identify high-risk areas and determine optimal resource allocation.

- Natural language processing (NLP) will assist in analyzing regulatory changes and aligning audit plans accordingly.

Opportunities for Auditors (Thomson Reuters Tax and Accounting, 2024)
- Save time by using AI to **automatically prioritize high-risk areas.**
- Incorporate NLP to continuously update audit plans based on changing regulatory requirements.

3. **AI-Driven Control Testing and Exception Analysis**

Future Impact
- AI will automate **control testing** through robotic process automation (RPA) and continuous control monitoring (CCM).
- Exception analysis will become more refined, reducing false positives and focusing audit efforts on genuine anomalies.

Opportunities for Auditors (TeamMate, 2024)
- Implement AI-powered tools to perform **real-time control testing.**
- Leverage AI for dynamic exception handling, improving audit quality and efficiency.

4. **NLP Understanding for Compliance Audits**

Future Impact
- AI-powered NLP will analyze regulatory documents, contracts, and policies to ensure compliance across various audit types.
- NLP models will identify inconsistencies, potential control gaps, and areas of non-compliance more effectively.

Opportunities for Auditors (IBM, 2024)
- Use AI to **automate regulatory compliance checks.**
- Integrate NLP to review and assess complex contracts and regulatory frameworks.

5. **Continuous Auditing and Real-Time Assurance**

Future Impact
- Auditors will transition from periodic audits to continuous auditing models powered by AI and data analytics.
- Real-time dashboards will provide auditors with ongoing insights into risk areas and control effectiveness.

Opportunities for Auditors (Darley, 2025)
- Deploy AI to develop **continuous auditing platforms** that provide real-time alerts and assurance.
- Enhance audit agility by identifying and addressing risks in near real time.

6. **AI-Powered Fraud Detection and Anomaly Detection**

Future Impact
- AI will improve **fraud detection capabilities** by analyzing vast amounts of structured and unstructured data to identify patterns that might indicate fraud.
- Deep learning models will refine anomaly detection processes, reducing false positives.

Opportunities for Auditors (Darley, 2025)
- Leverage AI to implement **fraud risk models** that continuously scan financial and operational data.
- Utilize AI to enhance fraud investigations and anomaly identification.

7. **Data Visualization and AI-Enhanced Reporting**

Future Impact
- AI will generate **dynamic, interactive audit reports** with actionable insights.
- Advanced data visualization tools will enable auditors to communicate findings more effectively with stakeholders.

Opportunities for Auditors (Pradeep, 2025)
- Use AI to create **customized dashboards** that provide stakeholders with real-time insights.
- Enhance audit communication through AI-generated reports that summarize key findings.

8. **AI Governance and Ethical AI Frameworks**

Future Impact
- The future of AI in auditing will require auditors to establish **ethical AI governance frameworks** that ensure fairness, transparency, and compliance.
- AI auditing frameworks will be essential to assess the ethical and operational implications of AI models.

Opportunities for Auditors (Nguyen & McKeown, 2024)
- Evaluate or develop AI governance policies that ensure **bias-free and transparent AI decision-making.**
- Participate in AI model audits to ensure compliance with regulatory standards and organizational policies.

9. **The Role of Auditors in an AI-Driven Future**
   - **Strategic Advisors:** Auditors will transition into **strategic advisory roles,** providing insights on AI governance, cybersecurity, and data privacy.
   - **AI Model Validators:** Auditors will provide assurance that AI models used in business operations are reliable, ethical, and aligned with organizational goals.

By embracing AI opportunities, auditors can enhance their effectiveness, provide greater value to stakeholders, and remain at the forefront of innovation in the rapidly evolving audit landscape.

> **Important Note:** While AI may often receive criticism due to potential risks and ethical concerns, it also offers numerous advantages that auditors should not overlook. To maximize its benefits, auditors should assess the associated risks and implement appropriate controls. As the cybersecurity threat landscape evolves, embracing AI will be essential to maintain high-quality audit work while ensuring timely and effective responses to emerging threats.

1.10 SUMMARY

This chapter focused on how internal and external audit plays a critical role in ensuring organizational resilience by evaluating processes, systems, and controls through established audit concepts and standards. First, the audit standards included the IIA Global Internal Audit Standards, ISACA frameworks, and the GAO Yellow Book. Beyond compliance, IA/OIG adds value by offering risk insights, process improvements, and strategic advice while maintaining independence. Second, the audit role spans planning, execution, continuous monitoring, and internal consulting, making it complex due to the involvement of multiple stakeholders, diverse audit types (financial, operational, IT, and compliance), and adherence to various frameworks. Third, as cybersecurity threats continue to evolve, the relevance of cybersecurity auditing grows, requiring auditors to assess and strengthen cyber controls, identify emerging threats, and align audits with dynamic risk environments. Fourth, looking ahead, the future of cybersecurity auditing will increasingly leverage AI to enhance efficiency, automate manual processes, and provide real-time risk insights, empowering auditors to perform high-quality work with speed and agility in a rapidly changing threat landscape.

Let's continue the cybersecurity audit journey by discussing partnerships in Chapter 2 – Building Partnerships for Success.

Chapter 2

Building partnerships for success

2.1 LEARNING OBJECTIVES

By the end of this chapter, readers will be able to:

1. **Define 3LoD** roles and responsibilities.
2. **Identify techniques for streamlining** risk assessments and ensuring consistency across the organization or government entity.
3. **Understand how to build partnerships** without jeopardizing audit independence.

2.2 OPENING INSIGHTS

The Three Lines of Defense (3LoD) model was formally introduced by the Institute of Internal Audit (IIA) in 2013 (Amblard-Ladurantie, 2023). The objective was to provide a consistent model across all internal audit (IA) and Office of Inspector General (OIG) programs. While IIA is often perceived as the prominent authoritative source across public and private sector, the 3LoD model was introduced in the financial services sector in late 1990s/early 2000s (Coppini & Moreira, 2024). Financial services firms adopted and implemented this structure in the early 2000s, with more robust requirements after the 2008 financial crisis. Previously, there were many risk functions, such as model and asset/liability risk management, but not a complete operational risk management function that included cybersecurity. Moreover, the existing risk management functions had different risk management frameworks (RMFs), preventing an aggregation of consistently rated information into an enterprise risk management (ERM) report. While there are varying 3LoD models, all provide a separation of duties.

In addition to frameworks, More (2022) provides a clear and concise 3LoD description:

- First Line of Defense (1LoD) owns the risks and controls and applies the framework as created by the second line of defense (2LoD).

DOI: 10.1201/9781003640301-3

- 2LoD owns the RMF (governance) and provides oversight to ensure compliance with that framework.
- 3LoD owns an independent assessment of the 1LoD and 2LoD risk management governance and execution.

Switching from the historical perspective, we can all agree that in today's complex regulatory environment, organizations and government entities must adopt a robust RMF that incorporates the **3LoD** to ensure effective governance and compliance. Streamlining **risk assessments** across business units helps identify, evaluate, and mitigate potential threats more efficiently, reducing redundancies and enhancing decision-making. **Building strong partnerships** across the three lines fosters collaboration, enhances communication, and ensures that risk management responsibilities are clearly defined and aligned with organizational objectives. At the same time, **maintaining audit independence** is essential to provide an objective evaluation of internal controls, ensuring the integrity and reliability of risk management processes.

Let's begin by expanding the brief 3LoD model information noted in the previous paragraphs. After describing the details of those three lines, we will delve into how each group can leverage from each other. This is intended to be a theoretical and conceptual approach with technical aspects provided in Chapters 3 through 5.

> **Pro Tip:** Tailoring the 3LoD framework to your organization or agency is important. There could be some nuances related to detailed requirements that need to be factored into how you partner with the 1LoD and 2LoD. If the 3LoD is mature, take the time to understand how it operates to determine the best approach for partnering. "*One size does not fit all*," Frank Zappa (n.d.).

2.3 THREE LINES OF DEFENSE

Effective risk management is critical for organizations and government entities navigating today's dynamic regulatory and legal landscape, and the **3LoD** model provides a structured approach to achieve this goal. This section explores how each line – operational management, risk and compliance functions, and IA/OIG – works together to identify, assess, and mitigate risks while maintaining clear roles and responsibilities. By fostering collaboration across these lines, entities can enhance their risk posture, improve decision-making, and ensure continuous oversight (IIA, 2020; Moyle, 2022; OCC, 2019). Additionally, this chapter highlights best practices for integrating the 3LoD model with governance frameworks to strengthen overall organizational resilience.

🛠 **Important Note:** While the **3LoD** model provides a comprehensive framework for internal risk management and control, it is essential to recognize that **external auditors are not part of the three lines.** External auditors operate independently from the entities and provide an objective assessment of financial statements and compliance with applicable laws and regulations. Their role is to offer assurance to stakeholders rather than participate in the entity's internal control processes, maintaining a necessary level of independence and objectivity.

The 3LoD offer many benefits to an entity (Hetler, 2023).

1. **Improved Risk Management:** By clearly defining roles and responsibilities, the model helps entities to identify, assess, and manage risks more effectively. This ensures complete coverage across the entity.
2. **Enhanced Governance:** The model promotes a structured and accountable approach to risk management, leading to stronger governance practices. A standardized governance framework ensures consistency.
3. **Greater Accountability:** Each line of defense is accountable for its own responsibilities, which helps to ensure that risks are managed effectively.
4. **Increased Efficiency:** By streamlining processes and roles, the model can help to improve the efficiency of risk management activities. Consider the lean management principles in Chapter 4 – Agility in Action: Rethinking Cybersecurity Audit as the foundation to this benefit.
5. **Better Compliance:** The model helps entities ensure that they are complying with relevant laws, regulations, and internal policies.

🎯 **Pro Tip:** Use these benefits and those that you identify to sell this concept to management and encourage collaboration and partnership, as necessary.

🛠 **Important Note:** Remember that all 3LoD are focused on risk management, each from a different perspective. This concept makes it easier to understand how collaboration and partnerships can be established, yet each line of defense maintains their own roles and responsibilities.

2.4 FIRST LINE OF DEFENSE (1LoD)

This line is responsible for the day-to-day management of operational risks and controls. This includes the business units and operational management who are directly involved in identifying and controlling risks within their area of responsibility (Astley & Regelbrugge, n.d.). Moreover, the **1LoD** in cybersecurity consists of the people, processes, and technologies that **own and**

manage risks as part of daily business operations. These are the individuals and teams responsible for implementing security controls, detecting threats, and ensuring compliance with security policies **before an attack escalates.**

2.4.1 First line of defense (1LoD) roles and responsibilities

The 1LoD has specific roles and responsibilities that are separate from the 2 LoD and 3LoD. As noted in the information below, the 1LoD is ultimately responsible for ensuring risks are managed by the organization or agency risk appetite statement.

Before going into more detail on the 1LoD, it is important to understand a risk appetite statement. A **risk appetite statement** defines the amount and type of risk an organization is willing to accept in pursuit of its objectives. It serves as a guiding principle for decision-making, helping leaders align strategic initiatives and operational activities with the organization's tolerance for uncertainty. A well-crafted risk appetite statement provides clarity to stakeholders by distinguishing between acceptable and unacceptable risks across key areas such as cybersecurity, compliance, financial exposure, and reputation. In the context of cybersecurity, for example, an organization might express low appetite for data breaches or regulatory non-compliance but a moderate appetite for adopting emerging technologies with manageable risks. Ultimately, the statement supports a balanced approach to risk-taking, reinforcing accountability and informing governance frameworks (Tozzi, 2025).

Key Characteristics of the 1LoD

1. **Operational Ownership of Security Risks:** Frontline personnel and IT teams managing security risks daily.
2. **Direct Implementation of Security Controls:** Applying security controls to protect data, networks, and applications.
3. **Detection and Response to Threats:** Actively monitoring and responding to security incidents.
4. **Adherence to Security Policies and Procedures:** Complying with established security guidelines.

Who is in the 1LoD?

The 1LoD includes employees and third-party service providers, information technology (IT) staff, and security teams that handle cybersecurity at an operational level:

1. **IT Operations and System Administrators**
   - Maintain and configure firewalls, intrusion detection system/intrusion prevention system (IDS/IPS), endpoint security, and other protective technologies.
   - Patch vulnerabilities and system updates.

⚖ **Example:** An IT administrator applies a **critical operating system security patch** to all servers to prevent exploitation of a known vulnerability.

2. **Cybersecurity Operations Teams**
   - Manage **Security Information and Event Management (SIEM)** systems.
   - Conduct **threat monitoring** and **incident response.**
   - Deploy and maintain **Multi-Factor Authentication (MFA)** and **Identity and Access Management (IAM)** controls.

⚖ **Example:** A Security Operations Center (SOC) analyst detects **anomalous login activity** from an overseas location and locks the account before a breach occurs.

3. **Business Units and End Users (First Human Layer of Defense)**
   - Employees follow cybersecurity policies and report suspicious activities.
   - Departmental managers enforce security practices within their teams.

⚖ **Example:** A finance employee identifies a **suspicious email** requesting wire transfer details and reports it as a **phishing attempt** instead of clicking the link or opening an attachment.

4. **Application and Software Developers**
   - Implement **secure coding practices** (e.g., input validation, encryption).
   - Follow Development Security Operations (DevSecOps) principles to integrate security into the Software Development Life Cycle (SDLC).

⚖ **Example:** A developer uses **parameterized queries** to prevent **Structured Query Language (SQL) injection attacks** in a web application.

5. **Cloud and Network Security Engineers**
   - Configure **secure cloud environments** (Amazon Web Services (AWS), Azure, Google Cloud).
   - Enforce **zero-trust security** by restricting access based on user identity and device security posture.

⚖ **Example:** A cloud engineer configures **S3 bucket encryption** and enables **least privilege access** to minimize data exposure.

Table 2.1 presents a comparative chart that highlights the 1LOD function responsibilities through examples. Note that this differs from the 1LoD staffing examples as presented above.

Table 2.1 1LoD function examples

Function	1LoD role
Prevent Threats	Implement firewalls, IDS/IPS, endpoint security, and email security filters
Monitor and Detect	Use SIEM and threat intelligence to identify anomalies
Respond to Incidents	Mitigate phishing attacks, malware infections, and unauthorized access attempts
Control Access	Enforce least privilege, MFA, and identity verification policies
Ensure Compliance	Follow industry regulations (National Institute of Standards & Technology (NIST), International Organization for Standardization (ISO) 27001, Federal Risk and Authorization Management (FedRAMP), etc.)

Table 2.2 describes the relationship between the other lines of defense. This highlights the unique roles and responsibilities, demonstrating a clear delineation between the roles. Note the independent and unique roles between the 3LoD.

Table 2.2 1LoD vs. other lines of defense

Line of defense	Primary focus	Who is involved?
1st Line (Operational Security)	Implement security controls and manage risks daily	IT, security engineers, system admins, end users, developers
2nd Line (Risk Management andCompliance)	Oversees security policies, governance, and compliance	Risk management teams, compliance officers, cybersecurity auditors
3rd Line (Independent Assurance)	Conducts independent security audits and assessments	Internal/external auditors, regulators, third-party assessors

Why is the 1LoD critical?

- Prevents security breaches before they escalate.
- Ensures day-to-day security operations run smoothly.
- Reduces attack surface through proactive controls.
- Acts as the first barrier against human errors and insider threats.

> 💡**Critical Thinking Moment:** Think about all the activities that the 1LoD conducts and how cybersecurity auditors can leverage from those activities. Cybersecurity auditing is more than ensuring compliance with policies, standards, and procedures; it is about independently evaluating the quality of management's cybersecurity activities.

2.4.2 First line of defense (1LoD) roles and responsibilities alignment with frameworks

It is important to understand more details about the **1LoD** responsibilities as they relate to various frameworks. The benefit of this understanding is in the event you need to use the information to sell the required concepts as part of the audit work. Several security frameworks define and reinforce the **1LoD** by establishing guidelines for **risk management, security controls, and operational security best practices.** Below, we break down key frameworks like **NIST Special Publication (SP) 800-53 (Rev. 5) (NIST, 2020b), ISO 27001 (ISO, 2022), Center for Internet Security (CIS) Controls (CIS, 2025), and FedRAMP** (FedRAMP, 2025), focusing on how they support 1LoD activities.

1. **NIST SP 800-53 (Rev. 5)**
   Why It Matters for 1LoD: NIST SP 800-53 (Rev. 5) provides **a structured approach to security controls**, ensuring organizations properly implement cybersecurity measures at the operational level (NIST, 2020b). Expanding upon that standard, Table 2.3 provides specific activities that 1LoD is required to execute. The objective is to convert the NIST SP 800-53 (Rev. 5) Control Families into actionable information that is related to an organization. This approach would be required for all NIST SP 800-53 (Rev. 5) Control Families when evaluating an organization's 1LoD process completeness.

Table 2.3 Key 1LoD controls from NIST SP 800-53 (Rev. 5)

Control family (NIST, 2020b)	1LoD activity	Example
Access Control (AC)	Enforce least privilege, MFA, and account management	System administrators set role-based access controls (RBAC) for a cloud platform
Audit and Accountability (AU)	Implement logging, SIEM, and monitoring of security events	SOC analysts review anomalous login attempts using a SIEM solution
Configuration Management (CM)	Maintain secure system configurations and patch management	IT teams apply Operating System (OS) security patches in a timely manner.
Incident Response (IR)	Implement incident response procedures, training, and exercises	Employees participate in a phishing awareness drill to test security awareness
System and Communications Protection (SC)	Secure data transmission with encryption (Transport Layer Security (TLS), Virtual Private Networks (VPNs), etc.)	Network engineers configure end-to-end encryption for sensitive communications

How It Supports 1LoD

- Establishes foundational **security controls** for IT and security teams to follow.
- Provides guidance for **employees, admins, and SOC teams** to proactively manage risks.
- Requires **real-time monitoring, logging, and auditing** of potential and actual security incidents.

2. **ISO 27001**
   Why It Matters for 1LoD: ISO 27001 is an **internationally recognized Information Security Management System (ISMS)** framework that mandates security controls for **risk management, access control, and operational security.** Like the NIST SP 800-53 (Rev. 5), ISO 27001 provides specific framework considerations specific to 1LoD. Table 2.4 provides examples for several of the ISO 27001 Control Domains. The objective is to convert the ISO 27001 Control Domains into actionable information that is related to an organization. This approach would be required for all ISO 27001 Control Domains when evaluating an organization's 1LoD process completeness.

Table 2.4 Key ISO 27001 Annex A controls for 1LoD

Control domain (ISO, 2022)	1LoD activity	Example
A.5 – Security Policies	Ensure security policies are followed at the operational level	Employees complete mandatory security training
A.9 – Access control	Implement authentication, authorization, and user account management	IT staff disable inactive user accounts after 90 days of inactivity
A.12 – Operations security	Secure system operations and apply secure configurations	IT teams implement logging and monitoring for unauthorized system access
A.16 – Incident management	Establish incident detection, reporting, and escalation processes	A SOC team investigates and contains a malware outbreak in a corporate network

How It Supports 1LoD

- Provides guidance to **employees and IT teams** for enforcing cybersecurity best practices.
- Establishes **incident handling procedures** for frontline security teams.
- Supports **encryption, identity management, and access control** for IT systems.

3. **CIS Controls**
   Why It Matters for 1LoD: CIS Controls provide **a prioritized set of cybersecurity best practices** for protecting systems against cyber threats. Like the NIST SP 800-53 (Rev. 5) and ISO 27001 provide specific framework considerations specific to 1LoD, Table 2.5 provides examples for several of the CIS Controls. The objective is to convert CIS Controls into actionable information that is related to an organization. This approach would be required for all CIS Controls when evaluating an organization's 1LoD process completeness.

Table 2.5 Key CIS controls for 1LoD (Version 8)

CIS Control (CIS, 2025)	1LoD activity	Example
CIS Control #1: Inventory and Control of Assets	Identify and manage IT assets	IT teams maintain an up-to-date inventory of devices and software
CIS Control #5: Account Management	Enforce identity and access controls	Admins apply least privilege policies to user accounts
CIS Control #8: Audit Log Management	Enable logging and SIEM integration	Security teams monitor failed login attempts and suspicious activities
CIS Control #14: Security Awareness & Training	Educate employees on cybersecurity threats	Employees undergo quarterly phishing simulation training

How It Supports 1LoD

- Focuses on **practical, operational security controls** that can be implemented by **IT, security teams, and employees.**
- Prioritizes **real-time monitoring, threat detection, and security** awareness.
- **Maps directly to NIST and ISO 27001** for structured security implementation.

4. FedRAMP

Why It Matters for 1LoD: FedRAMP ensures **federal cloud service providers (CSPs) comply with NIST security controls,** making it highly relevant for IT and cloud security teams. Like the NIST SP 800-53 (Rev. 5) and ISO 27001 provide specific framework considerations specific to 1LoD, Table 2.6 provides examples for several of the FedRAMP requirements. The objective is to convert FedRAMP into actionable information that is related to a Federal Agency. This approach would be required for all FedRAMP requirements when evaluating an organization's 1LoD process completeness.

Table 2.6 Key FedRAMP security requirements for 1LoD

FedRAMP requirement (FedRAMP, 2025)	1LoD activity	Example
Continuous monitoring	Maintain ongoing security visibility for cloud systems	SOC teams review real-time cloud security alerts
IAM	Restrict unauthorized access to federal cloud systems	Cloud engineers enforce zero-trust policies for remote users
Data Encryption (Federal Information Processing Standards (FIPS) 140-2)	Encrypt data at rest and in transit	IT staff enable FIPS 140-2 compliant encryption for sensitive federal data
Vulnerability Scanning	Perform continuous security scans	Security teams conduct weekly vulnerability scans on cloud environments

How It Supports 1LoD

- Provides **mandatory security controls** for **cloud engineers, IT teams, and SOC analysts.**
- Recommends **real-time monitoring, logging, and access control** for federal systems.
- Provides cloud security teams with **continuous compliance** with security policies guidance.

Building upon the previous framework tables and supporting information, Table 2.7 summarizes the framework focus areas and those in 1LoD who would use the framework. The objective of articulating this information is that the focus areas are slightly different. While not in Table 2.7, ISACA (2018) provides security controls within the COBIT 2019 framework, which can be used by 1LoD. This demonstrates the number of frameworks available for benchmarking an organization's 1LoD requirements.

Table 2.7 Summary table: how frameworks support 1LoD

Framework	Focus area	Who uses it in 1LoD?
NIST SP 800-53 (Rev. 5) (NIST, 2020b)	Government and private sector security controls	IT staff, SOC analysts, system administrators
ISO 27001 (ISO, 2022)	Global information security management	IT security teams, risk managers, developers
CIS Controls (CIS, 2025)	Practical, prioritized security best practices	IT, system admins, end users
FedRAMP (2025)	Federal cloud security compliance (but can be used in the private sector)	Cloud engineers, SOC teams, compliance officers

Why It Matters for 1LoD

- All these frameworks emphasize strong security controls that 1LoD teams implement daily.
- IT security teams, SOC analysts, and developers use these frameworks to protect data, systems, and users.
- Understanding these frameworks ensures your organization can effectively detect, prevent, and respond to cybersecurity threats at the operational level.

🎯 Pro Tips

- While FedRAMP is a Federal Agency requirement, private sector organizations can leverage from this framework to benchmark the 1LoD requirements for completeness.

- These frameworks can be uploaded into ChaptGPT requesting a comparison between these frameworks and management's policies, standards, and procedures. Consider the time savings of automating this review versus a manual review, with the latter being prone to human error.

2.5 SECOND LINE OF DEFENSE (2LoD)

The **2LoD** in cybersecurity provides oversight, guidance, and support to ensure that security and risk management practices are effectively implemented by operational teams (1LoD). This layer typically includes **cybersecurity policy makers, risk managers, compliance officers, and governance personnel** who develop cybersecurity standards, monitor control performance, interpret regulatory requirements, and provide risk-based advice. In addition, the 2LoD ensures that organizational cybersecurity efforts align with frameworks like **NIST RMF (RMF) (NIST, 2018), Federal Information Security Management Act (CISA, 2025), and ISO 27001** and that the 1LoD has the resources and direction needed to effectively manage cybersecurity risks.

2.5.1 Second line of defense (2LoD) roles and responsibilities

This line provides oversight and support to the 1LoD, ensuring that risks are identified, assessed, and managed effectively. This includes risk management and compliance functions, which monitor and challenge the 1LoD's risk management activities.

The **2LoD** plays a critical role in **cybersecurity governance, risk management, and compliance oversight**, ensuring that the organization's cybersecurity strategy is properly executed and aligned with regulatory requirements and enterprise risk appetite. It could be argued that the 2LoD is independent of the 1LoD, typically reporting to a Chief Risk Officer (CRO). Below are key **roles and responsibilities** of the 2LoD from a cybersecurity context.

Key Characteristics of the 2LoD

1. **Risk Governance Framework:** Establishes and maintains the risk management governance framework, which includes policies, standards, procedures, risk assessment templates, and reporting.
2. **Cybersecurity Risk Oversight:** Evaluates 1LoD risk assessments and may independently conduct risk assessments.

3. **Detection and Response to Threats:** May independently identify and evaluate emerging risks and compare against the 1LoD risk results.
4. **Independent Reporting:** Aggregates risk data and provides independent risk reporting to senior/executive management and the Board. For the Federal Government, this would be reporting to Senior Executive Service members and Agency Heads.

Who is in the 2LoD?

The 2LoD includes employees with the same technical expertise as the 1LoD with an emphasis on risk management skills who can execute cybersecurity at an operational level:

1. **Cybersecurity Risk Management Professionals**
   - Build out the cybersecurity risk management template that includes risk ratings.
   - Research and understand cybersecurity trends and emerging risks.
   - Conduct independent risk assessments.
   - Aggregate cybersecurity risk management reporting to demonstrate the risk against the cybersecurity risk appetite statement for evaluation.

⚖ **Example:** A cybersecurity risk analyst who conducts a risk assessment over the **cybersecurity incident response process** to determine if management's risk assessment is complete.

2. **Cybersecurity Compliance Professionals**
   - This could include legal and regulatory specialists who monitor for privacy and other requirements through the RMF.
   - Primarily partner with the other 2LoD risk professionals to provide the legal and regulatory lens to the cybersecurity domain area.

⚖ **Example:** A privacy officer who shares the relevant privacy laws and regulations for **third party risk assessment related to brokerage back office.**

3. **Policy and Standards Development**
   - Draft, maintain, and enforce cybersecurity policies, procedures, and standards.

- Ensure alignment with frameworks like **NIST SP 800-53 (Rev. 5)**, Federal Information Security Modernization Act (**FISMA**), **ISO 27001**, and agency-specific requirements.

⚖ **Example:** A cybersecurity risk manager drafts, maintains, and ensures compliance with the entity's **risk appetite statement.**

4. **Risk Management and Assessment**
   - Identify, analyze, and monitor cybersecurity risks across the enterprise.
   - Facilitate enterprise risk assessments and support the **Risk Executive Function.**
   - Maintain risk registers and support categorization and risk acceptance decisions.

⚖ **Example:** A cybersecurity risk analyst configures the risk management software to **capture all risks, controls, and supporting information.**

5. **Compliance Oversight**
   - Monitor adherence to internal policies, external regulations, and contractual security requirements.
   - Support continuous monitoring programs and track **Plan of Action & Milestones** (**POA&Ms**).
   - Assist in preparing for audits, inspections, and security assessments.

⚖ **Example:** A cybersecurity risk analyst compares risk assessment output results to the **risk appetite statement tolerances and thresholds.**

6. **Performance Monitoring and Reporting**
   - Define and monitor **Key Risk Indicators** (**KRIs**) and **Key Performance Indicators** (**KPIs**).
   - Analyze control effectiveness based on operational data and security metrics from 1LoD.
   - Report risk posture to senior leadership and stakeholders.

⚖ **Example:** A cybersecurity risk analyst compares the results of KRIs and KPIs against the **risk appetite statement tolerances and thresholds.**

7. **Advisory and Support Function**
   - Provide guidance to the 1LoD on implementing controls and managing risk.

- Interpret regulatory and framework requirements for operational teams.
- Offer training, awareness, and technical consultation on best practices.

⚖ **Example:** A cybersecurity risk manager provides **risk assessment training** to 1LoD personnel in preparation for the risk assessment execution.

8. **Liaison between 1LoD and 3Lod**
   - Serve as a bridge between operational implementers and independent auditors.
   - Facilitate communication during audits, helping translate operational language to compliance terms.
   - Help reconcile disagreements on control interpretation or risk severity.

⚖ **Example:** A cybersecurity risk manager attends all audit activity meetings between the 1LoD and 3LoD to provide **risk input as needed.**

9. **Documentation and Governance Support**
   - Maintain centralized documentation for policies, risk decisions, compliance evidence, and security governance processes.
   - Support governance bodies such as the Cybersecurity Steering Committee, **Change Control Boards**, or **Enterprise Risk Councils.**

⚖ **Example:** A cybersecurity analyst evaluates the **cybersecurity risk management policies, standards, procedures, and templates** against the NIST SP 800-53 (Rev. 5) framework.

In federal environments, 2LoD roles often include **Chief Information Security Officers (CISOs), Information Systems Security Managers (ISSMs), Enterprise Risk Officers,** and **Compliance Analysts** – all ensure that the cybersecurity program remains robust, well documented, and audit-ready.

2.5.2 Second line of defense (2LoD) roles and responsibilities alignment with frameworks

Let's think about the frameworks specific to the 2LoD, providing step-by-step information. Here's a structured breakdown of **2LoD roles and responsibilities,** mapped to common frameworks like **National Institute of**

Standards and Technology (NIST) RMF, NIST SP 800-53 (Rev. 5), ISO/ International Electrotechnical Commission (IEC) 27001, and FedRAMP. Table 2.8 describes how governance and risk management functions align with established standards. Note that those frameworks for 1LoD can be used for 2LoD, these2LoD do not require separate frameworks when building a cybersecurity risk program. The objective of Table 2.8 is to provide some ideas on how a benchmarking exercise could be conducted.

Table 2.8 2LoD roles and responsibilities associated with risk standards

2LoD role / responsibility	NIST RMF Alignment (NIST, 2018)	NIST SP 800-53 (Rev. 5) Controls (NIST, 2020b)	ISO/IEC 27001:2022 Alignment (ISO, 2022)	FedRAMP Alignment (FedRAMP, 2025)
Policy and Standards Development	Prepare / Implement / Monitor	PL-1 (Policy and Procedures), PL-2 (System Security Plan), PL-4 (Rules of Behavior)	A.5.1 (Policies for information security), A.5.2 (Review of policies)	CSP must provide documented security policies for authorization packages
Risk Management and Assessment	Categorize / Select / Monitor / Respond to Risk	RA-1 to RA-7 (Risk Assessment Family), PM-9 (Risk Executive Function)	A.6.1 (Actions to address risks), A.8.28 (Risk assessment for suppliers)	Continuous monitoring strategies and risk adjustments are essential
Compliance Monitoring and Reporting	Monitor / Assess	CA-1 (Security Assessment Policies), CA-2 (Control Assessment), CA-7 (Continuous Monitoring)	A.5.3 (Roles and responsibilities), A.18.2 (Compliance with policies and standards)	Ongoing assessment and authorization (Continuous Monitoring (ConMon))
Guidance and Advisory Support	Prepare / Implement / Monitor	AT-2 (Security Awareness Training), PM-14 (Testing, Training, and Monitoring), SA-8 (Security Engineering Principles)	A.7.2.2 (Information security awareness, education, and training)	Required to guide CSPs and internal teams on FedRAMP security control interpretation
Control Effectiveness Evaluation	Monitor / Assess / Respond	CA-7 (Continuous Monitoring), SI-4 (Information System Monitoring), AU-6 (Audit Review)	A.12.4.1 (Event logging), A.12.4.3 (Administrator and operator logs review)	CSPs and agency assessors regularly review system control effectiveness

(*Continued*)

Table 2.8 2LoD roles and responsibilities associated with risk standards (*Continued*)

2LoD role / responsibility	NIST RMF Alignment (NIST, 2018)	NIST SP 800-53 (Rev. 5) Controls (NIST, 2020)	ISO/IEC 27001:2022 Alignment (ISO, 2022)	FedRAMP Alignment (FedRAMP, 2025)
Risk Reporting to Leadership	Monitor / Respond / Authorize	PM-9 (Risk Executive), PM-11 (Mission/ Business Process Definition), CA-5 (Plan of Action & Milestones)	A.5.3 (Organizational roles), A.17.2 (Reporting information security events)	CSPs must submit monthly ConMon reports and incident notifications
Liaison between 1LoD and 3LoD	Monitor / Assess / Authorize	PM-15 (Contacts with Security Groups), CA-2 (Control Assessment Participation)	A.5.3 (Roles and responsibilities), A.15.1 (Information security in supplier relationships)	FedRAMP Program Management Office (PMO) facilitates communication between CSPs (1LoD) and Third-Party Assessment Organization (3PAO) auditors (3LoD)
Documentation and Governance Support	Prepare / Implement / Monitor	PL-2 (System Security Plan), PM-4 (Plan of Action & Milestones), AU-6 (Audit Review)	A.7.5 (Documented information), A.8.32 (Information life cycle management)	FedRAMP requires detailed authorization documentation (System Security Plan (SSP), POA&M, SAR)

Key Positive Takeaways

- **NIST RMF and NIST SP 800-53** (Rev. 5) place the 2LoD in monitoring, preparation, and guidance roles across all steps of the RMF life cycle.
- **ISO/IEC 27001** emphasizes policy maintenance, risk analysis, compliance verification, and top-level reporting as core 2LoD responsibilities.
- **FedRAMP** embeds 2LoD activities in ongoing assessments, documentation management, and liaison duties between operational and assessment teams.

2.5.3 How the NIST Cybersecurity Framework (CSF) aligns with risk management frameworks (like NIST RMF)

Important Note: The NIST Cybersecurity Framework (CSF) is a strategic, high-level framework that helps organizations **understand, manage, and communicate cybersecurity risks** at an enterprise level.

The **RMF**, particularly **NIST SP 800-37 (Rev. 2) RMF**, which provides guidelines for applying the RMF to information systems and organizations, and **NIST SP 800-53 (Rev. 5)**, which provides a **more detailed, operational framework** used to **implement** and **assess** specific controls at the system level, especially in the federal space.

The two complement each other:

- **CSF = Why and What you need to achieve** (outcomes and risk goals).
- **RMF = How you achieve it** (detailed controls and processes).

Table 2.9 describes how governance and risk management functions align with established standards. NIST CSF is a voluntary framework focused on managing and reducing cybersecurity risk at a high level, emphasizing business outcomes and continuous improvement. In contrast, NIST RMF is a mandatory process for federal agencies that provides a structured approach to selecting, implementing, and assessing security controls for information systems. While CSF is broader and flexible, RMF is more prescriptive and compliance-driven, especially for systems governed by FISMA. While CSF is not mandatory for federal agencies or private sector and RMF is not mandatory for the private sector, using these best practices is recommended because of the guidance quality.

Table 2.9 NIST CSF and RMF alignment overview

NIST CSF Component (NIST, 2024)	NIST RMF Alignment (NIST, 2018)	Explanation
Identify (ID): Understand the environment, assets, risks, and governance	**RMF Steps: Categorize, prepare NIST SP 800-53 (Rev. 5): PM-xx, RA-xx families**	RMF starts with preparing the organization and categorizing systems based on impact. CSF's "Identify" function mirrors this, focusing on asset management, risk management strategy, and governance
Protect (PR): Safeguards to ensure delivery of services	**RMF Step: Selectand implement controls NIST SP 800-53 (Rev. 5):AC, SC, IA, CM families**	RMF requires organizations to select and implement controls to protect confidentiality, integrity, and availability. CSF's "Protect" function aligns with technical and administrative safeguards like access controls and awareness training
Detect (DE): Identify cybersecurity events quickly	**RMF Step: monitor controls NIST SP 800-53 (Rev. 5):AU, SI families**	RMF mandates ongoing monitoring, log reviews, and anomaly detection. CSF's "Detect" function focuses on developing detection processes and continuous security monitoring

(Continued)

Table 2.9 NIST CSF and RMF alignment overview (*Continued*)

NIST CSF Component (NIST, 2024)	NIST RMF Alignment (NIST, 2018)	Explanation
Respond (RS): Take action against detected cybersecurity events	**RMF Step: monitor, respond** **NIST SP 800-53 (Rev. 5): IR family**	RMF's incident response planning and execution maps to CSF's "Respond," which involves response planning, communications, and analysis
Recover (RC): Restore services and resilience after incidents	**RMF Step: Monitor (Recovery Planning Controls)** **NIST SP 800-53 (Rev. 5): CP family**	RMF includes contingency planning and recovery strategies. CSF's "Recover" focuses on recovery planning, improvements, and communications

🎯 *Key Alignment Insights*

- **CSF gives you the high-level "why" and "what," RMF gives you the detailed "how."**
- **Both are risk-based:** CSF helps prioritize risk management activities at the business level, while RMF manages system-specific risks.
- **CSF can guide RMF implementation:** Organizations use CSF categories to **prioritize** which RMF controls to implement first, based on risk appetite and mission impact.
- **CSF is flexible across industries, RMF is mandatory for federal systems:** In federal government environments, CSF can support enterprise-level risk discussions, while RMF ensures compliance with FISMA and FedRAMP.

🏛 **Federal Government Example:** An agency might use **CSF** to set enterprise cybersecurity priorities (e.g., "improve incident response capability") and then use **RMF** to operationalize that goal by implementing specific controls like **Incident Reporting (IR)-4, IR-6.** This ensures that cybersecurity risks are continuously monitored through the **POA&M** process.

🔚 **Conclusion:** The NIST CSF and RMF frameworks are not competitors – these are **complementary tools.** CSF provides the strategic lens to manage cybersecurity risks at an organizational level, while RMF operationalizes that strategy with specific, actionable controls and processes. Together, these frameworks create a full-spectrum approach to cyber risk management that aligns with mission goals, regulatory requirements, and evolving threat landscapes.

2.6 THIRD LINE OF DEFENSE (3LoD)

The **3LoD** is typically composed of **independent auditors, assessors, and IA/OIG functions** who are separate from operational management (1LoD) and risk oversight functions (2LoD). Their job is to provide **objective, independent assurance** that risks are properly managed, security controls are appropriately designed to prevent or detect errors, and are effective, and governance processes are working as intended.

> 🛠 **Important Note:** The 3LoD **does not manage or operate controls** – their role is to independently evaluate whether the risk management and control environment, as maintained by the 1LoD and overseen by the 2LoD, is effective.

2.6.1 Third line of defense (3LoD) roles and responsibilities

- **Independence and Objectivity:** Operates **independently** from operational management (1LoD) and risk/compliance functions (2LoD) and free from conflicts of interest to ensure unbiased evaluations.
- **Provides Assurance on Effectiveness of Controls:** Validates whether cybersecurity policies, procedures, and controls are **adequately designed and effectively implemented.** Evaluates the efficiency of both preventive and detective controls. Confirms if risks are being properly managed and mitigated by the 1LoD and overseen by the 2LoD.
- **Conducts Independent Audits and Assessments:** Performs **formal audits, assessments, and evaluations** such as compliance audits, vulnerability assessments, penetration testing reviews, and control effectiveness audits. Supports regulatory audits (e.g., **FISMA, FedRAMP, Sarbanes-Oxley Act (SOX)** (Anastasiades & Fritchie, 2024), **Payment Card Industry Data Security Standard (PCI DSS)** (PCI Security Standards Council, 2018) and prepares audit reports for oversight bodies.
- **Evaluates Governance and Risk Management Processes:** Assesses the organization's overall **governance structure** and effectiveness of ERM frameworks. Reviews **risk registers, POA&Ms, and risk appetite statements** to ensure alignment with actual practices.
- **Provides Recommendations for Improvement:** Identifies control weaknesses, gaps, and areas of improvement. Issues **findings and recommendations** in audit reports to improve organizational security posture. Tracks remediation actions and follows up on previous findings.

- **Supports Regulatory and Stakeholder Confidence:** Provides assurance to **external regulators, customers, and stakeholders** that cybersecurity risks are effectively managed. Strengthens organizational credibility and trust with third parties and government agencies.
- **Periodic, Structured, and Formal Approach:** Conducts audits on a **planned, recurring basis,** typically following a risk-based audit plan. Uses **formal methodologies and standards** (e.g., IIA Standards, ISACA guidelines).

Table 2.10 provides example descriptions related to the audit standards noted in the previous paragraph. The objective is to expand on the general audit standard section name with actionable information. The descriptions are often referred to as procedures that would supplement a standard.

Table 2.10 Summary table: how 3LoD audit standard characteristics are defined

Characteristic	Description
Independence	Free from operational influence; reports to top leadership
Objective assurance	Evaluates effectiveness of controls and risk management
Formal audits and reviews	Performs structured audits, assessments, and testing
Governance oversight	Reviews risk appetite, governance structures, and compliance
Actionable recommendations	Provides findings and tracks remediation progress
Supports external assurance	Builds trust with regulators and stakeholders
Risk-based and periodic	Follows an audit schedule based on organizational risk

3LoD is the organization's independent control evaluator, providing unbiased assurance that risks are properly managed and controls are functioning as intended. It serves as a critical feedback mechanism to strengthen cybersecurity resilience and governance.

2.6.2 Third line of defense (3LoD) roles and responsibilities alignment with frameworks

Table 2.11 articulates a clear and structured explanation of how the various frameworks can provide information for 3LoD audit activities. Like the

1LoD and 2LoD, common cybersecurity and risk frameworks like **NIST RMF, NIST SP 800-53 (Rev. 5), ISO/IEC 27001**, and **FedRAMP** provide cybersecurity requirements for benchmarking an organizations IA/OIG program. It is important to note that the referenced frameworks are risk related; this does not include the various audit frameworks as noted in Chapter 1 – Understanding Audit Objectives, Expectations, Concepts, and Opportunities. The objective is to demonstrate that all 3LoD can leverage from the "risk" guidance.

Table 2.11 Summary table: how frameworks support 3LoD

3LoD role / responsibility	NIST RMF Alignment (NIST, 2018)	NIST SP 800-53 Rev. 5 Controls (NIST, 2020)	ISO/IEC 27001:2022 Alignment (ISO, 2022)	FedRAMP Alignment (FedRAMP, 2025)
Independent security assessment	**Assess controls:** Validating control effectiveness independently.	**CA-2: Control Assessment, CA-7: Continuous Monitoring, CA-5: Plan of Action & Milestones**	**A.9.3.1: Independent review of information security**	FedRAMP requires **3PAO** to perform independent assessments before authorization
Audit and reporting to leadership	**Authorize system:** Provide input to authorizing officials	**CA-7: Monitoring Controls, CA-5: POA&M AU-6: Audit Review, Analysis, and Reporting**	**A.5.3: Organizational roles and responsibilities, A.18.2.3: Technical compliance review**	FedRAMP requires independent security assessment reports (SAR) submitted to the Joint Authorization Board (JAB) or agency Authorizing Official (AO)
Findings and recommendations	**Assess:** Document findings, recommend corrective actions	**CA-5: Plan of Action & Milestones, PM-4: Risk Management Strategy**	**A.5.3: Roles and responsibilities, A.17.1: Information security continuity**	FedRAMP requires **POA&M** management following audit findings. Findings are prioritized and tracked to closure

(Continued)

Table 2.11 Summary table: how frameworks support 3LoD (*Continued*)

3LoD role / responsibility	NIST RMF Alignment (NIST, 2018)	NIST SP 800-53 Rev. 5 Controls (NIST, 2020)	ISO/IEC 27001:2022 Alignment (ISO, 2022)	FedRAMP Alignment (FedRAMP, 2025)
Verification of remediation / follow-up	**Monitor controls:** Validate remediation of deficiencies over time	**CA-7: Continuous Monitoring, SI-2: Flaw Remediation**	**A.12.6: Technical vulnerability management, A.8.32: Information life cycle management**	FedRAMP requires assessors to verify remediation of POA&M items before continuous authorization
Support for regulatory and external reviews	**Prepare for authorization and ongoing monitoring reviews**	**AU-11: Audit Record Retention, AU-6: Audit Review**	**A.18.2.2: Compliance with security policies and standards**	FedRAMP requires periodic assessment by 3PAO and support during JAB/agency reviews
Evaluate governance and risk management processes	**Prepare / Categorize / Monitor** Review risk strategy and control selection	**PM-9: Risk Executive Function, PM-11: Mission/ Business Process Definition**	**A.5.1: Leadership and commitment, A.5.3: Organizational roles**	FedRAMP assessors validate that cloud service providers follow governance procedures and security control selection aligns with system categorization
Promote continuous improvement	**Monitor:** Provide feedback loop for improving risk posture	**CA-7: Continuous Monitoring, PM-6: Risk Management Strategy Review**	**A.10.1: Continuous improvement of the ISMS**	FedRAMP continuous monitoring requires regular reporting and reassessments. Assessors support by identifying areas for ongoing improvement

🎯 *Key Positive Takeaways*

- **NIST RMF** positions the 3LoD in the assessment and monitoring steps, validating controls before and after system authorization.
- **NIST SP 800-53 (Rev. 5)** maps strongly to control assessment (CA-2), POA&M management (CA-5), and audit activities (AU-6, AU-11).
- **ISO 27001** explicitly calls for independent reviews and technical compliance audits, closely aligned with 3LoD functions.
- **FedRAMP** mandates a formal third-party assessment organization (3PAO), ongoing audit support, and remediation verification.

The 3LoD ensures through independent assessment and reporting that the risk management strategies and controls implemented by the organization (and overseen by the 2LoD) are effective, compliant, and continuously improved. Across all major frameworks, their role is critical to maintaining security assurance and regulatory trust.

2.7 BUILDING RELATIONSHIPS

2.7.1 Initial thoughts

Would you agree that all 3LoD are focused on risk management? That concept provides one commonality across all groups, identifying and assessing risk. The 2LoD would also be responsible for remediating significant risks, but 2LoD and 3LoD may provide recommendations. Since all three groups focus on risk management, there are a lot of common topics that the cybersecurity auditor can use to build relationships.

Taking that concept a step further, a salesperson once recommended that I read a book on how to develop "sales" skills. That recommendation came after I explained some challenges of convincing management to implement cybersecurity controls. In the event you may not have the time to read Schiffman's (2008) book, here is a quick summary: a *good salesperson is someone who focuses on building strong relationships, actively listens to customer needs, and demonstrates empathy. That person would also develop strong communication and negotiation skills, and maintain a positive and persistent attitude. Be honest, transparent, and always strive to add value to the customer* experience (Schiffman, 2008). Does this sound like good skills for a cybersecurity auditor? "Customer" can be replaced with "client," "stakeholder," or another name and still apply, would you agree?

Another critical piece of advice once offered to me was to be patient. It is not realistic to think that trust can be built overnight, it will take time. Below is a structured, professional list of **best practices** for cybersecurity auditors to build **productive, professional relationships** with the 2LoD (risk management and compliance teams):

2.7.2 Best practices for cybersecurity auditors building relationships with 2LoD

1. **Establish Regular Communication Channels**
   - **What:** Set up recurring touchpoints (monthly/quarterly) with 2LoD leadership and operational risk owners (1LoD).
   - **Why:** Proactive communication builds familiarity and shared understanding of priorities before audit activities begin.

⚖ **Example:** Quarterly alignment meetings to review updates to the risk register and discuss emerging cybersecurity threats.

2. **Understand and Respect 1LoD and 2LoD's Role**
   - **What:** Acknowledge that 1LoD owns the risks and business as usual activity and can provide institutional knowledge. Acknowledge that 2LoD provides oversight, guidance, and monitoring – not operational control.
   - **Why:** Clarifies responsibilities and avoids misunderstandings about independence.

⚖ **Example:** Create a clear Responsible-Accountable-Consulted-Informed (RACI) chart to differentiate responsibilities while demonstrating collaboration touchpoints.

3. **Leverage 2LoD Risk Assessments for Audit Planning**
   - **What:** Use 2LoD risk heat maps, risk appetite statements, and assessments to guide audit focus areas.
   - **Why:** Ensures audit work is risk-based and aligned with the organization's priorities.

⚖ **Example:** If 2LoD identifies ransomware as an increasing risk, IA includes incident response readiness in its audit plan.

4. **Collaborate During Control Walkthroughs and Risk Discussions**
   - **What:** Involve 1LoD and 2LoD in control walkthroughs to understand the intent and design of controls.
   - **Why:** Reduces audit friction and ensures correct understanding of how controls mitigate risks.

⚖ **Example:** Before testing incident response controls, 3LoD meets with 2LoD to clarify playbooks and escalation procedures.

5. **Align Risk Language and Reporting**
   - **What:** Use the same risk rating scales and terminology as 1LoD and 2LoD when presenting audit findings.
   - **Why:** Improves clarity and ensures consistency in risk communications to executive leadership.

⚖ **Example:** 3LoD collaborates with 1LoD and 2LoD to agree on a common risk lexicon to avoid confusion during reporting.

6. **Share High-Level Audit Insights Proactively**
   - **What:** Provide 1LoD and 2LoD with emerging themes and trends from audit activities (without compromising audit independence). Consider creating periodic touchpoints to discuss emerging themes and trends between all three groups providing information.
   - **Why:** Enables 2LoD to strengthen monitoring and preventive controls proactively.

⚖ **Example:** 3LoD shares anonymized insights about control gaps across audits to support enterprise risk monitoring.

7. **Maintain Professional Independence, But Avoid Isolation**
   - **What:** Engage with 1LoD and 2LoD openly while preserving audit independence through independent evaluation and analysis.
   - **Why:** Builds trust without compromising the objectivity of audit work.

⚖ **Example:** 3LoD documents interactions to preserve transparency and audit trail integrity.

8. **Participate in Risk and Governance Committees (as Observer)**
   - **What:** Attend risk management forums and steering committees as an observer and to ask questions or pose additional thoughts.
   - **Why:** Provides valuable insights into risk decisions while maintaining auditor independence.

⚖ **Example:** 3LoD attends Cyber Risk Council meetings to stay informed on risk appetite updates and mitigation strategies.

9. **Support Post-Audit Remediation Collaboration**
   - **What:** Coordinate with 2LoD on tracking remediation of audit findings.
   - **Why:** Improves follow-up effectiveness and closes the feedback loop between audit and risk monitoring.

⚖ **Example:** 3LoD participates in remediation tracking sessions led by 2LoD to validate progress.

10. **Promote a Culture of Shared Risk Ownership**
    - **What:** Reinforce the message that 1LoD, 2LoD, and 3LoD all play critical roles in cybersecurity.
    - **Why:** Encourages collaboration rather than viewing audits as adversarial.

⚖ **Example:** 3LoD uses post-audit debriefs to highlight areas where 2LoD's oversight improved audit outcomes.

Table 2.12 articulates additional benefits for building relationships across all 3LoD. Cybersecurity audit professionals may start out with a couple of approaches and expand that portfolio over time. This information can be shared with leaders as the relationship building expands. Cybersecurity audit professionals often need to demonstrate sales skills to effectively promote this approach.

Table 2.12 Summary table: benefits of building partnerships

Practice	Benefit
Regular communication	Builds trust and alignment
Respect roles and independence	Maintains professionalism and objectivity
Use risk assessment data	Enables risk-based audit planning
Control walkthroughs	Clarifies control design and risk intent
Align reporting language	Strengthens executive understanding
Share insights proactively	Helps 2LoD enhance oversight
Attend risk committees	Stay informed on enterprise risks
Coordinate on remediation	Enhances closure of audit findings
Promote shared ownership	Builds collaboration culture

🛠 **Important Note:** Cybersecurity auditors strengthen their effectiveness by building respectful, transparent, and risk-aligned relationships with the 2LoD. This collaboration enhances risk visibility, improves audit relevance, and fosters a culture of continuous improvement – all while maintaining essential independence.

2.7.3 First line of defense (1LoD) collaboration examples

Collaboration between the **1LoD** – the operational teams who manage cybersecurity day-to-day – and the **3LoD** – independent auditors and assessors – is crucial for building a strong, resilient security posture. Here are some **collaboration ideas** to enhance trust, transparency, and shared understanding between these two lines:

1. Conduct Pre-Audit Knowledge Sharing Sessions
    - **What:** 1LoD teams walk 3LoD through current systems, security controls, and recent changes.
    - **Why:** Builds a baseline understanding, reduces misunderstandings, and sets realistic audit expectations.

⚖ **Example:** The SOC team explains their detection logic and SIEM workflows to auditors prior to a security assessment control testing.

2. Share Dashboards and Metrics Transparently
    - **What:** Provide 3LoD with read-only access to security dashboards (e.g., patch status, MFA coverage, incident volume).

- **Why:** Allows auditors to independently assess maturity while giving credit to 1LoD's ongoing efforts.

⚖ **Example:** Vulnerability management KPIs from Tenable or Qualys are shared ahead of an audit.

3. **Involve 3LoD in Tabletop Exercises or Impulse Response (IR) Simulations.**
   - **What:** Invite auditors to observe or participate in incident response simulations or tabletop drills.
   - **Why:** Helps 3LoD evaluate response effectiveness and provides real-time insight into operational procedures.

⚖ **Example:** During a ransomware tabletop, 1LoD leads the simulation while auditors observe and provide post-exercise feedback.

4. **Co-Develop Remediation Plans**
   - **What:** Instead of auditors just listing findings, 1LoD and 3LoD collaborate on practical, risk-based solutions.
   - **Why:** Builds a shared commitment to security improvements and prioritization.

⚖ **Example:** After finding insufficient logging, both teams agree to phase in centralized log collection over three months.

5. **Host Post-Audit "Lessons Learned" Workshops**
   - **What:** Debrief findings and observations together to identify improvement opportunities.
   - **Why:** Encourages a culture of learning and continuous improvement, not blame.

⚖ **Example:** After a FedRAMP readiness review, both teams meet to align future control enhancements.

6. **Encourage Open Q&A during Control Reviews**
   - **What:** During walkthroughs, let 1LoD explain their intent and constraints; let 3LoD clarify audit criteria.
   - **Why:** Improves control accuracy and helps 3LoD avoid misinterpreting evidence or intent.

⚖ **Example:** 1LoD explains a compensating control for noncompliant legacy systems – auditors adjust the severity of the finding accordingly.

7. **Sharing Training and Awareness Materials**
   - **What:** 1LoD shares internal security awareness content or playbooks with 3LoD to demonstrate a security culture.

- **Why:** Gives auditors better insight into security maturity beyond just control checklists.

⚖ **Example:** SOC shares phishing simulation results and lessons learned from previous internal campaigns.

8. **Invite 3LoD to Observe Change Control or Change Advisory Board (CAB) Meetings**
   - **What:** Allow auditors to observe how the organization manages security during operational changes.
   - **Why:** Offers visibility into real-time risk management without interfering.

⚖ **Example:** 3LoD sits in on a CAB meeting where firewall rules are being reviewed.

9. **Maintain a Shared Audit and Risk Tracker**
   - **What:** Use a centralized system (e.g., Jira, Archer, ServiceNow) to track audit findings, 1LoD responses, and remediation timelines.
   - **Why:** Promotes accountability and ensures both teams stay aligned on priorities and progress.

⚖ **Example:** 3LoD uses the same risk register as 1LoD and 2LoD with a data field that only cybersecurity auditors can update with risk, control, or other attribute revisions.

10. **Build Relationships – Not Just Reports**
    - **What:** Regular check-ins, informal meetings, and cross-functional collaboration.
    - **Why:** Builds trust, reduces friction, and ensures both sides work toward shared goals.

⚖ **Example:** Monthly syncs between the CISO's team and IA/OIG create space for proactive conversations.

🎯 **Pro Tip:** The above are just some ideas, partner closely with the 1LoD to customize to your organization.

Here's a **federal example** of how the **1LoD** and **3LoD** can collaborate effectively within the context of the **RMF** and **FISMA/FedRAMP compliance**:

🏛 Federal Collaboration Example: RMF in Action

Scenario: An agency is preparing for a **FISMA annual assessment** and a **FedRAMP ConMon audit** for its cloud-based case management system hosted on AWS GovCloud (AWS, 2025b).

1LoD Role (Operational Teams): The **System Owner, Information Systems Security Officer (ISSO), and IT Security Team** are part of the 1LoD. They are responsible for:

- Implementing NIST SP 800-53 Rev. 5 controls (e.g., AC-2, AU-6, CM-6).
- Maintaining the **system security plan** (**SSP**), **POA&M**, and **continuous monitoring artifacts.**
- Performing monthly **vulnerability scans** and weekly **log reviews.**
- Updating the agency's **inventory and change control logs.**

3LoD role (Auditors and Assessors): The **Agency's OIG** and/or a **3PAO** serve as the 3LoD. They are responsible for:

- Independently evaluating the effectiveness of implemented controls.
- Reviewing evidence of **ongoing authorization activities** (in accordance with NIST SP 800-137).
- Identifying any residual risk, systemic issues, or control weaknesses.

Table 2.13 focuses on 1LoD and 3LoD interactions. The objective is to provide an example that can be applied in an organization. While this table reflects 1LoD and 3LoD, the 2LoD could also be involved, providing input from a risk Cmanagement approach.

Table 2.13 Collaboration in action: 1LoD and 3LoD

Collaboration point	What happens	Why it works
Pre-assessment sync	1LoD walks the OIG through recent control updates and discusses any known POA&Ms	Sets expectations, clarifies remediation timelines, and reduces friction
Control walkthroughs	1LoD demonstrates access controls (AC-2) and audit logging (AU-2) through live system walkthroughs	Provides clarity and transparency, helping auditors understand context
Joint review of evidence	Both parties review scan results, patch logs, and user access reviews during audit window	Ensures 3LoD sees real data and understands how it's maintained
Finding risk rating fiscussions	3LoD proposes a Moderate finding; 1LoD presents a compensating control. Risk level is downgraded	Demonstrates that 3LoD can be flexible when 1LoD provides justifiable risk mitigation
Shared remediation timeline	Teams agree on POA&M milestones and assign owners for each corrective action	Improves accountability and enables achievable compliance

Outcome

- The system passes the annual FISMA assessment with **only two minor findings.**
- 3LoD praises the 1LoD's responsiveness and maturity.
- The agency demonstrates **progress in continuous monitoring,** reducing the burden for future FedRAMP renewals.

Pro Tips

- Use RMF artifacts (SSP, security assessment report (SAR), POA&M) as shared collaboration tools – not just audit deliverables.
- Invite 3LoD early into the **Security Control Assessment (SCA)** planning process.
- Document everything in a shared tool to manage and track all cybersecurity management requirements (e.g., Enterprise Mission Assurance Support Service (eMASS) (DISA, n.d.) or Cybersecurity Asset Management (CSAM) (SentinelOne, 2025) to keep evidence aligned).

2.7.4 Second line of defense (2LoD) collaboration examples

Here's a clear description of how the **2LoD supports the 3LoD:** The **2LoD** supports the **3LoD** by providing critical oversight insights, governance documentation, and risk assessments that form the foundation for independent audits and evaluations.

2LoD functions — including compliance officers, risk managers, and cybersecurity governance teams – maintain and monitor the organization's risk posture, track control performance, and ensure policy adherence. This ongoing oversight enables the 3LoD (independent auditors and assessors) to focus on verifying the effectiveness of controls rather than spending time gathering basic operational evidence.

Additionally, 2LoD facilitates access to risk registers, POA&Ms, compliance reports, and continuous monitoring outputs, helping auditors conduct informed and efficient assessments. Throughout the audit life cycle, the 2LoD acts as a bridge between operational teams (1LoD) and auditors (3LoD), clarifying control interpretations, coordinating audit logistics, and supporting the remediation of identified issues.

Ultimately, by maintaining robust oversight and transparent reporting, the 2LoD enables the 3LoD to deliver objective assurance that the organization's cybersecurity risk management practices are effective and aligned with regulatory requirements.

The below summarizes the 2LoD role in a simple flow

2LoD Monitors & Governs → Provides Reliable Inputs → 3LoD Independently Verifies & Assures

🏛 **Bank Example:** Here's a **scenario-based example for a banking environment**, using the **NIST RMF** to demonstrate how cybersecurity governance works in a critical infrastructure sector like finance.

While banks are often subject to Federal Financial Institutions Examination Council (FFIEC), Gramm-Leach-Bliley Act (GLBA), PCI DSS, etc., many are adopting NIST RMF because of its maturity and because **NIST RMF scales well to critical infrastructure**, and some banking regulators recommend it (like the Office of the Comptroller of the Currency (OCC), Federal Reserve, and Federal Deposit Insurance Corporation (FDIC).

Scenario: Bank Implements NIST RMF for a New Online Banking Platform.

Background: A regional bank is launching a new **online banking platform** that allows customers to transfer funds, view statements, and set up bill payments. Because of its critical function and sensitive customer data, the bank's **CRO** mandates use of the **NIST RMF** to manage risks and demonstrate strong cybersecurity governance to regulators (e.g., OCC, FFIEC, FDIC).

Table 2.14 focuses on 1LoD, 2LoD, and 3LoD interactions using the NIST RMF as the risk assessment source. The same approach could be applied to other frameworks, such as NIST CSF. The objective of this table is to demonstrate that the partnership between all 3LoD ensures sufficient evaluation for a high-quality risk deliverable. While the NIST RMF was used to demonstrate the partnership, this approach can be applied to other frameworks.

Table 2.14 Collaboration in action: 1LoD, 2LoD, and 3LoD using NIST RMF

RMF Step (NIST, 2018)	Activity in the banking scenario	Who is involved? (lines of defense)
Step 0: Prepare	The bank's 2LoD Risk Management Team defines the risk appetite, business impact levels (High for Confidentiality, Integrity, Availability), and cyber risk strategy for the new platform	2LoD (Risk Management, Compliance) supports strategic prep; 1LoD (IT & security operations) provides system inventory
Step 1: Categorize system	The system is categorized as "High Impact" based on sensitivity of Personally Identifiable Information (PII), Payment Card Industry (PCI) data, and availability requirements. Risk register entries are created	2LoD helps categorize, 1LoD provides data flow mapping, 3LoD (IA/OIG) reviews categorization approach
Step 2: Select controls	Based on the categorization, the security architect selects appropriate controls from NIST SP 800-53 (Rev. 5) (e.g., AC-2 for access control, SC-12 for cryptography)	1LoD selects and implements controls; 2LoD reviews alignment with policy and risk appetite

(Continued)

Table 2.14 Collaboration in action: 1LoD, 2LoD, and 3LoD using NIST RMF (*Continued*)

RMF Step (NIST, 2018)	Activity in the banking scenario	Who is involved? (lines of defense)
Step 3: Implement controls	The IT Security team deploys MFA, encryption, logging, and secure coding practices. Developers apply Open Web Application Security Project (OWASP) guidance for secure web applications	1LoD (implementers) lead, 2LoD monitors progress and reviews evidence of implementation
Step 4: Assess controls	The bank contracts an external assessor to validate control effectiveness through penetration testing, control testing, and vulnerability scans	3LoD (IA/OIG) assesses, with 2LoD facilitating assessor access to evidence and environment
Step 5: Authorize system	The bank's Risk Committee, chaired by the CRO, reviews the Security Assessment Report (SAR), residual risks, and POA&Ms to make the authorization decision	2LoD prepares risk documentation and advises leadership; 3LoD provides independent assessment input
Step 6: Monitor controls (ongoing authorization)	Monthly vulnerability scans, quarterly user access reviews, and incident monitoring continue post-launch. Continuous monitoring dashboards feed into quarterly executive risk reports	1LoD operates controls, 2LoD oversees metrics and POA&M progress, 3LoD audits monitoring effectiveness

Outcome

- The platform goes live with **full risk-informed authorization.**
- The bank demonstrates strong governance to regulators, satisfying inquiries from **OCC.**
- Residual risks are logged in the enterprise risk register and tracked by **2LoD.**
- Continuous monitoring enables **early detection of phishing campaigns** targeting the platform, leading to swift mitigation.

Key Positive Takeaways

- **The 1LoD** (IT, developers, SOC) implements controls and manages risks day-to-day.
- **The 2LoD** (risk management and compliance) ensures alignment with regulatory expectations and monitors effectiveness.
- **The 3LoD** (internal/external audit) independently verifies the integrity and effectiveness of controls.
- **RMF structures the risk management life cycle** for critical banking systems, and **regulatory expectations** are met through clear documentation and oversight.

🏛 Federal Government Example: This example leverages from the FISMA execution, which all Federal Agencies are required to periodically execute.

Scenario: FISMA Annual Assessment for a Federal Agency. Here's a **scenario-based federal example** demonstrating how the **2LoD** supports the **3LoD** in the context of **FISMA** compliance.

Background: A federal agency is preparing for its annual **FISMA audit** conducted by the **OIG**, which serves as the **3LoD**. The agency's **Cybersecurity Risk Management Team** and **Compliance Office** act as the **2LoD**, while the **IT Operations, ISSO, and SOC teams** make up the **1LoD.**

Table 2.15 outlines the various FISMA audit stages and how each line of defense supports that audit activity. This table could be the foundation for the roles and responsibilities communication to ensure all participants agree to the roles.

Table 2.15 Collaboration in action: 1LoD, 2LoD, and 3LoD FISMA audit planning and execution

Stage (CISA, 2025)	2LoD action	How this supports 3LoD (OIG auditors)
Pre-audit preparation	The 2LoD compiles the latest risk register, POA&Ms, and continuous monitoring reports. A risk register is a structured document or tool used to identify, assess, prioritize, and track risks throughout a project, program, or organizational process, including their potential impacts, likelihood, mitigation strategies, and assigned responsibilities	Provides auditors with verified, up-to-date evidence of the agency's risk posture and remediation progress
Control interpretation	2LoD clarifies agency-specific control implementations (e.g., how AC-2 is applied in cloud environments)	Helps OIG auditors understand operational context and tailor their testing approach
Audit logistics coordination	The 2LoD schedules meetings between auditors and appropriate system owners, ensuring the right technical stakeholders (1LoD) are involved	Streamlines auditor access to operational teams and speeds up evidence collection
Evidence validation	2LoD reviews and pre-validates technical evidence from 1LoD (e.g., vulnerability scan outputs, incident logs) before submitting it to auditors	Reduces the likelihood of incomplete or inconsistent documentation during the audit
During the audit	2LoD supports auditors by answering policy and risk-related questions, and explains the risk rationale for accepted residual risks	Enhances auditor understanding of organizational risk decisions and control effectiveness
Post-audit remediation	After findings are issued, 2LoD works with 1LoD to coordinate corrective action plans in accordance with POA&Ms and reports progress to auditors	Ensures timely and accurate remediation tracking for audit follow-up reviews
Audit closure and lessons learned	2LoD conducts a post-audit debrief to document lessons learned and updates governance processes accordingly	Improves future audit readiness and builds a feedback loop between governance and independent assurance

Outcome

- The audit proceeds smoothly because 2LoD preemptively organized evidence and facilitated effective communication.
- OIG auditors complete their audits efficiently, issuing fewer findings due to proactive risk management.
- Identified findings are promptly tracked in the POA&M, with clear ownership and deadlines, satisfying OIG follow-up.

Why this matters?

In federal environments, especially under **FISMA**, this collaboration is essential because:

- Agencies must demonstrate **continuous monitoring and risk-informed decision-making.**
- The OIG relies on clear, validated information to assess effectiveness.
- 2LoD plays a vital role as **translator and facilitator**, bridging the gap between operational execution (1LoD) and independent evaluation (3LoD).

2.7.5 Third line of defense (3LoD) collaboration examples

When the **3LoD** – the independent auditors/assessors – collaborates effectively with the **1LoD** and **2LoD**, the organization becomes much more resilient, and audits become opportunities for improvement, not just compliance exercises.

Table 2.16 provides examples of how 1LoD and 3LoD can collaborate. The objective is to provide ideas that will build partnerships to ensure risk information is shared across the s2LoD. Face-to-face interactions typically yield better results than multiple emails (refer to the email and multi-tasking discussion in Chapter 4 – Agility in Action: Rethinking Cybersecurity Audit). While 1LoD is noted, their corresponding 2LoD personnel may participate in the collaboration ideas.

Table 2.16 Collaboration in action: 3LoD and 1LoD (Operational Teams)

Collaboration idea	Why it matters	Example
Pre-audit workshops or readiness reviews	Helps 1LoD prepare evidence and clarify expectations	IA/OIG holds a prep session with system admins and SOC to explain audit scope
Control walkthroughs	Enables auditors to understand the operational reality of control implementation	SOC analyst walks auditors through incident response playbook
Evidence validation sessions	Reduces audit findings by ensuring quality of control evidence	3LoD reviews vulnerability scan reports with IT ops before audit submission
Informal Q&A opportunities	Builds trust and demystifies the audit process for operational teams	Auditors offer office hours for 1LoD to ask questions before formal assessments
Post-audit lessons-learned workshops	Identifies areas of improvement and avoids repeat findings	After audit completion, 3LoD and 1LoD debrief on what worked and what to improve

Like Table 2.16, Table 2.17 provides examples of how 3LoD can collaborate with 2LoD. The 2LoD risk and compliance teams were specifically mentioned because those are typically the two main risk groups within 2LoD. The 2LoD may provide an independent and varying risk view from the 1LoD, thus having separate discussions can yield new information.

Table 2.17 Collaboration in action: 3LoD and 2LoD (risk and compliance teams)

Collaboration idea	Why it matters	Example
Risk assessment sharing	Aligns audit focus with known organizational risks	2LoD shares updated risk register with 3LoD to guide audit priorities
Control interpretation discussions	Ensures common understanding of policy intent and control design	3LoD clarifies with 2LoD how compensating controls meet risk objectives
Joint audit planning	Enables risk-based scoping of audit activities	2LoD helps IA/OIG prioritize audits of high-risk systems
Remediation tracking collaboration	Keeps findings resolution on track and transparent	2LoD uses POA&M management tools that 3LoD can access for updates
Regulatory update briefings	Keeps audits aligned with evolving compliance requirements	2LoD briefs 3LoD on changes in FISMA reporting expectations

Some of the previous collaboration examples could involve all 3LoD, but specific examples were not provided. Table 2.18 describes specific examples that would involve all 3LoD. The objective is to share the benefits of that partnership, which provides an in-depth risk discussion from different perspectives.

Table 2.18 Collaboration in action: across all three lines (1LoD, 2LoD, 3LoD together)

Collaboration idea	Why it Matters	Example
Integrated risk management workshops	Builds shared understanding of risks and controls	All three lines participate in a tabletop exercise for incident response
Audit kickoff meetings	Aligns goals, scope, and expectations before audits begin	3LoD hosts a kickoff with 1LoD and 2LoD to discuss scope and timelines
Control maturity reviews	Assesses how well controls are implemented and managed across lines	Joint sessions to rate control maturity and identify improvements
Enterprise risk reporting alignment	Ensures accurate, consistent risk reporting to leadership	All lines contribute to an executive risk dashboard

🔑 Key Principles for Effective Collaboration

- **Transparency:** Open sharing of information between lines reduces the risk of surprises during audits.

- **Respect for Roles:** Collaboration doesn't compromise independence – 3LoD can maintain objectivity while still engaging constructively.
- **Continuous Engagement:** Don't limit interaction to just audit time. Year-round collaboration strengthens control environments.
- **Shared Goal:** All three lines aim to protect the organization and ensure resilient cybersecurity practices.

🔚 **Conclusion:** The 1LoD, 2LoD, and 3LoD can collaborate effectively with the 1LoD and 2LoD by proactively engaging in risk discussions, offering pre-assessment guidance, validating evidence, and participating in continuous improvement activities – all while maintaining independence. This ensures that audits are meaningful, not mechanical, and that cybersecurity posture continuously strengthens.

2.8 STREAMLINING RISK ASSESSMENTS

2.8.1 Initial thoughts

Audit departments are required to implement and maintain an audit framework that includes risk assessments. There may be multiple risk assessments. An example is the annual audit planning risk assessment and individual audit risk assessment. The individual audit risk assessment is typically to assess risks that result in identifying controls associated with high inherent risks.

Let's begin this section by asking yourself the questions below. Consider these questions as you read through the subsequent paragraphs. Does the audit department have:

1. Multiple risk assessments?
   - Annual audit planning?
   - Quarterly refresher to audit plan?
   - Individual audits?
   - Special projects?
2. Unique risk assessments?
   - Does it include inherent and residual risks?
   - Are the risk ratings different?
   - Does it consider compensating controls?
3. Risk and control library that differs from management?
4. RMF that leverages from NIST RMF or other RMFs?

A previous employer created a unique audit risk assessment to evaluate the annual audit plan throughout the year, which was more like a mini audit. The ratings were vague without having a correlation between the rating number and the rating description. Often the ratings were intentionally kept the same quarter-over-quarter to avoid changing the audit schedule, which defeated the purpose of analyzing risks to determine if audit resources should be shifted to a higher risk area. Moreover, the risk assessment required obtaining evidence, some of which was not directly related to the risk title. And the results did not align with emerging threats and vulnerabilities. Last, in addition to a significant amount of time spent on this activity that did not add value, I would argue that this goes against lean management principles of maximizing resources. The lean management topic will be explored in Chapter 4 – Agility in Action: Rethinking Cybersecurity Audit, reflecting the relationships and differences.

First, risk assessments should be simple to complete. As one example, consider three to four risk ratings that have clear and concise explanations so that the user can accurately assign a rating. Require a rating explanation so an independent person can evaluate. And, require both inherent and residual risks and associated ratings. The objective is to ensure consistency across all areas so that the information can be aggregated.

Second, risk assessments should be automated. One previous employer did create Microsoft Excel based risk assessments, but this was to run through the process and determine the best automated solution. An automated risk assessment tool leverages from technology and data analysis to streamline risk identification, risk rating, controls, and residual risk ratings. An example implemented at a previous employer was Rivest, Shamir, and Adleman (RSA) Archer, which was selected because of the alignment with various frameworks that included NIST and ISO, and integrated with other applications (Archer, n.d.).

Third, maintain reporting that aggregates risk assessment information. As an example, the 2LoD aggregates the information into enterprise-wide reporting to understand risk concentration within the organization.

Perhaps you are thinking there is a potential for IA/OIG to leverage from 2LoD RMF. Does it make sense to have so many RMFs within one organization? Perhaps the 2LoD could have data fields that allow cybersecurity auditors the capability of entering independent risk ratings? The objective of these questions is to inspire collaboration with 2LoD that makes sense and reduces overall costs to the firm when all risk activity is independently established and executed.

> **Important Note:** All 3LoD are tasked with managing risk within risk appetite/risk tolerance levels. Collaborating makes sense to ensure consistency and efficiency.

2.8.2 How IA (3LoD) can leverage the 2LoD's risk assessment framework

First, Understand the Relationship

- The **2LoD** maintains the organization's **RMF**, conducts **ongoing risk assessments**, and monitors risks as part of ERM.
- The **3LoD (IA)** is independent but can use the outputs of 2LoD's work to **better target audits**, improve efficiency, and focus on the **highest risk areas.**

IA does **not duplicate** 2LoD's work – it **leverages it as input** for independent assurance activities. This collaboration or leveraging worked best when individuals have experience in both 2LoD and 3LoD roles.

2.8.2.1 Practical ways IA can leverage 2LoD risk assessment

1. **Risk-Based Audit Planning**
   - IA uses 2LoD's risk register, heat maps, and risk appetite statements to prioritize high-risk areas in the audit plan.

   ⚖ **Example:** If 2LoD flags third-party vendor risk as "High," International Association for Impact Assessment (IAIA) can schedule a focused audit on third-party risk management processes.

2. **Control Effectiveness Validation**
   - 2LoD monitors controls as part of their role, and IA can **test** and **independently validate** the effectiveness of these controls.

   ⚖ **Example:** 2LoD reports quarterly access review completion; IA tests a sample to confirm accuracy and control effectiveness.

3. **Avoid Duplication of Effort**
   - IA can rely on 2LoD's continuous monitoring activities and **focus on areas not regularly reviewed** by 2LoD.

   ⚖ **Example:** If 2LoD continuously monitors endpoint security controls, IA focuses on broader governance or incident response processes.

4. **Enhanced Risk Understanding**
   - By reviewing 2LoD's risk methodologies, audit teams gain a clearer view of how risks are identified, scored, and prioritized.

   ⚖ **Example:** IA aligns its control testing methodology with 2LoD's risk criteria to ensure audit findings are presented in similar risk terms.

5. **Focus on Emerging Risks**
   - 2LoD often tracks emerging threats (like ransomware or third-party service provider attacks). IA can proactively plan audits around these risks.

   ⚖ **Example:** 2LoD flags an increase in social engineering attacks – IA includes phishing resilience in the upcoming audit scope.

6. **Validate the RMF Itself**
   - IA can use 2LoD outputs to **assess the effectiveness of the RMF.**

⚖ **Example:** Audit reviews if 2LoD consistently updates the risk register, evaluates risks per policy, and integrates risk outputs into decision-making.

2.9 INFORM AUDIT REPORTING AND EXECUTIVE DISCUSSIONS

Effective audit reporting translates complex findings into clear, actionable insights that support executive decision-making. By aligning results with organizational goals and risk priorities, auditors can drive strategic conversations with leadership. Timely, concise, and value-focused communication enhances the relevance of the audit function and fosters informed governance.

- Using 2LoD's risk language and risk heat maps aligns IA reports with a common language that senior leadership would recognize.

⚖ **Example:** IA references enterprise risk ratings in the audit report to articulate alignment with strategic priorities.

Table 2.19 expands the above information by providing specific outcomes, which includes efficiently and effectively achieving the IA action without starting from the beginning of the risk assessment process. The objective is to work smarter, not harder, yet challenge the information by the cybersecurity audit professional using critical thinking skills.

Table 2.19 Summary table: streamlining IA risk assessments

IA action	Leverage from 2LoD risk assessment	Outcome
Risk-based audit planning	Use risk register and heat maps	Audit focuses on high-risk areas
Control validation	Review 2LoD monitoring outputs	Efficient, targeted testing
Avoid duplication	Identify areas already monitored by 2LoD	Resource-efficient audits
Emerging risk focus	Use 2LoD's threat tracking	Proactive audit coverage
Risk methodology alignment	Understand 2LoD's scoring model	Consistent risk communication
Audit of risk framework	Use 2LoD process artifacts	Assurance over risk management effectiveness
Reporting alignment	Integrate risk heat maps into audit reports	Improved executive understanding

🔚 **Conclusion:** IA (3LoD) can maximize value by leveraging 2LoD's risk assessment framework for smarter, risk-based audit planning and execution – all while maintaining independence and providing objective assurance that 2LoD's risk processes are robust and effective.

2.10 ACHIEVING AUDIT STANDARDS

Chapter 1 – Understanding Audit Objectives, Expectations, Concepts, and Opportunities discussed Independence and objectivity from a theoretical perspective, which cybersecurity auditors must understand and maintain. Think about those audit standards and the relationship with building partnerships without deviating from those standards. For example, for cybersecurity audits to be effective, auditors must operate independently from the systems, processes, and teams they assess. Independence ensures objective findings, unbiased recommendations, and stronger security overall.

Let's expand on Chapter 1 – Understanding Audit Objectives, Expectations, Concepts, and Opportunities by exploring collaboration examples. For this collaboration example, IA (3LoD) uses risk assessment outputs from the 2LoD to strengthen the **audit planning, scope**, and **focus**, ensuring that audit engagements target the areas of **highest risk exposure** and **emerging threats.**

Table 2.20 provides a collaboration example focused on risk assessments. The objective is to provide an idea on how to avoid potential independence and other audit standard concerns when partnering with the 1LoD and 2LoD teams. For purposes of this discussion, several audit standards are provided, this is not intended to be an exhaustive analysis of all audit standards.

Table 2.20 Collaboration in action: 1LoD and 2LoD risk assessment

Step	2LoD responsibility (risk assessment role)	3LoD benefit (audit leveraging) and audit standard compliance examples
Maintain risk register	Maintain and update enterprise risk register with evolving risks, likelihood, and impacts	Use risk register to compare against audit analysis and prioritize audit engagements toward high-risk areas **Independence Audit Standard** is met because the auditor independently analyzes and challenges the risk register information and may expand upon or modify the risks for audit purposes **Reporting and Findings Audit Standard** is met when the auditor documents the risk register review and variance discussion with 2LoD
Conduct enterprise risk assessments	Regularly assess and report risk landscape, emerging risks, and residual risks across the organization	Inform risk-based audit planning, evaluating audit activity scope to the enterprise risk profile **Independence Audit Standard** is met because the auditor independently evaluates the risk assessment input and results, potentially challenging that information **Materiality Audit Standard** is achieved when the auditor evaluates and assigns a risk rating with supporting rational

(*Continued*)

Table 2.20 Collaboration in action: 1LoD and 2LoD risk assessment (*Continued*)

Step	2LoD responsibility (risk assessment role)	3LoD benefit (audit leveraging) and audit standard compliance examples
Evaluate control effectiveness (continuous monitoring)	Monitor and report on the effectiveness of operational controls mitigating top risks	Identify and evaluate control areas requiring independent testing and validation **Independence Audit Standard** is met because the auditor independently evaluates the control effectiveness testing approach and results, potentially challenging that information **Documentation and Evidence Audit Standard** is achieved when the auditor creates a worksheet memorializing the evaluation
Share emerging risk insights	Report on new threats (cyber, regulatory, operational)	IA adjusts audit focus to proactively address emerging risks **Independence Audit Standard** is met because the auditor independently evaluates the risk threat intelligence processes and activities, potentially challenging that information **Reporting and Findings Audit Standard** is met when the auditor provides a separate report on variances to 2LoD threat intelligence reporting, which may require remediation. The latter would result in achieving the **Continuous Monitoring and Follow-Up Audit Standard** because management would be required to implement a remediation plan
Post-audit activity risk calibration	Review audit findings and update risk assessments based on results	Creates feedback loop where audit results inform future risk assessments **Independence Audit Standard** is met because the auditor will independently validate risk assessment remediation plans **Documentation and Evidence Audit Standard** is achieved because the auditor documents the audit results so that an independent individual can reperform the activity

Pro Tip: Consider creating a risk collaboration table or checklist that expands upon the information in Table 2.20. Use the table or checklist to confirm audit standard compliance as part of all audit activities.

In addition to Table 2.20, the examples below provide details on why certain activities would comply with audit standards.

1. **Reviewing Policies and Procedures**
   Cybersecurity auditors may review governance documents as part of an internal consulting engagement. The objective is to evaluate that governance document before it is approved and communicated to various stakeholders.

Why Is It not a Concern?

- Evaluating security policies (e.g., access control, incident response), risk appetite statement, and other governance documents does not involve implementing them. In addition, management is not required to accept all comments.
- Auditors are verifying compliance with established frameworks (e.g., NIST, ISO 27001), not creating policies.
- The auditors providing comments would not audit those governance documents.

⚖ **Example:** An auditor assesses an organization's **data classification policy** to ensure it aligns with NIST SP 800-53 (Rev. 5) standards.

2. **Conducting Risk Assessments**

Why Is It not a Concern?

- Auditors assess risk but do not make business decisions on how to address those risks. This applies to evaluating management's risk assessments.
- Their role is advisory, providing risk ratings and recommendations.

⚖ **Example:** An auditor identifies risks in a **cloud migration project** but does not select security tools or approve the migration readiness.

3. **Assessing Compliance with Regulations and Frameworks**

Why Is It not a Concern?

- Auditors check for compliance but do not create or enforce regulations.

⚖ **Example:** An auditor reviews a company's **FedRAMP authorization package** for compliance with NIST SP 800-53 (Rev. 5).

🎯 **Key Positive Takeaways**

Audit activities remain independent as long as auditors **evaluate and verify controls** without being involved in their **implementation, enforcement, or decision-making.** IA/OIG can leverage from the existing internal and external RMFs without jeopardizing independence because they don't own the implementation and execution elements.

2.11 ARTIFICIAL INTELLIGENCE – CHAT GENERATIVE PRE-TRAINED TRANSFORMER (CHATGPT) SNEAK PEEK (OPENAI CHATGPT 4o, 2024)

Chat Generative Pre-Trained Transformer (ChatGPT) was used for purposes of this book because it consistently provides more functionality and information. This conclusion was made after researching the information provided or using my subject matter expertise to confirm reliability. Other AI large language models include Microsoft Copilot, Google Gemini, Meta Llama, and many others (Kerner & Lutkevich, 2025). Refer to Chapter 5 – Harnessing Artificial Intelligence: Enhancing Cybersecurity Audits through Automation and Insight for more information on Generative AI.

⚠ **Caution:** Confirm that the Generative AI tool is secure and approved by audit management before executing prompts.

Generative AI Example:s

- *"Describe how cybersecurity auditors can effectively collaborate with first-line cybersecurity professionals to strengthen security controls and compliance. Provide specific examples or best practices."*
- *"How can cybersecurity auditors collaborate with first-line cybersecurity professionals to enhance security operations and compliance? Provide examples aligned with NIST SP 800-53 (Rev. 5), ISO 27001, or CIS Controls."*

Pro Tips

- Practice executing ChatGPT prompts by considering the questions or queries you may have. Consider follow-up instructions, including requesting more information as recommended by ChatGPT at the end of the information provided.
- Consider attending prompt engineering courses, such as those offered through Coursera.

2.12 SUMMARY

This chapter focused on building partnerships in relation to the **3LoD Model.** This 3LoD model in cybersecurity provides a structured approach to risk management and cybersecurity governance. The **1LoD** consists of operational teams, including IT staff, system administrators, developers, and employees, who implement security controls, monitor threats, and respond to incidents. The **2LoD** includes risk management, compliance, and governance teams that oversee security policies, ensure regulatory adherence, and provide guidance to 1LoD. The **3LoD** is composed of independent auditors and assessors who conduct objective evaluations, ensuring that security measures are effective and properly implemented. This layered approach enhances cybersecurity resilience by integrating proactive risk management, oversight, and independent assurance.

Pro Tip: Leverage from this chapter when thinking about agility and artificial intelligence. Remember that agility and AI are intended to streamline the collaboration and partnership across all 3LoD.

You made it to the end of this chapter! Let's continue the cybersecurity audit journey by discussing partnerships in Chapter 3 – How to Influence Behaviors and Culture.

Chapter 3

How to influence behaviors and culture

3.1 LEARNING OBJECTIVES

By the end of this chapter, readers will be able to:

1. **Define organizational culture** and explain its relevance to the internal audit (IA) function and broader enterprise risk and compliance environments.
2. **Analyze how organizational culture influences audit processes**, including audit planning, stakeholder engagement, and reporting effectiveness.
3. **Evaluate the types of organizational cultures that best support agile audit practices and artificial intelligence (AI) adoption**, identifying enablers and barriers to innovation and automation.
4. **Explain the relationship between culture and change management**, and how cultural dynamics can either facilitate or hinder successful transformation initiatives.
5. **Differentiate between behavior change and culture change** and describe strategies for managing both in the context of audit modernization and digital transformation.
6. **Develop a culture and behavior change management strategy** aligned with organizational goals, audit objectives, and innovation readiness.

3.2 OPENING INSIGHTS

Chapter 2 – Building Partnerships for Success – discussed how to build partnerships with all three lines of defense personnel. This chapter takes that partnership building to the next level. Not all organizations or agency personnel are eager for IA or Office of Inspector General (OIG) to change their practices, especially when those individuals have been audited in the past and know the routine. In addition to technical and trust building skills, internal auditors need to understand how to evaluate culture and the role that culture plays in the audit work. This may seem like going above and beyond what auditors should be required to do, but it will make the audit work more enjoyable and rewarding in the long run. It will boost audit team productivity, morale, communication, and helps manage risks, cut audit costs, and enhance customer experience.

DOI: 10.1201/9781003640301-4

As you read through this chapter, think about your firm or agency, what specific culture or behavior attributes have you identified? How has that impacted the audit work? Perhaps it hindered progress or reduced the value added to the audit work. An information technology (IT) audit role was assigned to me before I had any IT experience. I spent time with the development and operation team members asking them to "brag" about the work they did, including what they enjoyed most and least. Letting them share their experiences not only builds trust, but it also allowed me to think about the risks associated with the work they executed through a mutual discussion. The collaboration instilled a sense of ownership. While this may fall into building relationships, it also applied an understanding of human behavior that was influenced by the organization's culture.

Figure 3.1 outlines a seven-step process for driving intentional cultural transformation within an organization. It begins with assessing the current culture to identify prevailing norms and values, followed by observing and analyzing existing behaviors linked to that culture. The next step is to define the desired culture and behaviors aligned with organizational goals, then identify the gaps and root causes preventing change. From there, leaders can design a tailored culture and behavior change strategy, implement and reinforce new practices, and finally, monitor progress to ensure adaptability and sustainability over time. This model emphasizes a structured, iterative approach grounded in awareness, alignment, and continuous improvement. The iterative element relates to working with new teams, leaders, employees, and others. That effort should not be an ongoing requirement for repeat audit areas.

Figure 3.1 Understanding and modifying culture and behaviors.

3.3 CULTURE DEFINITION

Think about the culture from a corporate/agency and IA/OIG perspective. There could be nuances for those two cultural environments that need to be considered. The goal of understanding the culture is to determine the best approach to achieving agility and AI objectives by incrementally working on cultural change as necessary. There is a caveat that some cultural changes may not occur, and you need to determine the best approach to still achieve the desired agility and AI objectives. Both approaches will be discussed in this chapter.

> **Pro Tip:** Leverage from a culture or behavior audit conducted by your organization or agency. Culture or behavior audits are usually conducted by an audit team that focuses on human resources, legal or compliance, or other group that owns the corporate/agency culture (IIA, 2024a). A culture audit provides an objective view of an organization's culture that in turn can be used to understand the best approach for transforming cybersecurity audits. You may also find that a culture survey was conducted providing beneficial behavior or cultural information.

3.3.1 Corporate culture

Corporate culture refers to the shared values, beliefs, behaviors, and norms that shape how employees and management interact within an organization and how the organization conducts its business. It reflects the company's identity and influences everything from decision-making and communication styles to dress codes, work hours, and employee engagement.

Key Elements of Corporate Culture (Cameron, 2011; Denison, 1990)

- **Core Values:** The guiding principles and ethics that the company stands by (e.g., tone at the top, integrity, innovation, accountability).
- **Norms and Behaviors:** Expected ways of behaving, both formal and informal, such as collaboration or risk-taking.
- **Communication Style:** Whether the culture supports open, transparent communication or a more hierarchical structure.
- **Work Environment:** The tone of the workplace, which can be competitive, supportive, fast-paced, etc.
- **Symbols and Rituals:** Includes company slogans, ceremonies, dress codes, and office layout that represent the culture.
- **Leadership Style:** How leaders interact with staff – authoritative, participative, or servant leadership, for instance.

Why Corporate Culture Matters: Corporate culture affects employee satisfaction, retention, productivity, brand reputation, and the ability to attract talent. A strong, positive culture can drive performance and innovation, while a toxic culture can lead to high turnover and reputational damage.

3.3.2 Audit culture

Audit culture primarily relates to IA/OIG leadership and managers who may be hesitant to migrate to **Agility** or **AI tools** for a variety of strategic, cultural, technical, and organizational reasons. Below are key **reasons for resistance,** organized into thematic categories:

1. **Cultural and Mindset Barriers**
    - **Comfort with Traditional Audit Models:** Many leaders built their careers on linear, risk-based audit planning and are deeply invested in standardized frameworks and waterfall methodologies.
    - **Fear of Losing Control or Oversight:** Agile approaches decentralize planning and empower audit teams to self-organize, which may feel threatening to hierarchical leadership structures.
    - **Skepticism Toward AI:** Concerns that AI lacks transparency or explainability (i.e., "black box" decision-making) can lead to mistrust in AI-generated insights.
2. **Knowledge and Skill Gaps**
    - **Lack of Understanding of Agile Principles:** Agile is often misunderstood as chaotic or informal, rather than iterative and value driven.
    - **Limited Familiarity with AI Capabilities:** Without a strong understanding of AI's strengths (e.g., anomaly detection, predictive analytics), leaders may not see its relevance to audit objectives.
    - **Training Deficiency:** Leadership and staff may lack technical training to use or oversee AI tools effectively, making adoption risky.
3. **Resource Constraints**
    - **Budget Prioritization:** Agile transformation and AI implementation require upfront investments in tools, training, and pilot programs – resources that may not be immediately available.
    - **Competing Priorities:** Cybersecurity threats, regulatory audits, or talent shortages may take precedence, delaying innovation efforts.
4. **Perceived Risk**
    - **Regulatory and Reputational Risk:** Concerns that reliance on AI tools could result in audit errors or non-compliance if the technology fails or is misunderstood. The industry faces regulations that prevent or restrict AI adoption due to inadequate AI safeguards.

- **Loss of Objectivity or Independence:** Some leaders may believe that adaptive audit planning or automated analytics could compromise the auditor's independence or impartiality.

5. **Organizational Resistance**
   - **Change Fatigue:** If the organization has undergone multiple transformations recently, leadership may delay further change to stabilize operations.
   - **Lack of Executive Buy-In:** Without visible support from the board or senior executives, audit leaders may be reluctant to champion agile or AI initiatives.
   - **Fear of Job Redundancy:** Implicit concern that adoption of AI may lead to downsizing, leading to subtle or overt resistance from leadership protecting their teams or functions.
6. **Lack of Clear Return on Investment (ROI)**
   - **Uncertainty Around Value:** Agile and AI tools promise efficiency and insights, but if benefits are not clearly quantified or communicated, leadership may question the return on investment.
   - **Failed or Inconclusive Pilots:** Past experiences with partial agile adoption or AI tools that didn't meet expectations can sour leadership on future attempts.

Why Audit Culture Matters: Audit culture matters because it directly shapes the effectiveness, credibility, and impact of the IA/OIG function. It defines how auditors think, behave, and interact – not just within the audit team, but across the entire organization. Audit culture matters because it's the foundation of how IA/OIG delivers trust, adapts to change, supports ethical behavior, and enables business resilience. It is not just *how* audits are conducted – but *why* and *with what mindset* – that defines audit's value to the organization. Think about the benefits that auditees will observe by employing Agility and AI.

> 🛠 **Important Note:** Understanding "why" individuals react or behave in a certain way, such as rooted in the culture, is important because cybersecurity auditors need to find an approach that will achieve the Agility and AI goals. That approach may need to be tailored depending on an individual's behavior or group culture. As noted in Chapter 2 – Building Partnerships for Success, relationships are important to achieve quality audit objectives.

3.3.3 Google versus traditional finance firm culture

Let's do a review of two different IA/OIG cultures: Google and a traditional finance firm, the latter could represent a government agency. This side-by-side example contrasts **Google's innovation-driven culture** with a **traditional finance firm's formal environment:**

🏛 *Google's Innovation-Driven Culture (Whittaker, 2024)*

- **Workplace Atmosphere:** Open, casual, and collaborative. Employees are encouraged to speak up, share ideas freely, and experiment without fear of failure.
- **Dress Code:** Informal attire – jeans, t-shirts, and hoodies are common.
- **Leadership Style:** Flat hierarchy with accessible leadership. Managers act as coaches and facilitators rather than directors.
- **Decision-Making:** Decentralized and data driven. Cross-functional teams test and iterate quickly.
- **Innovation Approach:** Employees are encouraged to spend time on passion projects (e.g., the 20 percent-time rule, which leads to products like Google Mail (Gmail)).
- **Office Design:** Open spaces, lounges, nap pods, and creative zones to inspire ideation and collaboration.
- **Communication Style:** Informal and transparent – frequent all-hands meetings, digital platforms for idea sharing.

🏛 *Traditional Finance Firm's Formal Environment (Lindenfeld-Hall, 2022)*

- **Workplace Atmosphere:** Structured, disciplined, and hierarchical. There's a strong emphasis on procedure, precision, and risk management.
- **Dress Code:** Formal attire – suits, ties, and professional attire are the norm.
- **Leadership Style:** Top-down and risk averse management. Decisions are made by senior executives and communicated down the management chain.
- **Decision-Making:** Cautious and compliance driven. Emphasis on minimizing risk and following established protocols.
- **Innovation Approach:** Conservative. Innovation is more incremental and subject to extensive approval and regulatory review.
- **Office Design:** Cubicles or individual offices with a more traditional layout and limited personalization.
- **Communication Style:** Formal and measured – written memos, scheduled meetings, and controlled information flow.

> **Quick Summary:** Google fosters **experimentation, speed, and creativity** in a relaxed and supportive environment, while a traditional finance firm prioritizes **structure, discipline, and control** within a formal and risk-averse culture. Each approach aligns with the organization's goals and the nature of its industry.

Going beyond corporate culture, let's look at the **IA culture at Google (under Alphabet Incorporated),** which blends traditional audit rigor with the company's hallmark culture of **innovation, transparency, and agility.** While the exact inner workings aren't fully public, based on corporate disclosures, industry benchmarks, and employee insights, here's a description of how IA likely operates within Google's unique environment (Google, n.d.a, n.d.b).

Google's IA Culture: A Fusion of Innovation and Oversight

1. **Risk-Based and Technology-Driven**
   - IA functions are **data-driven** and focus on **key risks** tied to innovation, privacy, cybersecurity, and regulatory compliance (especially given Google's global operations).
   - Google leverages **AI, automation, and advanced analytics** to perform continuous auditing, detect anomalies, and analyze massive datasets across its platforms (e.g., Search, Ads, Cloud).
2. **Agile and Collaborative**
   - IA teams likely follow **agile methodologies** – conducting shorter, iterative audits focused on real-time insights rather than long traditional audit cycles.
   - There is a **strong emphasis on partnering with business units**, not just policing them. Auditors are expected to advise teams on how to manage risk while still rapidly innovating.
3. **Transparency and Ethical Standards**
   - IA at Google supports a **"speak-up" culture**, where ethical concerns or risks can be reported without fear.
   - As part of Alphabet's (Google's parent company) broader **ethics and compliance program**, audit plays a role in evaluating controls over AI ethics, data use, and responsible innovation.
4. **Flat Structure and Empowerment**
   - Like the rest of Google, the IA team likely operates in a **less hierarchical** structure. Team members are empowered to challenge assumptions, share insights across teams, and contribute to solutions.
5. **Cross-Disciplinary Talent**
   - Auditors come from **diverse professional backgrounds** – tech, data science, cybersecurity, privacy law, and finance – to better understand complex products and operations.
   - This diversity supports an audit culture that's more **consultative than confrontational**, adding value beyond compliance.

Quick Summary: Google's IA culture reflects the company's broader ethos: bold innovation with built-in accountability. It is forward-thinking, technologically advanced, and collaborative, aligning with the demands of auditing a fast-paced, data-heavy tech ecosystem.

Not all firms are like Google, but incremental change is possible. The objective is to embed innovation and creativity within individual audit activities, then communicate the benefits.

3.4 HOW CULTURE INFLUENCES AUDIT PROCESSES

Culture influences audit processes at every stage – from planning and execution to communication and follow-up – by shaping how auditors approach their work, how stakeholders engage with them, and how risks and issues are perceived and addressed.

How Culture Influences Audit Processes

1. **Risk Identification and Assessment**
   - **Cultural Influence:** An open, risk-aware culture encourages transparency and the early identification of issues.
   - **Impact on Audit:** Auditors receive **more accurate and complete information** from stakeholders, allowing for better scoping and prioritization.
   - **Contrast:** In risk-averse or blame-oriented cultures, individuals may withhold information or downplay issues, leading to **incomplete risk** assessments.
2. **Audit Planning and Scoping**
   - **Cultural Influence:** An innovative culture supports agile planning and responsiveness to emerging risks.
   - **Impact on Audit:** Audit plans can be **dynamic, collaborative**, and aligned with business strategy.
   - **Contrast:** In rigid or highly bureaucratic cultures, audit plans may be **inflexible**, driven by checklists, and not reflective of evolving priorities based on risk profile.
3. **Fieldwork and Execution**
   - **Cultural Influence:** A collaborative culture fosters cooperation and access to data and personnel.
   - **Impact on Audit:** Fieldwork is **more efficient and effective**, with fewer barriers to documentation, interviews, walkthroughs, and testing.
   - **Contrast:** In siloed or mistrustful environments, auditors may face **resistance, delays, or obstruction.**
4. **Issue Identification and Reporting**
   - **Cultural Influence:** A culture that values transparency and learning from mistakes promotes honest reporting.
   - **Impact on Audit:** Auditors can deliver **constructive, forward-looking recommendations** that are more likely to be accepted and acted upon.

- **Contrast:** In politically sensitive cultures, findings may be **censored, softened, or challenged**, leading to watered-down reports and unresolved risks.

5. **Follow-Up and Continuous Improvement**
   - **Cultural Influence:** Cultures that value accountability and continuous improvement treat audits as opportunities to learn and grow.
   - **Impact on Audit: Remediation happens faster**, and lessons learned are shared across the organization.
   - **Contrast:** In compliance-only cultures, there may be **minimal engagement in root cause analysis**, with fixes aimed only at "closing the audit issue" rather than systemically improving controls.

Table 3.1 describes the positive and negative audit impact for the cultural traits noted. The objective is to achieve the positive audit impact to ensure the cybersecurity audit professional has full access to information and evidence for control testing. The objective of describing the negative audit impact is to understand that impact and note for learning how to address through the concepts presented in this chapter.

Table 3.1 Examples of cultural traits that influence auditing

Cultural trait	Positive audit impact	Negative audit impact
Transparency	Openness to discuss risks and share documentation	Concealment or selective disclosure
Accountability	Stakeholders own remediation actions	Finger-pointing, lack of follow-through
Innovation mindset	Support for agile audits and new technologies	Resistance to data analytics or non-traditional methods
Tone at the top	Leadership models ethics and audit value	Leadership dismisses audit or is defensive toward findings
Collaboration	Cross-functional support for audit activities	Audit viewed as adversarial or intrusive

Quick Summary: Culture doesn't just influence audit – it defines the environment in which audit operates. A strong, ethical, and open culture **amplifies audit's impact**, while a weak or defensive culture **limits its effectiveness** and creates blind spots in risk management. This may lead to a reduction of shareholder value and in extreme cases, entity going out of business. As one example, Enron's corporate culture, shaped by its Chief Executive Officer, promoted unethical behavior, excessive risk-taking, and a lack of transparency and accountability, ultimately leading to the company's collapse and significant investment losses for shareholders (Free et al., 2007). A similar toxic culture could also hinder IA and OIG teams from adopting agile methodologies and leveraging AI tools due to resistance to change, fear of oversight, or lack of leadership support.

3.5 WHAT CULTURE WORKS BEST WITH AGILITY AND AI

Admittedly, the Google culture would be preferable because of the innovation and creative culture that inspires all associates. There are other firms that have the same philosophy. One of my previous employers was very similar to Google, even had a fire pole that went from the second to the first floor in the technology building as noted in Chapter 1 – Understanding Audit Objectives, Expectations, Concepts, and Opportunities. There were ping pong and pool tables that inspired thoughtful discussions. Moreover, the audit team was not perceived as the enemy and was involved in many leadership and management meetings. While I did not know it at the time, I was able to apply agile concepts within my audit team.

Let's think more about what culture works best with Agility and AI. All cultures will work with Agility and AI. Why is this believed to be true? First, you may find colleagues that practice the agile methodology. Second, you may find many cybersecurity teams using AI tools. Exploring this a bit further, the culture that works best with **Agility concepts** and **AI tools** is one that embraces **collaboration, adaptability, experimentation, and data-driven decision-making.** This type of culture encourages continuous learning, rapid iteration, and ethical responsibility – enabling IA/OIG teams to **respond quickly to emerging risks** and **leverage AI effectively** for deeper insights. However, this ideal culture may not be observed in all organizations, thus, cybersecurity audit approaches must consider challenging cultures.

Table 3.2 presents a comparative chart that highlights the desired support for each of the cultural traits noted. The objective of providing these cultural traits with support ideas is to encourage the reader to think about when success is achieved for your organizational/audit culture.

Table 3.2 Key cultural traits that support agility and AI in IA/OIG

Cultural trait	How it supports agility	How it supports AI adoption
Collaboration	Promotes cross-functional teamwork and faster iterations	Encourages shared ownership of data and insights
Transparency	Supports real-time feedback and open two-way communication	Facilitates clear understanding of AI inputs and outputs
Adaptability	Embraces change and reprioritization based on risk	Allows for AI tool evolution and refinement
Experimentation	Encourages testing new audit methods (e.g., agile sprints)	Supports piloting and scaling AI-driven audits
Learning orientation	Fosters retrospective learning and continuous improvement	Promotes skill development in data science and AI ethics

(Continued)

Table 3.2 Key cultural traits that support agility and AI in IA/OIG (*Continued*)

Cultural trait	How it supports agility	How it supports AI adoption
Data-driven thinking	Decisions are based on analytics and metrics	Aligns with AI's predictive and prescriptive capabilities
Psychological safety	Empowers team members to question status quo	Enables candid feedback on AI limitations and risks
Ethical awareness	Ensures responsible innovation and use of technology	Supports fairness, explainability, and accountability in AI use

Agile + AI-Enabling Culture in Practice

Let's convert the theory into actionable practice. The example below is related to an innovative culture that reflects the associated benefits. The objective is to understand the success factors so that a future state vision can be developed.

- Teams are **comfortable with ambiguity** and quick iterations instead of rigid, step-by-step audits.
- There is **support from leadership** to explore new tools like robotic process automation (RPA), machine learning models, and predictive analytics.
- Auditors feel **empowered to suggest improvements**, raise concerns about AI bias, and contribute to more intelligent risk assessment processes.
- **Continuous feedback loops** drive both audit quality and AI model refinement.

⚠ **Caution:** Confirm that the Generative AI tool is secure and approved by audit management before executing prompts.

Generative AI Example: Imagine an audit team using an AI model to detect anomalies in procurement data:

- In a **rigid culture**, auditors may distrust the model or ignore its outputs.
- In an **agile, innovation-oriented culture**, auditors analyze the anomalies, provide feedback to improve the model, and incorporate findings into real-time assurance efforts.

Pro Tips

- Practice executing Generative Pre-Trained Transformer (ChatGPT) prompts by considering the questions or queries you may have. Consider follow-up instructions, including those recommended by ChatGPT at the end of the information provided.
- Consider attending prompt engineering courses, such as those offered through Coursera that are created by reputable institutions, such as Google.

Quick Summary: The most effective culture for Agility and AI is one that combines **openness, flexibility, and accountability** – where innovation is encouraged, learning is continuous, and ethical guardrails are in place. Think about those groups within your organization that exhibit one or more of the previously mentioned traits. Is it possible that you could begin the Agility and AI journey by partnering with those who already exhibit one or more of the desired culture and behavior attributes?

3.6 HOW CHANGE MANAGEMENT IS INFLUENCED BY CULTURE

Technology-based change management is the common thought when change management is mentioned. However, there are other use cases for change management, such as cultural change management. While transitioning may be perceived as changing an organization's goal, the objective is to change the "how" in achieving the goal. Alignment with the firm/agency and audit goals would remain the same. It is about changing the audit practices by using agility and AI.

Culture has a profound influence on **cultural change management** because it shapes **how change is perceived, communicated, and adopted** across an organization. An organization's existing culture can **either accelerate or hinder** the success of change initiatives, including those related to adopting agility, AI, or IA/OIG transformation (Cameron & Quinn, 2011; Hiatt, 2006; Kegan & Lahey, 2001; Kotter, 1996; Lencioni, 2016; Schein, 2010).

🔄 *How Culture Influences a Cultural Change Management Approach*

1. **Determines Readiness for Change**
    - A culture that values **learning, innovation, and adaptability** is naturally more open to change.
    - In contrast, cultures rooted in **risk aversion, hierarchy, or tradition** often resist change, requiring more time and effort to shift mindsets.

    🏛 **Culture Example:** In a transparent and empowering culture, staff may ask, "How can we make this work?" In a fearful culture, they may ask, "Will I lose my job?"

2. **Shapes Communication Strategy**
    - **Open cultures** respond well to transparent, participatory communication, such as town halls and two-way feedback loops.
    - **Top-down, formal cultures** may require structured, hierarchical communication, such as memos from leadership or policy-driven rollouts.
    - **Trust in leadership** and a history of follow-through impact whether change messages are believed or ignored.
3. **Change in Leadership Style Influencers**
    - In **collaborative cultures**, change can be led through **coalitions, champions, and peer influencers.**

- In **centralized cultures**, change may rely on **executive mandates** and compliance-based enforcement.
- Culture impacts **who have credibility** in driving change (e.g., senior leaders vs. subject-matter experts).

4. **Affects Stakeholder Engagement**
   - In inclusive cultures, employees are **invited to co-create** the change, which increases buy-in.
   - In rigid or siloed cultures, stakeholders may be **excluded or resistant**, slowing down the process or causing friction.
   - Cultural norms define **how resistance is expressed** – directly through questions or passively through disengagement.
5. **Drives Adoption Behaviors**
   - Cultures that reward **experimentation, agility, and recognition** will reinforce new behaviors aligned with the change.
   - Cultures focused on **compliance, status quo, or individual performance** may cause people to revert to old habits unless incentivized otherwise.

Table 3.3 presents four different negative cultural traits and the associated impact. The objective of this table is to define the impact so that cybersecurity auditors can use the terminology and impact within a Generative AI tool to determine the best approach for influencing change.

Table 3.3 Example negative cultural trait impacts

Cultural trait	Impact on change management
Hierarchy and control	Requires formal approval and gradual rollout; change is top-down
Innovation and openness	Encourages quick adoption; supports iterative feedback and evolution
Fear of failure	Slows adoption; requires safe zones and visible leadership support
Accountability culture	Enhances follow-through on change initiatives; drives sustainable change

Quick Summary: **Culture is both the lens and the lever** in cultural change management. It determines **how you introduce change, how fast it spreads, who leads it, and how well it sticks.** A successful cultural change strategy must:

- **Understand and respect the current culture.**
- **Identify what elements to preserve or evolve.**
- **Design interventions aligned with how people think, behave, and connect.**

Pro Tip: Write down the three bullets above and remember these tips as you progress in your Agility and AI journey.

3.7 DEFINING CULTURE AND BEHAVIOR CHANGE MANAGEMENT STRATEGY

In today's workforce, five generations: Traditionalists (1925–1945), Baby Boomers (1946–1964), Generation X (1965–1980), Millennials (1981–2000), and Generation Z (2001–2020) coexist, each bringing distinct values, communication styles, and priorities. Traditionalists emphasize loyalty, hierarchy, and personal recognition, while Baby Boomers favor teamwork, hard work, and direct communication. Gen Xers, shaped by skepticism and independence, value flexibility and work-life balance. Millennials seek meaningful experiences, responsive leadership, and digital collaboration. Finally, Gen Z is highly tech-savvy, entrepreneurial, and mission-driven, preferring personalization and rapid innovation (Purdue Global, n.d.).

These generational differences significantly influence organizational culture. They can lead to misunderstandings in communication preferences (e.g., face-to-face vs. instant messaging (IM)), divergent expectations around hierarchy and autonomy, and varying levels of comfort with change and technology. Leaders who recognize and embrace these differences, through agile communication methods, tailored development opportunities, and inclusive decision-making, can foster a culture that leverages generational strengths rather than allowing them to create silos or conflict.

> ⚠ **Caution:** Confirm that the Generative AI tool is secure and approved by audit management before executing prompts.

Generative AI Examples

- Example prompt use: "*How can I influence behavior change among Baby Boomers in the workplace when introducing new technology or processes?*"
- Example prompt use: "*What strategies are most effective for encouraging Baby Boomers to adopt new habits or behaviors in a professional setting, especially related to digital transformation?*"
- Example prompt use: "*What are the best ways to influence Gen X employees to adapt to new organizational changes or technologies?*"
- Example prompt use: "*How can I motivate Gen X professionals to change established work habits while respecting their experience and independence?*"

3.7.1 Behavior role in culture change management

The previous sections discussed the types of culture and why individuals are hesitant to change. Understanding why the culture may prevent Agility and AI progress is important before looking for solutions. Why do you include behavior? Behavior is both a **reflection of culture** and a **driver of culture** – they are deeply interconnected and mutually reinforcing (Denison, 1990; Heskett, 2012).

1. **Behavior Reflects Culture:** Culture can be thought of as the "*way we do things around here*." It is made visible through patterns of behavior, including how people interact, make decisions, handle conflict, and respond to change. When we observe behaviors such as collaboration, accountability, or resistance, we see culture in action.
   🏛 **Examples**
   - If a culture values transparency, behaviors like open communication and information sharing will be common.
   - If a culture tolerates risk aversion, employees may avoid speaking up or experimenting with new ideas.
2. **Behavior Reinforces and Shapes Culture:** While culture shapes expected behaviors, repeated behaviors – especially those modeled or rewarded by leadership – reinforce and evolve the culture over time. This is why behavior change is often the first tactical step in culture transformation. What gets **rewarded, recognized**, or **tolerated** becomes embedded, which is a mechanism of reinforcement. For example, if leaders consistently acknowledge proactive problem-solving, those behaviors will spread gradually cultivating a culture of innovation or ownership.
3. **Behavioral Consistency = Cultural Strength:** Strong, healthy cultures show **alignment between values and behaviors** across levels and departments. Misalignment, such as a stated value of collaboration but competitive individual behavior, can signal cultural dysfunction.

🔙 **Quick Summary:** Behavior is the **visible manifestation of culture** and the **lever through which culture is changed**. To shift culture, organizations must target key behaviors – especially those demonstrated by leaders, reinforced in systems, and shared through norms. Sustainable culture change is achieved not by slogans, but by cultivating consistent, observable, and rewarded behaviors across the organization.

- **Culture is enacted and reinforced through behavior.**
- **Leader and peer behaviors** send strong signals about what is expected and acceptable.
- **Changing culture requires changing behavior** – through role modeling, incentives, feedback loops, and consistent reinforcement.

3.7.2 Auditor as a change agent

Now that different cultures and behaviors with associated benefits and opportunities have been described, it is time to think about how IA/OIG can change those cultures and behaviors. In essence, cybersecurity auditors need to be change agents. A **change agent** is an individual or group that actively facilitates, leads, or drives change within an organization. Change agents play a crucial role in helping organizations transition from a current state to a desired future state by **influencing attitudes, behaviors, processes, and structures.**

> 📖 **Definition:** A **change agent** is someone who champions, manages, or implements change by engaging stakeholders, overcoming resistance, and ensuring that change initiatives align with strategic goals and cultural values (Garvin & Roberto, 2005; Hiatt, 2006; Keller & Aiken, 2008; Rogers, 2003).

Table 3.4 provides change agent examples. The objective is to provide ideas on who change agents could be within your organization. Every organization and agency have nuances, including specific role titles and responsibilities that you may not be able to alter. Identify those individuals who exhibit the desired culture and behaviors that support agility concepts and AI technology.

Table 3.4 Types of change agents

Type	Description
Internal change agent	Employees, managers, or IA/OIG leaders who understand the organization's culture and politics
External change agent	Consultants, advisors, or external auditors who bring fresh perspectives and objective insights
Formal change agent	Individuals officially tasked with change (e.g., project managers, transformation leads)
Informal change agent	Influential individuals who drive change through personal credibility and leadership

🔑 *Key Roles and Responsibilities of Change Agents*

- **Communicate Vision:** Translate the purpose of the change into clear, motivating messages.
- **Build Trust and Credibility:** Earn the respect of stakeholders and act as a liaison between leadership and employees.
- **Identify and Overcome Resistance:** Understand the root causes of resistance and tailor approaches to mitigate it.
- **Model Desired Behaviors:** Act as a role model by adopting the behaviors and mindset expected of others.
- **Facilitate Training and Engagement:** Provide resources, guidance, and encouragement to help others adopt the change.
- **Monitor Progress and Feedback:** Track milestones, adapt strategies, and provide updates on progress and lessons learned.

🤓 Traits of an Effective Change Leader

A change leader is an individual who drives and champions transformation within an organization by inspiring others, challenging the status quo, and guiding teams through uncertainty. Unlike traditional managers who focus on maintaining stability, a change leader embraces innovation and actively seeks improvement opportunities aligned with strategic goals. They communicate a clear vision, build trust, and address resistance by listening to concerns and involving stakeholders in the process. Effective change leaders balance empathy with decisiveness and possess the resilience to navigate setbacks while maintaining momentum toward desired outcomes. Their leadership is essential in fostering a culture that adapts, evolves, and thrives in dynamic environments. Specifically, change leaders typically exhibit the following leadership styles.

- Strong **communication** and **interpersonal** skills
- High **emotional intelligence** and empathy
- Trustworthy leader
- Resilience and **ability to manage conflict**
- Credibility and influence within the organization
- Strategic thinking with a focus on long-term impact
  Example (IA/OIG Context): In a traditional audit department transitioning to agile auditing and AI tools, a **change leader** might be:
    - An **audit manager** championing data analytics and agile planning
    - An **internal influencer** training others on emerging tools
    - A **consultant** helping redefine the audit charter and processes
    - A **cross-functional team leader** pilots new audit method

Quick Summary: Change leaders or agents are the catalysts that transform ideas into action and resistance into momentum. They are vital to achieving **successful, sustainable change,** especially when navigating shifts in culture, technology, or strategy. **Change leaders or agents are critical enablers of transformation,** acting as catalysts who:

- Influence behavior and mindset
- Build trust and engagement
- Sustain momentum through communication and modeling
- Align change with organizational culture and strategy

3.7.3 Culture change management strategy

Understanding the change leader or agent's role is important because that individual will create a formal or informal culture change management strategy. Remember that culture includes individual behaviors. The following information is related to a formal strategy, but the content can be tailored to individuals or groups within the organization or agency. A **culture change management strategy** is a structured approach used to intentionally shift an organization's norms, values, and behaviors to align with strategic goals. This strategy is crucial when organizations adopt new technologies (like AI), embrace agile practices, restructure, or face significant market or compliance pressures. Below is a comprehensive description of such a strategy:

1. **Define the Purpose and Desired Culture**
   Begin by articulating **why** culture change is needed. Link the desired culture to strategic business goals (e.g., innovation, agility, customer focus, compliance). Describe the **target cultural attributes** and related behaviors in clear, observable terms.

   Example: Move from a compliance-driven audit (e.g., check the box) culture to an innovation-driven audit culture that embraces continuous learning, proactive risk assessment, and technology integration.

2. **Assess the Current Culture**
   - Leverage from an existing **culture audit** or conduct a **culture audit** using surveys, interviews, focus groups, and behavioral observations. If the latter is required, make sure to include the requisite subject matter experts. Identify:
     - Dominant values and beliefs
     - Behavioral norms
     - Leadership styles
     - Symbols, language, and rituals
     - Alignment or gaps with the desired culture
   - This establishes a baseline and helps detect cultural strengths and obstacles.
3. **Identify Cultural Gaps and Change Readiness**
   - Analyze where the current culture **diverges from the desired state**, including:
     - Behavioral misalignments
     - Leadership resistance
     - Incentives that reward the wrong behaviors
   - Assess organizational **readiness for change**, including change fatigue, trust levels, and past transformation experiences.
4. **Engage Leadership and Key Influencers**
   - Cultural transformation must be **led from the top** and **reinforced from the middle**. Engage:
     - Executives who will champion the change and model desired behaviors
     - Middle managers to translate change into operational language
     - Informal influencers ("culture carriers") who shape peer norms
   - Provide leaders with coaching on **cultural storytelling**, behavioral modeling, and trust-building.

5. **Communicate with Purpose and Consistency**
   - Develop a compelling **culture change narrative** that connects hearts and minds. Specifically, communicate:
     - Why the culture is changing.
     - What the new culture looks like.
     - How employees will be supported during the transition.
     - How employees will benefit from the culture change (e.g., learn new skills, enhance career development and promotions).
   - Use multiple channels (e.g., town halls, storytelling, visual symbols) and repeat key messages frequently.

6. **Align Systems, Structures, and Incentives**
   - Embed the new culture into:
     - Performance management systems (e.g., evaluation criteria)
     - Hiring and onboarding (e.g., cultural fit and values-based selection)
     - Recognition programs (e.g., awards for collaborative innovation)
     - Policies and processes (e.g., workflows that support agility or inclusion)
   - Make sure internal systems **reward and reinforce** the behaviors you want to see.

7. **Develop Capabilities and Tools**
   - Equip employees with the skills and mindsets needed for the new culture through:
     - Leadership development programs
     - Behavioral workshops
     - Psychological safety training
     - Agile and AI tool training, if relevant
   - Provide **safe-to-fail** environments that allow experimentation and learning.

8. **Monitor Progress and Adapt**
   - Measure culture change using:
     - Culture surveys and behavioral indicators
     - Engagement and retention metrics
     - Adoption rates for new practices
   - Track successes and setbacks. Use insights to recalibrate tactics, refine messaging, and respond to resistance. And celebrate visible wins to sustain momentum.

9. **Sustain the Culture Over Time**
   - Cultural change is not a one-time project; it requires **reinforcement and evolution**. Maintain momentum by:
     - Institutionalizing the new behaviors
     - Refreshing leadership alignment
     - Continually engaging employees in improvement efforts
   - Establish rituals, stories, and symbols that **anchor the new culture**.

Quick Summary: An effective culture change strategy is both **top-down and bottom-up**, blending **formal systems change** with **informal behavioral shifts**. It focuses not only on what needs to change but also on **how to influence beliefs, habits, and symbols** that define the employee experience.

Generative AI Example – ChatGPT Sneak Peak

⚠ **Caution:** Confirm that the Generative AI tool is secure and approved by audit management before executing prompts.

Submitted the following within ChatGPT

Example prompt use: "*Describe how to modify someone's behavior. The behavior is defiant and not wanting to share information with the auditor.*"

ChatGPT said (OpenAI ChatGPT 4o, 2024)

"*Modifying **defiant behavior** – especially when someone **refuses to share information with an auditor** – requires a thoughtful, respectful, and strategic approach. The goal is not only to obtain the needed information but to **transform the underlying resistance into cooperation**, ideally without escalating conflict.*"

Table 3.5 provides some ideas of why an individual may not be willing to change their behavior or the culture within their group. Before changing behavior, assess *why* the individual is defiant. The objective of this table is to describe some common defiance root causes.

Table 3.5 Understanding the root cause of defiance

Root cause	Behavioral expression
Fear of exposure or repercussions	Defensive, evasive, or stonewalling
Lack of trust in auditors	Withholding, undermining credibility
Cultural or political dynamics	Passive resistance, information hoarding
Misunderstanding of audit purpose	Dismissive or disengaged responses
Power imbalance or ego conflict	Challenging authority, asserting control

Steps to Modify Defiant Behavior in an Audit Context

Leveraging from the root cause of defiant behavior and your unique observations as noted in Table 3.5, apply that information to the behavior modification ideas below.

1. **Build Psychological Safety and Trust**
   - **Approach:** Use empathy and respect to reduce perceived threat.

- **Action:** Privately explain the auditor's role as a partner, not a "gotcha" investigator. Reinforce confidentiality and ethical handling of information.
- **Tone:** Calm, curious, and nonjudgmental.

🤓 **Example:** "*I understand audits can feel uncomfortable. My role isn't to assign blame, but to help improve controls so that your team is protected and supported.*"

2. **Clarify the Purpose and Value of the Audit**
   - **Approach:** Reframe the audit as a tool for improvement, not punishment.
   - **Action:** Explain the benefits of transparency (e.g., risk mitigation, process improvement, regulatory alignment).
   - **Tone:** Collaborative, value-oriented.

🤓 **Example:** "*Your input is critical in helping us ensure this process is efficient and resilient. This isn't about fault, it's about identifying opportunities.*"

🛠 **Important Note:** You just witnessed a basic ChatGPT discussion. The request was written as if you were talking to another person. Note the detailed information provided in the ChatGPT session. Chapter 5 – Harnessing Artificial Intelligence: Enhancing Cybersecurity Audits through Automation and Insight will provide more details on ChatGPT and other tools.

3.7.4 Traditional to innovative and forward-thinking IA/OIG

Transforming a traditional IA/OIG department into an **innovative and forward-thinking function** and **management trusted advisor** requires a deliberate cultural and operational shift. It would take time and require incremental "wins" to demonstrate the values. Here's a structured approach you can use to guide that transformation, which is grounded in agility, technology, and value-driven auditing.

🗺 Transformation Roadmap for an Innovative IA/OIG Department

1. **Redefine the Audit Mission and Mindset**
   Goal: Shift from "compliance enforcer" to "strategic advisor."
   - **Update the IA/OIG charter** to emphasize risk advisory, data-driven insights, and forward-looking assurance.
   - Promote a **culture of curiosity and continuous learning,** encouraging auditors to ask not just "Is it compliant?" but also "Is it effective, scalable, and resilient?"
   - Reinforce that audit is a **partner to the business,** not a roadblock.

2. **Leverage Technology and Automation**
   Goal: Improve audit efficiency, coverage, and insight through modern tools.
   - Implement **audit analytics platforms (e.g., Audit Command Language (ACL), Interactive Data Extraction and Analysis (IDEA), Power Business Intelligence (BI), or Tableau) for continuous monitoring and data visualization.**
   - **Introduce automation and RPA to handle repetitive audit tasks like control testing and sampling.**
   - **Explore AI/Machine Learning** (ML) for anomaly detection, fraud risk modeling, and predictive insights.
3. **Adopt Agile Audit Methodologies**
   Goal: Increase flexibility, responsiveness, and stakeholder engagement.
   - Break down audits into **shorter sprints** with regular stakeholder check-ins and adaptive planning.
   - Use **Agile audit planning** with quarterly risk reassessments rather than static annual plans.
   - Deliver insights in **real time** or near-real time, not just in formal reports at the end.
4. **Build Cross-Functional Capabilities**
   Goal: Strengthen team skillsets to match modern risk landscapes.
   - Upskill auditors in:
     - **Data analytics and visualization**
     - **Cybersecurity and privacy**
     - **Cloud and emerging tech risks**
     - **Soft skills** like communication, storytelling with data, and influencing
   - Consider hiring or rotating in talent from **IT, data science, risk management**, or business operations.
5. **Enhance Stakeholder Value**
   Goal: Deliver insights that help the business innovate safely.
   - Focus audit objectives on **strategic priorities** (e.g., digital transformation, Environmental, Social, and Governance (ESG) framework, AI governance).
   - Provide **actionable recommendations**, not just findings.
   - Foster **ongoing communication** with stakeholders, using dashboards or short executive summaries to keep leadership informed.
6. **Encourage a Culture of Experimentation**
   Goal: Normalize innovation within the audit function.
   - Launch **pilot audits using new techniques** (e.g., agile audits, control automation reviews).
   - Reward creative problem-solving and risk foresight.
   - Host **"innovation labs" or workshops** to brainstorm audit process improvements.

7. **Measure and Celebrate Progress**
   Goal: Reinforce the value of change and maintain momentum.
   - Establish **key performance indicators (KPIs)** like audit cycle time, stakeholder satisfaction, analytics adoption, and innovative ideas implemented.
   - Celebrate early wins, such as detecting a critical issue earlier than in traditional cycles.
   - Share success stories within the organization to show audit's evolving role.

Quick Summary: Think of this transformation not just as a change in *tools* or *methods*, but as a change in **identity** – from "auditor of the past" to "trusted navigator of the future."

3.7.5 IA/OIG innovation maturity model

Let's switch from a current state behavior and culture to a future state that achieves the benefits previously mentioned. One tool to identify and manage a future state would be a maturity model. Maturity models are a common tool to identify the desired maturity of a program. There is a maturity model for AI described by many different sources (refer to Chapter 5 – Harnessing Artificial Intelligence: Enhancing Cybersecurity Audits through Automation and Insight). This model would be beneficial for agreeing upon and communicating the desired maturity that would support Agility and AI within your organization. Table 3.6 is an innovation maturity model example that is related to behavior and culture. The objective of this example is to inspire the reader to think about how this could relate to influencing behavior and culture changes. Like the previous discussions, understanding individuals is important to identifying the best approach for influencing change. This type of table could be used as a communication to support behavior or culture changes.

Table 3.6 IA/OIG innovation maturity model

Maturity level	Focus	People	Processes	Technology
Level 1: Traditional	Compliance and controls	Generalists, limited tech skills	Annual plan, static scope	Manual tools (spreadsheets, Word)
Level 2: Developing	Risk-based auditing	Risk-aware, early analytics use	Basic risk assessments	Sampling tools, limited analytics
Level 3: Integrated	Advisory + risk-focused	Cross-skilled teams	Agile risk reassessments	BI dashboards, process mining
Level 4: Innovative	Strategic insight and foresight	Data scientists + auditors + subject matter experts (SMEs)	Continuous auditing, agile audits	RPA, AI/ML, real-time analytics
Level 5: Leading edge	Transformation enabler	Proactive, innovation champions	Embedded assurance, predictive risk	AI governance, cloud-native platforms

🎯 **Pro Tip:** Consider focusing on the People aspect first because individuals influence the maturity for the Processes and Technology.

The next step after finalizing an Innovation Maturity Model is to draft an implementation plan. The reader may recognize that this process loosely aligns with a system development life cycle. The objective is to formalize the plan and ensure agreement, such as what is described in Table 3.7. That table provides a high-level overview of an implementation plan. Every organization and agency have their own requirements, this table is intended to be a starting point that also inspires critical thinking for relevance to your environment.

Table 3.7 Phased implementation plan

Phase	Timeline	Key objectives
Phase 1: Assess and align	Month one–three	• Conduct IA/OIG maturity assessment • Revisit audit charter and mission • Identify strategic goals and stakeholder needs
Phase 2: Upskill and explore	Month three –six	• Launch training in agile, analytics, and tech risk • Hire or rotate in specialized talent • Start using basic data visualization tools (e.g., Power BI)
Phase 3: Pilot innovation	Month six –twelve	• Conduct agile audit pilots (e.g., cloud security or AI ethics) • Begin RPA or analytics use in one–two audits • Collect stakeholder feedback
Phase 4: Operationalize	Year two	• Institutionalize agile audit planning • Implement continuous auditing in critical areas • Develop dashboards and self-service tools for business units
Phase 5: Optimize and scale	Year three +	• Embed predictive analytics • Integrate with AI governance and ESG risk programs • Benchmark innovation impact on audit KPIs

★ Success Factors

- **Tone from the top:** Leadership must support risk-taking and innovation in audit.
- **Balance innovation and assurance:** Use tech responsibly without losing core audit principles.
- **Celebrate wins:** Promote early results to build momentum and stakeholder buy-in.

As the maturity model is developed, think about what an innovative audit culture would look like. An **innovative IA/OIG culture** may represent a modern shift in how IA/OIG functions operate and deliver value. It moves beyond traditional notions of compliance and control testing, embracing agility, technology, collaboration, and forward-thinking risk advisory.

📋 Innovative IA/OIG Culture – Key Characteristics

1. **Forward-Looking and Strategic**
   - Focuses on **emerging risks** (e.g., AI, (ESG, digital transformation) rather than just past transactions.
   - Advises on **strategic initiatives** and provides real-time insights to support decision-making.
2. **Agile and Adaptive**
   - Uses **agile auditing** to reprioritize audits based on dynamic risk landscapes.
   - Delivers **quick, iterative insights** rather than lengthy reports after static audits.
3. **Technology-Enabled**
   - Leverages **data analytics, RPA, AI,** and **real-time monitoring** to automate control testing and deepen analysis.
   - Uses visualization tools and dashboards to communicate results more clearly and impactfully.
4. **Collaborative and Embedded**
   - Operates as a **partner to the business,** embedded in transformation and innovation efforts.
   - Promotes **two-way communication,** mutual respect, and shared ownership of risk.
5. **Curiosity and Learning-Oriented**
   - Encourages a **growth mindset** – auditors are inquisitive, experimental, and comfortable navigating ambiguity.
   - Promotes **cross-training** in areas like cybersecurity, data science, cloud computing, and ESG reporting.
6. **Ethics and Culture Champions**
   - Actively evaluates and promotes **organizational culture, tone at the top,** and **ethical behavior.**
   - Supports a **speak-up culture** and psychological safety within the audit team and the organization.

🏛 Traditional IA/OIG Culture – Key Characteristics

1. **Retrospective and Compliance-Focused**
   - Emphasizes testing past transactions, adherence to policies, and regulatory compliance.
   - Often measures value in terms of audit coverage and number of findings.

2. **Linear and Static Planning**
   - Follows an annual audit plan with little room for flexibility or real-time reallocation.
   - Audits are executed in full cycles and delivered as comprehensive end-of-engagement reports.
3. **Manual and Labor-Intensive**
   - Heavy reliance on interviews, walkthroughs, and sample-based testing.
   - Limited use of technology beyond spreadsheets or basic audit management software.
4. **Siloed and Reactive**
   - Operates at arm's length from business units.
   - Tends to focus on identifying what went wrong rather than how to improve or prevent it.
5. **Rule-Oriented and Risk-Averse**
   - Conservative approach, with less room for experimentation or innovation
   - Focused on enforcing standards rather than enabling innovation

Expanding upon the innovative and traditional culture characteristics, Table 3.8 summarizes those differences. The objective of presenting this information is for awareness as you seek to influence a change from a traditional to innovative culture.

Table 3.8 Key innovative and traditional culture differences

Aspect	Traditional audit culture	Innovative audit culture
Focus	Compliance, controls, and historical data	Strategic risks, future foresight, advisory
Approach	Static, checklist-based	Agile, iterative, and adaptive
Technology use	Minimal	Extensive (AI, analytics, dashboards, RPA)
Mindset	Risk-averse, rule-following	Curious, collaborative, risk-aware
Relationship with business	Independent and siloed	Embedded and consultative
Skills emphasis	Auditing, accounting	Multidisciplinary (tech, cyber, data, business)
Reporting	Formal reports, end-of-cycle delivery	Real-time insights, visual dashboards

💡**Critical Thinking Moment:** You may find a direct correlation between **Table 3.8. Key Innovative and Traditional Culture Differences** and **Table 3.3. Example Negative Cultural Trait Impacts** and **Table 3.5. Understanding the Root Cause of Defiance.**

Conclusion: An **innovative IA/OIG culture** embraces change and enables audit teams to be **proactive risk advisors** and **value creators,** rather than just compliance enforcers. It's a cultural mindset shift supported by the right tools, talent, and tone from the top.

🛠 **Important Note:** The maturity model and ideal IA/OIG group is relevant to those firms/agencies that have leaders who support this initiative. If this is not supported, individuals can leverage from some of this information to execute informal changes through a one-on-one relationship.

3.8 NAVIGATING RESISTANCE: LEADERSHIP STRATEGIES AND REAL-WORLD CHANGE SCENARIOS

3.8.1 Change resistors

The previous section provided an example of an individual who refused to support the audit team. The objective of this section is to further explore those who hinder change, who are often described as **change resistors** or **resistors to change**. Depending on their motivations and behaviors, they can be categorized in a few nuanced ways:

General Description

- Individuals or groups who **oppose, delay, or undermine organizational changes** due to fear of the unknown, loss of control, perceived threats to job security, or lack of understanding of the change's purpose.
- They may **actively or passively resist**, either through vocal opposition, non-compliance, withdrawal, or spreading doubt and negativity.

Types of Change Resistors

- **Skeptics:** Doubt the effectiveness or necessity of the change; often demand evidence or clarity before buying in.
- **Traditionalists:** Prefer the status quo and are uncomfortable with new approaches that disrupt established routines.
- **Fearful:** Concerned about losing status, job relevance, or comfort with familiar tools/processes.
- **Saboteurs:** Actively work against change efforts due to personal grievances, distrust of leadership, or belief the change is harmful.
- **Overwhelmed:** Not inherently against change, but struggle to adapt due to change fatigue or lack of support/training.

Common Traits

- Low trust in leadership
- Lack of involvement in the change process
- Limited understanding of the change rationale
- Perception that past changes failed or caused harm

3.8.2 Strategies for change resistors

This section strikes a perfect balance between psychological insight, leadership application, and practical engagement. Resistance to change is a natural human and organizational response. It is often seen as a barrier, but when properly understood, resistance can offer valuable insight into organizational dynamics, communication breakdowns, and cultural tensions. Rather than viewing resistance as an obstacle, forward-thinking leaders and auditors should view it as a signal – one that, when addressed constructively, can lead to more sustainable and well-supported change outcomes.

This section explores the psychology behind resistance, common behavior patterns, and leadership strategies that can be applied to real-world change scenarios. The goal is to provide a practical framework for navigating resistance in the context of digital transformation, AI adoption, and agile audit practices (Hiatt, 2006; Kotter, 1996; Lewin, 1947; Schein, 2010).

3.8.3 The psychology of resistance

Understanding the root causes of resistance is essential for designing effective change interventions. Resistance is often driven by:

- **Fear of the Unknown:** Individuals may worry about how changes will affect their roles, skills, or relevance.
- **Loss of Control or Influence:** Change can disrupt decision-making authority or long-held responsibilities.
- **Comfort with the Status Quo:** Familiar routines provide a sense of stability, even if they are inefficient.
- **Distrust in Leadership:** Lack of transparency or poor communication fosters skepticism.
- **Change Fatigue:** Repeated changes without clear benefits can exhaust even the most adaptive employees.

These reactions are well explained by models such as **Lewin's Change Management Model** (Unfreeze – Change – Refreeze) and the **Kubler-Ross Change Curve** (Sounding Board Staff, n.d.), which reflects emotional responses from denial to acceptance. Recognizing these stages helps leaders meet employees where they are in the transition.

Table 3.9 organizes the resistor profile with behavioral traits and underlying concerns. Like many of the previous sections, the objective of this table is show the various traits as part of understanding how to influence behavior or cultural changes. This is like understanding the root cause of a control gap so that appropriate remediation can be identified and implemented.

Table 3.9 Types of resistance and associated behaviors

Resistor profile	Behavioral traits	Underlying concern
The skeptic	Challenges assumptions; questions data	Fear of failure or insufficient evidence
The traditionalist	Defends legacy systems and past methods	Comfort with familiarity; reluctance to adapt
The saboteur	Actively undermines change; spreads dissent	Feeling excluded or mistrust of leadership
The passive resistor	Avoids meetings; minimally complies	Fatigue or disengagement from the process
The overwhelmed	Emotionally withdrawn; anxious or frustrated	Cognitive overload; lack of support or clarity

💡**Critical Thinking Moment:** You may find a correlation between Tables 3.3, 3.5 and 3.9.

Leadership Strategies to Address Resistance

Like the other behavior and culture sections of this chapter, leaders play a pivotal role in transforming resistance into engagement. The following approaches are essential:

- **Engage Early and Build Trust:** Include stakeholders in the planning and pilot phases to increase buy-in and reduce surprises.
- **Communicate with Clarity and Purpose:** Reinforce the *why* behind the change repeatedly. Link changes to strategic goals, job impact, and long-term value.
- **Acknowledge Fears and Emotions:** Use empathetic communication to validate concerns. Avoid dismissing emotional reactions as irrational.
- **Create a Network of Change Champions:** Empower early adopters and respected peers to advocate for the change and share success stories.
- **Invest in Skills and Support:** Provide relevant training, resources, and time to learn new tools or systems. Resistance often masks a lack of preparedness.
- **Recognize and Reward Progress:** Publicly acknowledge efforts, adaptability, and improvements to reinforce desired behaviors.

🌍 *Real-world change scenarios*

Case Study 1: AI Implementation in IA/OIG: An IA/OIG team introduced AI-powered analytics to automate repetitive testing. Senior cybersecurity auditors feared being replaced by technology. Thus, leadership responded by framing AI as a tool for augmentation, not replacement. Workshops were held to retrain staff on data interpretation, and early adopters were given platforms to showcase insights derived from AI outputs. Within six months, resistance significantly dropped.

Case Study 2: Agile Audit Transformation: A traditional audit department shifted to agile sprints and shorter reporting cycles. Team leads accustomed to detailed annual planning resisted the new cadence. Thus, the Chief Audit Executive initiated a phased rollout, starting with one pilot team. Weekly retrospectives and peer mentoring supported the transition. Feedback loops were built in, allowing skeptics to influence the final agile structure.

Case Study 3: Shifting Risk Ownership to the First Line: A financial services firm realigned its risk governance model, shifting accountability to front-line managers. Resistance emerged as managers felt unprepared. Thus, the Risk Office partnered with department heads to co-develop KPIs and created a digital dashboard for real-time visibility. A cultural campaign reframed risk ownership as empowerment. Resistance turned into engagement once practical tools were in place.

Lessons Learned and Recommendations

- Resistance is not a roadblock, it is feedback.
- Effective change leadership requires emotional intelligence, patience, and the ability to translate strategy into shared purpose.
- Tailor strategies to the source and type of resistance. One-size-fits-all approaches often fail.
- Foster a culture of psychological safety so that employees can express concerns without fear of retaliation or marginalization.
- Change is most successful when people feel part of the process from the beginning, not just subject to it.

Reflection Questions

- Think of a recent change initiative you experienced. What type of resistance emerged, and how was it handled?
- How do you identify potential change champions within your team or organization?
- What leadership behaviors build trust during uncertain transitions?

3.9 ACHIEVING AUDIT STANDARDS

Chapter 1 – Understanding Audit Objectives, Expectations, Concepts, and Opportunities discussed independence and objectivity from a theoretical perspective, which cybersecurity auditors must understand and maintain. Now think about those audit standards and influencing behavior and culture change without deviating from those standards. For example, for cybersecurity audit professionals to successfully encourage use of agility and AI requires those professionals to comply with organizational requirements.

> **Pro Tip:** Use the behavior and culture concepts in parallel with building partnerships. There is a close relationship between the two and like agility, these are concepts and do not require a framework.

Let's expand on Chapter 1 – Understanding Audit Objectives, Expectations, Concepts, and Opportunities and the Pro Tip above by considering approaches noted for each scenario below to address behavior or culture scenarios.

> **Scenario 1:** The risk and control owner does not agree with the cybersecurity auditor's higher risk rating.

Independence and Objectivity, Risk-Based Approach, and Materiality Audit Standards: To convince an individual that a **higher risk rating** is appropriate, follow a clear, evidence-based, and collaborative approach. Note the authoritative sources, which could include internal policies and procedures. Articulate how the cybersecurity audit professional arrived at the conclusion.

> **Communication Example:** Based on the likelihood of this vulnerability being exploited and the potential impact to our operations and data, this warrants a higher risk rating under National Institute of Standards and Technology (NIST) guidelines. While I understand your concern about resource implications, underestimating this risk could leave us exposed. Let's look at the criteria together and ensure we're making the most informed decision possible.

> **Scenario 2:** The risk management professional does not agree that an AI system could be used to automate the risk assessment process.

Independence and Objectivity and Internal Controls Audit Standards: The cybersecurity audit professional must **normalize innovation** in audit and risk practices by highlighting trends across industry and government **reframe technology** as a compliance enabler, not a disruptor, and **empower professionals** to retain control while adopting smarter tools. Below are some examples of communication.

- **Communication Example:** As audit standards emphasize independence and objectivity, AI can actually strengthen our compliance by reducing human biases and applying consistent logic to every assessment.
- **Communication Example:** Internal controls standards support the use of tools that reduce human error and increase consistency. An AI system doesn't remove oversight – it enhances our ability to identify and manage risk reliably.
- **Communication Example:** AI-driven assessments can be fully aligned with National Institute of Standards and Technology (NIST) and audit standards, provided that humans remain responsible for oversight and validation. This ensures independence and preserves our accountability.
- **Communication Example:** Let's test the tool in a limited setting to validate its reliability and compare it with traditional assessments. We can evaluate if it enhances our objectivity and internal control compliance.

3.10 SUMMARY

This chapter focused on how to influence behaviors and culture, exploring the crucial relationship between organizational culture, individual behavior, and the transformation of IA/OIG practices through agility and AI. The chapter begins by defining culture within both corporate and IA/OIG contexts, emphasizing how shared values, leadership styles, and communication norms directly influence audit effectiveness and stakeholder engagement. As a refresher, a strong, adaptive culture fosters transparency, collaboration, and openness to innovation – conditions that are essential for successfully implementing agile methodologies and AI-driven audit tools.

Throughout the chapter, readers learn that cultural readiness plays a pivotal role in shaping how audit teams plan, execute, and report. Cultures that are rigid or rooted in hierarchy may resist change and limit audit scope, while those that value continuous learning and cross-functional collaboration enable auditors to be more agile and data-driven. A recurring theme is that behavior is both a reflection and a driver of culture, and lasting culture change begins with changing behaviors, especially those modeled and rewarded by leadership.

In addition, the chapter professes that IA/OIG as essential change agents, capable of driving cultural transformation through influence, trust-building, and proactive communication. To achieve that objective, a detailed culture change management strategy is presented, outlining nine steps ranging from defining the desired culture and assessing readiness to aligning systems and sustaining change over time. This strategy is supported by a maturity model and implementation roadmap designed to help IA and OIG departments evolve from traditional, compliance-focused units into innovative, forward-thinking partners in organizational success.

Importantly, the chapter also addresses resistance to change. It categorizes common resistor types – such as skeptics, traditionalists, and saboteurs – and offers leadership strategies for converting resistance into constructive dialogue. Case studies illustrate how real-world audit teams overcame cultural and operational pushbacks when adopting AI and agile methods.

In summary, Chapter 3 – How to Influence Behaviors and Culture provides a practical, psychology-informed framework for reshaping culture and behavior within the IA/OIG functions. It underscores that successful transformation is not just about tools or processes, but about the mindsets and habits that define how auditors interact with others and deliver value.

You made it to the end of this chapter! Let's continue the cybersecurity audit journey by discussing agile concepts in Chapter 4 – Agility in Action: Rethinking Cybersecurity Audit.

Chapter 4

Agility in action

Rethinking cybersecurity audit

4.1 LEARNING OBJECTIVES

By the end of this chapter, readers will be able to:

1. **Define agility and describe its core principles**, including how these principles support dynamic risk environments and align with the audit mission and strategic objectives.
2. **Compare agile auditing with the traditional waterfall methodology**, highlighting differences in process flow, stakeholder engagement, and responsiveness to change.
3. **Apply agile concepts to audit planning and execution**, including iterative delivery, backlog management, cross-functional collaboration, and value-driven reporting.
4. **Examine how agility enables the integration of artificial intelligence (AI) into audit practices**, enhancing adaptability, insight generation, and alignment with evolving audit strategies.

4.2 OPENING INSIGHTS

The need for agility in auditing did not originate within the cybersecurity audit profession but was adopted as audits increasingly came to be viewed as projects. This transition made sense because cybersecurity and technology auditors work closely with cybersecurity and information technology (IT) teams, often auditing areas that inherently require a structured project management approach. The same business problem solved for technology personnel applies to cybersecurity auditing. Specifically, the cybersecurity audit objective is to be collaborative, deliver incremental results, reduce administrative hours, and focus on high-risk cybersecurity areas.

What are the Agile origins? The Agile Manifesto for Software Development was introduced in 2001 (Highsmith, 2001), while the Institute of Internal Auditors (IIA) (2018) published an Agile Auditing Manifesto much later in

DOI: 10.1201/9781003640301-5

2018. This significant gap reflects nearly two decades during which cybersecurity auditors could have benefited from applying agile concepts to improve efficiency.

Why reach that conclusion? The original Agile Manifesto introduced many important ideas, including Scrum, which emphasizes incremental software deployments that continuously add value throughout the life cycle of a major project. These concepts resonated with the Internal Audit and Office of Inspector General (IA/OIG) communities because audits are also project-based efforts, as previously mentioned. The Agile Manifesto principles (which includes Scrum concepts) consists of (Agile Manifesto, n.d.; Amazon Web Services, n.d.a):

1. Collaborating with auditees and other stakeholders throughout the audit activity life cycle.
2. Changing audit focus when higher risk areas are identified.
3. Communicating results early in the audit activity to obtain feedback and confirm potential high-risk remediation.
4. Aligning audit activities with those inspired by change who support agile concepts and AI.
5. Using face-to-face for most activities, encouraging an open dialogue and discussion for brainstorming and finalizing information (more information on this in the "agile contradiction" section). Consider a brief daily meeting to discuss progress, address questions, and brainstorm on upcoming activities.
6. Using the "simplicity" concept to reduce administrative and increase analysis and value-added results.
7. Conducting a lesson learned with all relevant stakeholders to discuss what worked well and what could be enhanced.

In addition to the Agile Manifesto, many books and articles have been written on agile auditing. These resources frequently refer to "Agile Methodology" as the foundation due to its project management capabilities. While these books provide valuable insights, the repeated mention of "agile auditing" can unintentionally convey the idea of a rigid framework or methodology rather than a flexible concept. This perception often leads organizations to invest significant time and effort into building a formalized Agile Audit Framework, which can result in resistance – a challenge discussed in Chapter 3 – How to Influence Behaviors and Culture. Moreover, the effort may not yield the desired results or be abandoned.

Many firms that initially pursued building an Agile Audit Framework eventually abandoned the effort for various reasons. A recurring theme in these cases was that team members viewed the approach as "a process rather than a mindset." This process-driven thinking often led to the creation of extensive documentation on how to perform "agile audits," which missed the broader objective (Fedele & Narayanan, 2025).

Instead of focusing on constructing an agile framework, organizations should focus on "being agile." The goal is to embrace agile concepts with simplicity and flexibility, rather than formalizing them into another burdensome structure. This chapter emphasizes the value of agility and how adopting this mindset can make cybersecurity auditing more dynamic, engaging, and fun.

> **Real-World Scenario:** At a previous employer, the organizational culture was innovative, creative, and inclusive. Cybersecurity audit professionals were actively involved in strategic discussions, project meetings, and other key initiatives, enabling them to obtain information firsthand and contribute proactively to organizational goals. This culture supported the use of agile concepts without requiring changes to audit governance documents, which reduced administrative overhead and increased value-added outcomes.

Agile concepts

Agile concepts emphasize flexibility, collaboration, and continuous improvement by breaking audit activities into smaller, manageable cycles called sprints. In addition, agile concepts prioritize adaptive planning, rapid execution, and ongoing evaluation to deliver incremental value and meet evolving cybersecurity auditor expectations. Expanding upon the Agile Manifesto principles presented in the previous section, the following provides context specific to cybersecurity audit activities. Key characteristics include (Association for Project Management (APM), n.d.; Mendix, n.d.):

- **Iterative and Incremental:** Control testing is delivered in small, usable segments known as *iterations* or *sprints*, typically lasting 1 –4 weeks. This provides quicker discussion and confirmation of potential risks. It also provides quicker prioritization and changes to higher risk areas.
- **Customer Involvement:** Frequent feedback from cybersecurity and technology stakeholders, and audit management to ensure the audit activity aligns with audit activity requirements.
- **Communications:** Frequently, concise, and clearly articulated meeting agenda.
- **Cross-Functional Teams:** Agile relies on teams that include diverse roles working collaboratively, such as cybersecurity professionals, AI developers, cybersecurity auditors, technology auditors, privacy auditors, and other personnel, depending on the cybersecurity audit activity.
- **Reserve Prioritization:** Audit activity prioritizations may change, maintain a dynamic reserve log, and periodically review the reserve prioritization to ensure the highest risk areas are addressed first.
- **Continuous Improvement:** Teams conduct regular retrospectives to evaluate what went well, what didn't, and how agility and lean management concepts can improve.

- **Minimal Viable Product (MVP):** Emphasizes delivering the high-risk control testing results when preliminary results indicate a potential issue.
- **Time-Boxed Work Cycles:** Fixed durations for control testing to help control scope and maintain focus.

🌍 **Real-World Scenario:** Without explicitly labeling the cybersecurity audit work as "agile," those concepts were applied at a previous employer. The firm faced resource constraints, necessitating innovative and lean management approaches to deliver value in cybersecurity domains. This was challenging due to the evolving nature of technology, making meetings with cybersecurity and technology professionals crucial. Roundtables were employed to identify efficiencies and technical information, which often included external subject matter experts to explore cybersecurity risk areas.

💡**Critical Thinking Moment:** Keep the "concept" and "principle" approaches in mind as you execute audit activities. Think about how those concepts can be readily applied to audit activities without developing a framework. Brainstorm with other audit colleagues to develop best practices.

🎯 **Pro Tip:** Professional organizations offer valuable networking opportunities to connect with cybersecurity professionals from diverse perspectives and backgrounds. Networking can be instrumental in identifying participants for roundtable discussions.

🛠 **Important Note:** When building AI applications, the agile concepts can be applied by following the Agile Manifesto, which outlines technology project-specific principles and requirements. Remember to use that information as concepts and approach, not build out a governance framework.

4.3 AGILITY CONTRADICTION

Agile contradiction are practices that negate the agile, agility, and lean management principles and concepts. Why is this important? These practices have been commonly observed in many audit groups and are known to consume significant administrative hours without delivering the desired results.

The three primary administrative-intensive practices are:

- Excessive use of emails
- Continuously reading or accessing email accounts
- Multitasking

Each of these activities detracts from the efficiency, focus, and adaptability that agility and lean management aim to promote. These contradictory practices can consume a great deal of time and result in increasing the administrative hours or non-value add outcome.

4.3.1 📧 Excessive use of emails

Think about a time when you spent more than an hour composing or responding to an email. How many follow-up messages were required to clarify the information? Was the original email lengthy, covering multiple topics or complex details? Was the requested action ultimately completed, or did it require further clarification?

The reliance on lengthy email communication became even more prevalent during the COVID-19 pandemic, as most cybersecurity auditors shifted to remote work environments. As you read through this section, reflect on some of your own experiences with long or complex emails and consider how they impacted efficiency and outcomes.

4.3.1.1 👥 When cybersecurity audit discussions should occur instead of using email

Audit discussions (whether informal or formal meetings) should take place **in lieu of using email** when:

1. **Audit Planning:** Discussing both the annual and individual cybersecurity audit activities can be part of the standing or other meetings.
2. **Emerging Threats:** Sharing emerging cybersecurity threats and other related information.
3. **Complex or Sensitive Issues Are Involved:** Topics involving major findings, significant risks, reputational concerns, or sensitive personnel matters should be discussed verbally to ensure full context, tone, and confidentiality are preserved.
4. **Clarifications Are Needed Quickly:** If there is ambiguity, confusion, or a high potential for misinterpretation, real-time conversations (in person, via call, or video meeting) are better to ensure immediate clarification.
5. **Negotiations or Disagreements Arise:** Discussing audit ratings, recommendations, or management responses is better done live to collaboratively resolve differences and prevent escalation or misunderstanding that written tone might exacerbate.
6. **Relationship Building and Trust Are Important:** Discussions allow cybersecurity auditors to build rapport and trust with stakeholders, which is critical for audit effectiveness, cooperation, and future engagements.
7. **Preliminary or Draft Information Is Being Shared:** Early-stage findings, working papers, or preliminary conclusions should be verbally

discussed before being formally documented to prevent premature conclusions being misused or misunderstood.

8. **Urgency or Timeliness Matters:** When action is needed quickly (e.g., urgent control failure, time-sensitive compliance issue), discussions are more efficient than waiting for email responses.
9. **Delivering Negative or Difficult Messages:** Delivering significant deficiencies, audit issues requiring management action, or critical feedback should be handled face-to-face (or at least voice-to-voice) to appropriately convey tone and seriousness.

🎯 **Pro Tip:** Use discussions for anything complex, sensitive, time-sensitive, or relational considering the goal of building relationships. Reserve emails for confirmations, documentation, and simple, non-controversial communications.

4.3.1.2 ✏ Cybersecurity audit planning communication checklist

Determining the best communication mechanism – whether a meeting or an email – is essential for maximizing efficiency, clarity, and engagement. Using the wrong format can lead to misunderstandings, wasting time, or missed opportunities for input. By selecting the most appropriate method, teams can ensure timely decision-making, minimize disruptions, and promote a more productive work environment. Cybersecurity audit planning is provided below as an example communication channel evaluation, expanding upon the information in the previous section. Apply this same type of checklist for the other examples previously noted or for specific scenarios related to your organization.

- **Use a Discussion (Meeting/Call) if:**
  - The topic is sensitive, high-risk, or involves confidential issues.
  - The topic requires participation of multi-disciplinary experts.
  - Clarification is needed to avoid misinterpretation.
  - You're sharing preliminary or draft findings.
  - Disagreements or negotiation of ratings/responses are expected.
  - You are engaging a new or unfamiliar stakeholder.
  - Building rapport and trust is important for audit success.
  - Time sensitivity requires immediate response or alignment.
  - You're delivering negative or corrective feedback.
- **Use an Email if:**
  - You are confirming meeting outcomes, timelines, or expectations.
  - The message is informational with no expected debate.
  - You are distributing finalized documents (e.g., audit plan, scope memo).
  - The content is non-sensitive and doesn't require context or tone.
  - You need a documented response or approval for audit trail purposes.

As a last thought on this topic, many cybersecurity auditors rely on emails to deliver document or information request lists for audit activities, including planning, testing, and reporting phases. These lists are typically developed based on the auditor's understanding of the information needed to support the audit objectives. While some requested items may be self-explanatory, such as a copy of a policy document, others may require additional context to ensure clarity and efficiency. Thus, it is important to think through the best alternative to maximize efficiency.

> **Real-World Scenario:** In a previous cybersecurity audit role, a documented request list was required, typically maintained within a repository, and governed by a service level agreement (SLA) that stipulated a three business day response time. In practice, many auditees would submit a follow-up query on the third day, prompting the cybersecurity auditor to provide clarification or additional details, effectively restarting the three business day SLA with each exchange. This process not only consumed significant time through the repeated writing and rewriting of request list information but also led to continuous timeline extensions, ultimately delaying the initiation of control testing and prolonging the overall audit cycle.

4.3.1.3 *Information request list guidance*

The objective of this section is to introduce agility-focused strategies for developing and managing information request lists, promoting more effective communication and reducing unnecessary administrative effort.

4.3.1.4 ? *When to use an audit document or information request list instead of a discussion*

Use a **formal request list** *in lieu of discussion* when:

1. **Standard or Repeatable Information Is Needed**
    - Examples: policies, procedures, prior audit reports, access logs, contracts, organizational charts
    - These items can be clearly listed and retrieved without verbal clarification.
2. **You Need a Clear Audit Trail**
    - Documented requests provide traceability, deadlines, and accountability – especially important in regulated environments.
3. **Multiple Items Are Requested across Departments**
    - A centralized list avoids confusion and ensures consistency in communication across stakeholders.
4. **You Want to Minimize Interruptions or Back-and-Forth**
    - Listing all needs at once reduces repeated ad hoc follow-ups and allows the auditee to prepare materials efficiently.

5. **Deadlines and Delivery Dates Must Be Tracked**
   - A formal request list can set expectations for when each document is due, which supports audit scheduling and avoids delays.
6. **Pre-Audit Preparation**
   - It's a best practice to send a document request list *before* fieldwork begins so the auditee has adequate time to gather information.
7. **Project Status Tool/Report**
   - Provides input for periodic audit status reports.
   - Identifies potential delays and roadblocks due to lack of timely availability of artifacts

Use a **discussion** *in lieu of formal request list when:*

1. The request involves **subjective or qualitative input** (e.g., "How does your team decide on risk prioritization?").
2. The item is **not clearly defined,** and **clarification is needed.**
3. You're asking for **explanations, walkthroughs,** or **interviews.**
4. You're requesting **access to sensitive systems or data** and need to understand context first.

> 🎯 **Pro Tip:** Always follow up a discussion with written confirmation if documents are promised. That keeps your audit trail clean, and expectations aligned.

4.3.2 📧 Strategies for managing and prioritizing emails

In cybersecurity auditing, email is a critical communication tool. However, the constant review and immediate response to incoming emails can create major interruptions, fragment attention, and reduce the ability to focus on higher-priority activities – a direct contradiction to agile and lean management principles and concepts. Effective email management strategies emphasize minimizing disruptions by adopting disciplined reading and prioritization practices. Key techniques include:

📅 Scheduled Email Review Times: Designating specific times during the day to check and respond to emails, rather than reacting immediately to each notification, helps preserve focus on critical audit tasks and reduces context switching.

- Set 2–3 designated times per day to check and respond to emails (e.g., 10:00 AM, 2:00 PM, 4:30 PM).
- Avoid checking emails first thing in the morning if critical work needs full attention.
- Block email time on your calendar to establish a consistent routine.

🚦 Prioritization Frameworks and Triage Approach: Applying frameworks such as the Eisenhower Matrix (urgent vs. important) enables auditors to quickly assess which emails truly require immediate attention and which can be deferred (Priority, n.d.). Quickly scanning the inbox to categorize emails (respond immediately, schedule for later, delegate, or archive) allows professionals to manage time more efficiently without becoming trapped in reactive email cycles.

- **Urgent and Important:** Respond immediately or within the hour.
- **Important but Not Urgent:** Schedule a specific time to reply.
- **Urgent but Not Important:** Delegate or forward as appropriate.
- **Neither Urgent nor Important:** Archive, delete, or defer indefinitely.

Resist the urge to answer immediately. Ask: *Does this need my attention right now?* or *can this wait for the next review window?*

Additional email strategies include those below. Identify those that work the best for you and begin applying, even if you only apply one or two as a starting point. These complement the practices previously noted.

🔔 Notification Management: Turning off automatic pop-up notifications and sounds reduces the temptation to interrupt higher-value work for non-urgent messages.

- Turn off pop-up and sound notifications.
- Check the inbox intentionally, not reactively.

📢 Setting Expectations: Communicating standard email response times with colleagues and clients helps manage expectations and reduces the pressure to respond instantly.

- Inform stakeholders of standard response times (e.g., "Responses will typically be provided within twenty-four (24) hours.").
- Reinforce that immediate responses are not guaranteed unless flagged as urgent.

≡ Use Templates for Common Replies: Save time responding to frequent inquiries by preparing simple response templates. Standardize document or information request lists to minimize back-and-forth clarification.

🗁 Clear Email Organization Systems: Using folders, flags, or labels to sort emails by priority or project allows for more strategic reading and responding, focusing first on high-impact communications.

- Create a priority folder with project or other audit activity subfolders.
- Move the emails after reading and addressing.

By managing when and how emails are read, and resisting the urge to constantly monitor the inbox, cybersecurity auditors can improve their efficiency, maintain deeper focus on audits and project work. That in turn will better align with agile principles that prioritize value-driven, uninterrupted work.

4.3.3 Maximizing focus: Reducing the multitasking burden in cybersecurity audits

Multitasking assumes that an individual can effectively divide their attention between multiple activities. In the audit profession, it is common for individuals to be assigned to multiple audit engagements simultaneously. This can be manageable when the cybersecurity auditor allocates dedicated blocks of time to focus on one task at a time. For example, setting aside four hours of uninterrupted time to concentrate on a single audit task promotes deeper focus, higher-quality work, and greater efficiency.

Why is reducing multitasking important (American Psychological Association, 2006; Harvard Business Review, 2010; Ophir et al., 2009)?

1. **Divided attention** often leads to reduced accuracy and increased errors.
2. **Despite the perception** of getting more done, frequent task-switching consumes additional cognitive energy and time, lowering overall productivity. Switching between tasks creates a "cognitive switching penalty," where the brain must refocus each time, wasting time and mental energy.
3. **Continuous interruptions** can delay deliverables and extend audit timelines.
4. **Deep work** – a sustained, focused effort on a single task – often produces higher-quality audit results.
5. **Reducing multitasking supports agility** principles and concepts by emphasizing responsiveness, quality, and focus on value-driven activities.
6. **Dividing attention across multiple tasks** increases the likelihood of mistakes. Complex or detailed tasks especially suffer because they require sustained focus, which multitasking disrupts.
7. **Constantly shifting attention strains the brain**, leading to quicker exhaustion. This fatigue can impair decision-making, critical thinking, and memory over time.
8. **Information processed during multitasking** is less likely to be stored in long-term memory. People multitasking often retain less information and struggle to recall details later.
9. **Creativity often requires** deep focus and uninterrupted thought. Multitasking fragments attention, preventing the brain from making deeper connections that spark innovation.
10. **Multitasking can increase feelings** of pressure and overwhelm. The mental overload of handling several tasks at once can activate stress

responses, which, over time, negatively impacts both mental and physical health.

11. **In personal or professional interactions**, multitasking (e.g., checking a phone during a conversation) can signal disinterest, harming trust and communication quality.

4.4 AGILE AND LEAN MANAGEMENT PRINCIPLES

Agility is one concept that greatly benefits cybersecurity auditors; another valuable concept is lean management. While agile concepts primarily focus on project management, lean management methodology emphasizes business process efficiencies, which are indirectly related to managing projects. This creates an opportunity for cybersecurity auditors to leverage principles from both approaches to enhance audit effectiveness and efficiency.

It was previously noted that agility efforts sometimes fail because cybersecurity auditors become overly focused on processes, and lean management also emphasizes process improvement. Although this might initially appear contradictory, the true objective of understanding lean management is to identify complementary concepts that can strengthen agility, not replace it with rigid process control. The objective of this section is to highlight lean management principles that, like agility concepts, can be adapted by cybersecurity auditors to drive value, reduce administrative burden, and support a more flexible, responsive audit environment.

4.4.1 Lean management principles

Lean management principles seek to maximize value while minimizing waste, enabling entities to improve efficiency and continuously enhance processes (Do, 2017). The core lean management principles include:

- **Identify Value:** Understand the stakeholder values and ensure that all processes align with delivering that value.
- **Map the Value Stream:** Analyze the entire workflow to identify and eliminate non-value-added activities or inefficiencies.
- **Create Flow:** Streamline processes to ensure a smooth and continuous flow of work, minimizing delays and bottlenecks.
- **Establish Pull:** Implement a demand-driven system where work is initiated based on customer needs, reducing overproduction and inventory.
- **Pursue Perfection:** Continuously refining and improving processes through feedback and collaboration, striving for operational excellence.

By applying these principles, entities can enhance quality, reduce costs, and deliver greater value to their customers. For cybersecurity professionals, these benefits convert to higher audit activity quality, reduced administrative time allowing for more analysis, and providing value added information to management.

> **Real-World Scenario:** In a previous role, a manager would review audit reports multiple times, often requiring numerous modifications. There were instances where subsequent feedback reverted the audit report wording back to its original phrasing. This iterative process reflected a pursuit of perfection rather than maintaining focus on the primary audit report objectives and ensuring alignment with control testing results. While tools like Generative Pre-Trained Transformer (ChatGPT), Google Gemini, or Microsoft Co-Pilot were not available at that point in my career, leveraging AI-driven writing assistance today could significantly streamline the audit reporting process, saving time while maintaining clarity, consistency, and alignment with audit goals.

4.4.2 Relationship between agility and lean management

Lean management and agile are both methodologies aimed at improving efficiency, reducing waste, and increasing responsiveness, but they focus on different aspects of organizational performance and operate in slightly different contexts. Lean management was originally inspired by the Toyota Production System (Kanban Zone, n.d.; Liker, 2004) and later widely adopted across industries, including service sectors like cybersecurity auditing (Liker, 2004).

Lean management is not about working faster, it's about working smarter, with a relentless focus on what matters most (Womack & Jones, 2003). Table 4.1 articulates the lean management principles, the purpose of those principles, and a cybersecurity auditor example. The objective is to inspire the reader to think about more cybersecurity auditor examples that employ *working smarter not harder.*

Table 4.1 Lean management principles explained

Principle	Purpose	Example for cybersecurity auditors
Identify value	Focus only on what adds value to the auditee and organization	Reporting risks that truly matter
Map the value stream	Find and eliminate waste	Streamlining audit request processes
Create flow	Smooth progression without disruptions	Reducing delays between testing and reporting
Establish pull	Work on demand, not by arbitrary schedules	Starting fieldwork when documentation is ready
Pursue perfection	Continuous improvement of culture	Regularly refining audit methodologies

Let's further explore the similarities and differences between agility and lean management.

Key Similarities

1. **Focus on Efficiency:** Both lean management and agility aim to streamline processes, eliminate waste, and increase value to the auditee and auditor.
2. **Continuous Improvement:** Both emphasize continuous improvement. Lean management focuses on eliminating inefficiencies, while agile focuses on iterative development and adapting to changes.
3. **Customer-Centric:** Both approaches are driven by the goal of delivering value to the auditee and organization. Lean does this by reducing waste, while agile does this through responsiveness and frequent feedback loops.
4. **Collaborative:** Both methodologies encourage collaboration within teams and with stakeholders to improve processes and outcomes.

Key Differences

1. Core Objective
    - **Lean Management:** The primary goal is to eliminate waste (non-value-adding activities) and improve efficiency in processes, often through optimizing resource allocation and minimizing unnecessary steps. Think about eliminating control testing for cybersecurity risks rated "low."
    - **Agility:** The focus is on adaptability and flexibility, responding quickly to changes and customer needs, typically in dynamic and uncertain environments (e.g., software development, innovation sectors). Higher risks may arise requiring a shift in control testing or planning for another cybersecurity domain.
2. Approach to Change
    - **Lean Management:** Lean focuses on incremental, steady improvements to existing control testing and other cybersecurity audit activities. Change is typically planned and methodical, aiming for sustained optimization over time. This is good for the annual audit planning, but agility would be better for ongoing cybersecurity audit focus evaluation.
    - **Agility:** Agile embraces change as a constant, with iterative cycles allowing for rapid adjustments based on new risk information, auditee/stakeholder feedback, and shifting cybersecurity audit priorities.
3. Scope of Application
    - **Lean Management:** Lean originated in manufacturing (Toyota Production System (Kanban Zone, n.d.; Liker, 2004) but has been adapted to a variety of industries. It typically focuses on process optimization across the entire value stream, such as production,

third-party service provider, and operations. This is relevant to some cybersecurity audit practices, such as the email efficiency noted in a previous section of this chapter.
- **Agility:** Agile originated in software development (Agile Manifesto) but has since been adapted across industries, particularly in product development, project management, and cybersecurity auditing. Agile is often more focused on teams, projects, and flexibility in workflows.

4. **Methods and Practices**
   - **Lean Management:** Lean uses tools such as Value Stream Mapping (McLaughlin, 2025), Kaizen (continuous improvement) (US EPA, 2024), 5S: sort, set, shine, standardize, and sustain (workplace organization) (Lean Production, n.d.), Kanban (visual work management) (McLaughlin, 2025), and root-cause analysis to reduce waste. Tools would not be required for cybersecurity auditing; the objective is to keep it simple (Lean Process Improvement LinkedIn Community, n.d.).
   - **Agility:** Agile uses concepts like Scrum, Kanban, and XP (Extreme Programming) with practices such as sprints, backlogs, daily stand-ups, retrospectives, and continuous delivery. Cybersecurity auditing leverages from concepts within these frameworks, such as stand-up meetings noted within the Scrum framework.
5. **Timeframe and Decision-Making**
   - **Lean Management:** Lean often focuses on long-term process efficiency, reducing lead times, and delivering value through structured optimization of resources.
   - **Agility:** Agile emphasizes short-term, iterative cycles where decisions are made quickly and can change depending on the results of each iteration, enabling rapid adaptation to external changes or new insights.
6. **Employee Involvement**
   - **Lean Management:** Lean often encourages bottom-up involvement in process improvement, involving employees at all levels in identifying waste and contributing to continuous improvement efforts.
   - **Agility:** Agile heavily emphasizes team autonomy, self-organization, and constant communication to ensure that teams remain flexible and responsive to changes and feedback.

In conclusion, while **lean management** focuses on eliminating waste and improving efficiency in processes, **agility** emphasizes adaptability and the ability to quickly respond to changes. Both are complementary in many contexts but focus on different dimensions of cybersecurity auditing. Organizations often blend elements of both to create a more efficient and responsive environment.

4.5 AGILE AND TRADITIONAL AUDIT APPROACH

Are you convinced that agility is the best audit approach? If not, read more about the traditional audit approach, which is often associated with the waterfall methodology. A traditional audit methodology is a structured approach to reviewing records, documents, and processes to verify accuracy, compliance, and effectiveness. It often involves manual reviews, statistical sampling, and on-site audit practices like analytical tests, observations, and interviews. While effective in the past, traditional methods can struggle to keep pace with the complexity and volume of data in today's digital environment.

Waterfall **methodology** is a linear and sequential approach to project management and development that involves distinct phases such as requirements, analysis, design, coding/implementation, testing, operation/deployment, and maintenance (Kirvan, 2024). In the context of **cybersecurity auditing**, these steps can be aligned with the audit process. Here's how each phase of the waterfall methodology corresponds to cybersecurity auditing activities:

1. **Requirements Phase → Audit Planning and Scoping**
   In the waterfall methodology, the **requirements** phase involves gathering and documenting the initial requirements for the project. In the context of a cybersecurity audit:
   - **Audit Planning:** The auditor establishes the audit's objectives, scope, and criteria. This includes identifying the specific security controls and systems to be reviewed, the audit methodology, and any relevant compliance or regulatory frameworks, e.g., National Institute of Standards and Technology (NIST), International Organization for Standardization (ISO) 27001, General Data Protection Regulation (GDPR).
   - **Audit Scoping:** Identifying the key assets, data, and processes to be evaluated based on the organization's risk landscape and audit objectives.
2. **Analysis Phase → Risk Assessment and Information Gathering**
   The **analysis** phase in the waterfall methodology involves understanding the system and its requirements, often using tools like flowcharts or models. In cybersecurity auditing:
   - **Risk Assessment:** Analyzing potential risks associated with the organization's cybersecurity posture. This includes understanding threat vectors, vulnerabilities, and the impact of security breaches on the organization.
   - **Information Gathering:** Collecting data about the current security environment, including reviewing documentation, conducting interviews with key personnel, and collecting logs and network diagrams. This provides an understanding of the existing security controls and potential gaps.

3. **Design Phase → Control Framework Design and Audit Plan Development**
   The **design** phase focuses on creating the system architecture or the blueprint of the project. In a cybersecurity audit, this phase involves:
   - **Control Framework Design:** Developing a framework of the controls that will be evaluated during the audit. This may involve mapping controls to specific cybersecurity standards and frameworks.
   - **Audit Plan Development:** Detailed planning of audit steps, including testing procedures, timelines, resources, and roles. The audit plan is the blueprint that will guide the audit activities.
4. **Coding/Implementation Phase → Control Testing and Evidence Collection**
   In the waterfall methodology, **coding/implementation** is where the system or solution is built and put into action. In the cybersecurity audit process:
   - **Control Testing:** Conducting the audit by testing security controls and assessing their design and effectiveness. This includes reviewing access controls, network defenses, security monitoring systems, etc., to ensure they are designed, implemented, and function correctly.
   - **Evidence Collection:** Gathering evidence during the testing phase to support audit findings. This could involve analyzing system logs, conducting vulnerability scans, reviewing user access records, and interviewing personnel.
5. **Testing Phase → Audit Evaluation and Analysis**
   In the **testing** phase, the system is evaluated for correctness and performance. In a cybersecurity audit:
   - **Audit Evaluation:** Analyzing the results of control testing and evaluating the effectiveness of security measures. This involves identifying weaknesses, vulnerabilities, and any non-compliance with policies or regulatory requirements.
   - **Findings Analysis:** Determining the significance of findings, such as high-risk vulnerabilities or gaps in compliance, and assessing their potential impact on the organization's security posture.
6. **Operation/Deployment Phase → Reporting and Recommendations**
   In the **operation/deployment** phase, the system is deployed and put into use. In cybersecurity auditing:
   - **Audit Reporting:** Documenting the audit findings, including the results of control testing, identified vulnerabilities, risks, and compliance issues. The audit report is typically presented to senior management or the board for further action.
   - **Recommendations:** Providing actionable recommendations for improving the cybersecurity posture, closing identified gaps, and enhancing the effectiveness of existing controls. This may involve suggesting new tools, processes, or training programs.

7. **Maintenance Phase → Follow-up and Continuous Monitoring**
   The **maintenance** phase in the waterfall methodology involves maintaining the system after deployment. For cybersecurity auditing:
   - **Follow-up Audits:** Scheduling follow-up audits or assessments to ensure that the corrective actions have been implemented and are effective.
   - **Continuous Monitoring:** Recommending ongoing monitoring of cybersecurity controls, ensuring continuous compliance with security policies and frameworks, and adapting to evolving threats and vulnerabilities. This may also include periodic vulnerability assessments or security testing.

Does the above sound familiar? Can you visualize all the administrative work required in the above?

4.5.1 Understanding waterfall methodology approach: Pros and cons

As previously mentioned, the waterfall methodology is a linear approach with stages (requirement gathering, design, implementation, testing, deployment, and maintenance). The previous section detailed the extensive work required in an audit activity. In addition to the previous information let's consider the pros and cons (Kirvan, 2024).

✚ *Pros of Waterfall in Auditing*

- Clear structure and predefined phases.
- Easy to understand and manage, especially in regulated environments.
- Documented progress at each stage for tracking.

✖ *Cons of Waterfall in Auditing*

- Inflexibility when new issues or risks arise.
- High dependency on initial planning; late-stage changes can be costly.
- Doesn't always align with fast-paced, agile environments.

The waterfall methodology's structured and sequential approach was traditionally mirrored in cybersecurity auditing, where each phase builds upon the previous one, ensuring that thorough preparation, testing, and evaluation are carried out. While the methodology focuses on a linear progression, cybersecurity audits may involve iterative steps for continuous improvement and follow-up, especially when addressing new threats or changes in the organization's environment. Thus, waterfall methodology is not necessarily the best option for cybersecurity audits where cybersecurity threats continuously evolve and present new vulnerabilities.

🌍 **Real-World Scenario:** A previous employer required template formats through an established waterfall methodology. That template often required entering the same data in three or more different sections. It was common to receive quality assurance comments because the information may be changed in one section but not another. In addition, there was no value added to entering the information in multiple different locations within the same document.

4.6 AGILE AUDIT TEAM

Now that we have explored agility, lean management, and traditional audit methodologies, let's switch to audit team composition and approach. Traditional cybersecurity audit activities usually result in team members being assigned based on number of hours and timeline availability. That assignment usually results in conflict because audit activities may not meet the proposed timeline and managers of one cybersecurity audit team may have a different audit approach, that is, that person may not embrace agility.

The success of an audit team embracing agility concepts, especially in a traditionally structured field like cybersecurity auditing, relies heavily on the willingness of team members to embrace change, be innovative, and adapt to new methods. However, it's not uncommon for some auditors to be hesitant about adopting agile practices, as they may be more comfortable with the established, rigid processes they are used to. This resistance can stem from a variety of factors, such as fear of uncertainty, a lack of understanding of agility's benefits, or simply the preference for a more predictable, linear approach to auditing. Consider the resistance information in Chapter 3 – How to Influence Behaviors and Culture as you read through the remainder of this chapter.

4.6.1 Agile cybersecurity audit pod

My preference for audit teams is using the "agile cybersecurity audit pods" concept (IIA, 2018). This concept ensures continuity and building agility concept expertise. The same individuals are maintained in the "pod" for the entire year and work on cybersecurity audit assignments together. Like agility concepts, the pod is given autonomy to make decisions and change the scope based on new information. Lastly, the team members receive coaching and guidance throughout so that the agility skillsets are developed without interruption (IIA, 2018).

That said, **patience and understanding** are key when working with individuals who may be resistant to change. Drawing from Table 3.5 and Table 3.9 in Chapter 3 – How to Influence Behaviors and Culture, you can employ the following strategies to help shift the mindset of team members and foster an environment where agility concepts can take root:

1. **Cultivate a Safe Environment for Experimentation:** Encourage a culture of experimentation where team members feel comfortable trying new approaches without fear of failure. Start with small pilot projects or limited scope areas where agile concepts can be tested. When auditors see the benefits of these approaches, they are more likely to be open to adopting them more broadly.
2. **Lead by Example:** As a leader or advocate for agility, it's essential to demonstrate the value of agile practices through your own actions. Show how agility improves outcomes, whether through faster decision-making, enhanced collaboration, or more efficient auditing practices. Seeing someone else take the lead can inspire others to follow suit.
3. **Provide Education and Training:** Many auditors may resist agility simply due to a lack of understanding. Offering training sessions on agile concepts (Scrum, Kanban, etc.) and explaining how these concepts align with cybersecurity auditing can bridge that knowledge gap. Share success stories from other industries or auditing firms where agility has led to improvements in performance, efficiency, and risk management.
4. **Emphasize the Positive Impact of Agility:** Highlight the concrete benefits of agile concepts for cybersecurity auditing, such as quicker identification and response to threats, improved adaptability to changing regulations or risks, and more effective collaboration with other teams (IT, security, compliance). When auditors see how these practices can directly enhance their work, they may be more inclined to adopt them.
5. **Foster Collaboration and Open Communication:** Agile concepts thrive on collaboration and continuous communication. Organize regular meetings or discussions where auditors can share their experiences, concerns, and successes with agile practices. This helps break down silos and fosters a team-oriented culture that encourages innovation and problem-solving.
6. **Show Gradual Results:** Change takes time, and success doesn't happen overnight. Make sure to track and celebrate incremental improvements as they occur. Whether it's completing an audit faster, identifying new risks, or improving client satisfaction, showcasing these results can help win over skeptics and prove the value of agility.
7. **Encourage Ownership and Accountability:** In an agile environment, team members are often empowered to take ownership of their tasks and outcomes. Encourage auditors to take responsibility for specific aspects of the audit process, whether it's a particular control or an area of investigation. When they see the impact of their decisions and have the autonomy to innovate, they are more likely to embrace agile concepts.
8. **Be Patient and Supportive:** As previously mentioned, **patience** is key. Some team members may take longer to warm up to the idea of agility.

It's important to be patient and offer ongoing support as they transition. Recognize that not all auditors will immediately see the benefits, but with time, exposure, and a supportive environment, many will become more receptive to agility.

9. **Align Agility with Organizational Goals:** Show how agile concepts align with broader organizational goals, such as increasing efficiency, improving security posture, or enhancing client relationships. By tying agility to the larger vision of the organization, auditors may be more inclined to support its adoption as they see its alignment with organizational success.

Pro Tip: Compile the information from Tables 3.2 **and** 3.9 **in** Chapter 3 – **How to Influence Behaviors and Culture, tailor it to your organization, and determine the best approach to achieve the strategies outlined above by linking cultural and behavioral traits to the corresponding strategies. Strive to obtain feedback to identify changes to your agile approach as necessary.**

4.6.2 Scaling agility in cybersecurity auditing: From one pod to multiple pods

Consider scaling agility within your cybersecurity audit team. Start with a **single pod** in the first year and gradually expand to **multiple pods** in the second year, you're creating a structured path for the team to adapt and grow. Here's how this phased approach could unfold, with a focus on leveraging lessons learned and fostering collaboration across pods:

First Year: One Pod – Laying the Foundation

- **Focus on Fundamentals:** In the first year, the team focuses on establishing the core agile concepts and practices within the initial pod. This would allow the team to learn and experiment with agile concepts in low-risk, controlled environment.
- **Building Trust and Collaboration:** The initial pod will have the opportunity to build strong working relationships, understand team dynamics, and become familiar with agile practices such as sprints, daily standups, retrospectives, and collaborative decision-making.
- **Documenting Lessons Learned:** Throughout the year, document key challenges, successes, and improvements. This could include feedback on agile practices, audit process improvements, and insights into adapting agile to the cybersecurity audit environment.
- **Focus on Results and Metrics:** Measure the success of the agile practices in terms of improved audit outcomes, faster response times, and better collaboration. Use these metrics as a foundation for making the case for expanding agile practices in the second year.

Second Year: Scaling with Multiple Pods

- **Expansion to Multiple Pods:** In the second year, the team can expand to multiple pods, each focused on specific aspects of the cybersecurity audit process (e.g., risk assessment, control testing, compliance verification). The original pod leaders (those who led the first-year pod) can serve as mentors and leaders for the new pods.
- **Leverage Knowledge Sharing:** The key advantage of expanding to multiple pods is the opportunity for **information sharing**. The original pod leaders can share best practices, pitfalls to avoid, and lessons learned. Regular cross-pod meetings can be scheduled to ensure that all pods are aligned on goals, methodologies, and approaches.
- **Cross-Pod Collaboration:** Encourage collaboration between pods on larger or more complex audit projects. This allows each pod to bring its unique strengths to the table, while also learning from the experience of other pods. For example, if one pod develops a new methodology for control testing, it can be shared across all pods for adoption and refinement.
- **Iterative Improvements:** Each pod will likely have unique challenges as it adapts to agile practices. However, by having leaders who have already gone through the transition in the first year, they can help steer the newer pods, guiding them through obstacles and encouraging iterative improvements.
- **Inter-Pod Communication:** Establish a forum for information sharing across all pods to prevent silos and promote consistency in approaches.
- **Continuous Feedback Loop:** In this phase, continuous feedback from all pods should be encouraged through regular retrospectives and team assessments. The feedback from each pod can help refine the agile approach as a whole and allow for adjustments in real-time.

Benefits of the Pod Scaling Approach

- **Smoother Transition:** By starting with one pod and gradually expanding, the transition to agility is more manageable, and the original pod members can act as champions to help ease others into the new methodology.
- **Mentorship Opportunities:** The experienced pod leaders will have the opportunity to mentor newer team members, promoting leadership development and a sense of ownership.
- **Faster Adoption Across the Organization:** The knowledge gained from the first pod will provide a strong foundation for the rest of the organization, ensuring that the expansion to multiple pods is informed by the lessons learned and is more likely to succeed.
- **Fostering a Culture of Agility:** By scaling in this manner, the entire team will have a shared experience of working in agile environments, which

can strengthen the organizational culture and commitment to continuous improvement.

- **Improved Efficiency and Innovation:** As multiple pods operate, the competition between pods to improve processes and share insights will drive innovation and efficiency, ultimately benefiting the entire organization's audit outcomes.

Actionable Pod Creation Steps

- **Select Pod Leaders Early:** Identify and train potential leaders from the original pod to take on leadership roles in the second year. These individuals should be well versed in agile concepts and comfortable mentoring others.
- **Create Knowledge-Sharing Mechanisms:** Set up systems (e.g., collaborative platforms, shared documentation, cross-pod meetings) that will facilitate information sharing and collaboration across pods.
- **Track and Measure Success:** Establish metrics for measuring the success of each pod's agile adoption, including audit outcomes, team satisfaction, and time-to-completion of audit processes.
- **Foster an Agile Mindset:** Continuously reinforce the importance of an agile mindset – one that values flexibility, continuous improvement, and openness to change – through training, feedback loops, and leadership examples.

Conclusion: In summary, by starting small with one pod and expanding based on lessons learned, you are creating an environment where agility can be scaled sustainably across the cybersecurity audit team. The leadership and knowledge-sharing aspects will be critical to this growth, ensuring that each new pod benefits from the experiences of the original group while also contributing fresh ideas and perspectives. Lastly, cybersecurity auditors and other cybersecurity professionals may be inspired to join a pod.

Real-World Scenario: A re-assignment to another technology audit team disclosed that each cybersecurity and technology audit team conducted audit activities in a silo, with no communication between the multiple groups. This resulted in the same control testing in two or more audits. The Agile Audit Pod Leader using agile and lean management concepts would have reduced the duplication, which in turn would have allowed for more cybersecurity audit coverage.

4.6.3 Success metrics for agile cybersecurity auditing

In agile cybersecurity auditing, success is measured not only by traditional audit outcomes but also by how well the audit process embraces agility's concepts of flexibility, responsiveness, and stakeholder collaboration. Key success metrics include:

1. **Audit Cycle Time Reduction**
   - Measure the time taken from audit planning to audit report delivery.
   - Successful agile audits show reduced cycle times without compromising audit quality.
   - Enable the expansion of audit coverage from saved time.
2. **Incremental Delivery of Findings**
   - Track how often interim findings or observations are shared throughout the audit process.
   - Success is indicated by regular, actionable feedback to stakeholders rather than a single final report.
3. **Stakeholder Engagement and Satisfaction**
   - Collect feedback from auditees and leadership after each sprint or audit iteration.
   - High satisfaction scores and positive feedback on collaboration, responsiveness, and value indicate success.
4. **Adaptability to Change**
   - Monitor how quickly the audit team can pivot or reprioritize audit activities in response to emerging risks or changes in scope.
   - A high rate of successful mid-audit adaptations without significant disruption is a key agile success indicator.
5. **Value-Added Observations**
   - Evaluate how many audit findings are considered "value-add" (proactively identifying opportunities for improvement, not just compliance gaps).
   - Success is seen when audits contribute to strengthening cybersecurity posture beyond minimum compliance.
6. **Sprint Retrospective Implementation Rate**
   - Track the percentage of improvement ideas identified during retrospectives that are implemented in subsequent audit iterations.
   - High implementation rates show a learning, continuously improving audit culture.
7. **Team Collaboration and Empowerment**
   - Assess team dynamics: self-organization, communication quality, and decision-making autonomy.
   - Successful agile audit teams demonstrate shared ownership of outcomes and effective collaboration without heavy top-down management.
8. **Risk Coverage Efficiency**
   - Measure the percentage of high-priority risks covered during each sprint or short cycle.
   - Effective agile audits maximize high-risk coverage early and often.
9. **Reduction in Rework or Audit Finding Disputes**
   - Monitor the number of reworks or disputes over audit findings due to misunderstanding or misalignment with stakeholders.
   - Agile auditing should reduce the rework rate because of continuous stakeholder involvement and communication.

10. **Continuous Monitoring Integration**
    - Track the integration of continuous monitoring techniques into the audit process.
    - Success is indicated when audits leverage real-time data feeds or automated testing to support ongoing assurance.

> **Pro Tip:** While this list provides many ideas, consider focusing on two or three metrics as part of the pilot. The objective of using agility concepts is to reduce administrative hours and non-value-added activity. These metrics are intended to mature the agile cybersecurity auditing program.

4.7 ACHIEVING AUDIT STANDARDS

Chapter 1 – Understanding Audit Objectives, Expectations, Concepts, and Opportunities discussed Independence and objectivity from a theoretical perspective, which cybersecurity auditors must understand and maintain. Think about those audit standards, building partnerships, and influencing behavior and culture change without deviating from those standards. For example, for cybersecurity audit professionals to successfully encourage use of agility and AI requires audit professionals to comply with organizational requirements.

> **Pro Tip:** Use the behavior and culture, and building partnership concepts in parallel with applying agile concepts. There is a close relationship between the three domains, and these are concepts that do not require a framework.

Let's expand on Chapter 1 – Understanding Audit Objectives, Expectations, Concepts, and Opportunities and the Pro Tip above by considering approaches noted for each scenario below that align with agile concepts.

> **Scenario 1:** The cybersecurity audit team is executing a threat intelligence audit. Daily stand-up meetings are conducted with all business partners during the audit planning phase.

Independence and Objectivity and Risk-Based Approach Audit Standards: The stand-up meeting is led by the cybersecurity audit team to ensure that the requisite information is obtained. The meeting is short, focusing on a key topic and running for less than 15 minutes. Below is an agenda example with three key topics:

1. Yesterday's accomplishments
2. Audit activity plans for today
3. Foreseen impediments or blockers

> **Scenario 2:** The cybersecurity audit team is initiating a third-party risk audit. This requires building a cross-functional team that includes all the required subject matter experts.

Independence and Objectivity Audit Standard, and Documentation and Evidence Audit Standards: A cybersecurity auditor maintains independence by clearly defining their role as objective evaluator rather than a participant in the team's operational decisions. When recommending or identifying cross-functional teams, the auditor bases suggestions on risk assessments, control requirements, and organizational needs, not personal preferences or internal politics. By documenting criteria for team selection and avoiding involvement in team management or execution, the auditor ensures impartiality and preserves audit integrity.

4.8 SUMMARY

This chapter focused on agile and lean management concepts. While these concepts are not unique to cybersecurity auditing, introducing agility to a cybersecurity audit team requires a combination of education, example-setting, and a gradual shift in culture. By fostering a safe, collaborative, and open environment, while also demonstrating the tangible benefits of agile practices, auditors who are initially hesitant may begin to see the advantages of adopting an agile approach. As they observe the positive results and learn from their peers, they will likely become more motivated to embrace agility, eventually leading to greater innovation, improved audit outcomes, and a more dynamic audit team overall.

This chapter explored how cybersecurity auditors can integrate agility and lean management principles to enhance audit effectiveness, efficiency, and responsiveness. It discusses the differences and synergies between lean and agile principles and concepts, emphasizing that while agility enhances project adaptability, lean management drives business process efficiency. In addition, recognizing that many cybersecurity auditors may initially resist change due to a focus on rigid processes, the chapter stresses the importance of influencing behavior and fostering a culture of innovation. Techniques for managing change, building pilot "pods" of agile auditing teams, and leveraging lessons learned are outlined as practical strategies. By aligning individual behaviors with organizational goals and applying incremental improvements, cybersecurity auditors can gradually transform their audit culture, leading to more adaptive, forward-thinking IA/OIG functions.

You made it to the end of this chapter! Let's continue the cybersecurity audit journey. You are now prepared to apply agile and lean management concepts, along with the foundational knowledge from the previous chapters, as we move into Chapter 5: Harnessing Artificial Intelligence: Enhancing Cybersecurity Audits through Automation and Insight. In the next chapter, we will explore how AI is transforming the future of cybersecurity auditing.

Chapter 5

Harnessing artificial intelligence

Enhancing cybersecurity audits through automation and insight

5.1 LEARNING OBJECTIVES

By the end of this chapter, readers will be able to:

1. **Define key concepts,** explaining essential artificial intelligence (AI) terminology relevant to cybersecurity auditing, including machine learning (ML), natural language processing (NLP), generative AI (GenAI), and AI governance.
2. **Evaluate AI models to determine the most appropriate model for specific cybersecurity audit activities,** emphasizing higher-order cognitive skills (evaluation and determiçnation), aligns with Bloom's taxonomy, and better reflects an applied learning outcome in an auditing context.
3. **Validate AI models and address risks,** explaining the importance of AI model validation in auditing applications; identify key validation techniques and controls to ensure model accuracy, reliability, and fairness; and recognize the risks mitigated through validation, including bias, data quality issues, model drift, lack of transparency, and compliance breaches.
4. **Assess AI readiness,** describing the AI maturity model and evaluating an organization's current AI maturity level in the context of audit planning and execution.
5. **Apply AI use cases to cybersecurity auditing,** identifying and categorizing AI use cases that support the cybersecurity audit function. Map AI use cases to the annual audit plan, individual audit engagements, and continuous auditing processes.
6. **Demonstrate how AI-enabled auditing aligns** with the audit standards by integrating risk assessment, evidence collection, and reporting processes that promote agility, influence ethical behaviors and organizational culture, and foster collaborative relationships across stakeholder groups.

Pro Tip: As you progress through this chapter, you may identify multiple ideas and opportunities relevant to your cybersecurity audit environment. Document them in a "parking lot" for later evaluation, then prioritize based on audit risk, regulatory impact, and organizational relevance.

DOI: 10.1201/9781003640301-6

5.2 OPENING INSIGHTS

AI is rapidly transforming the landscape of cybersecurity auditing by enhancing auditors' ability to analyze vast datasets, detect anomalies, and automate routine tasks. As organizations adopt AI technologies to strengthen their security posture, cybersecurity auditors must develop a foundational understanding of AI terminology, models, and practical applications.

This chapter provides a comprehensive overview of AI concepts tailored to the auditing profession and for the AI novice. It introduces the AI maturity model to assess organizational readiness, explores real-world AI use cases across annual audit planning, individual audit engagements, and continuous auditing, and examines how these applications align with both the Institute of Internal Auditors (IIA) Standards for the Professional Practice of Internal Auditing (IIA Standards) and agile auditing principles. Readers will also gain insights into the ethical and compliance considerations that must be addressed when integrating AI into audit processes. Equipped with this knowledge, cybersecurity auditors can confidently leverage AI to enhance audit quality, efficiency, and adaptability in an evolving digital environment.

Also, the focus of this chapter is on how auditors can adopt AI to improve efficiency, accuracy, and agility within their own practices. The reader will learn about various AI models that provide an immediate return on audit time. That discussion will be followed by AI governance and oversight, to preserve the AI output integrity. This is distinct from evaluating or auditing AI systems deployed by the first and second lines of defense (1LoD and 2 LoD). Instead, the emphasis is on practical AI use cases.

In addition, this chapter is designed to offer a wide range of AI use cases to illustrate how cybersecurity auditors can integrate AI into their work. However, like the evolving nature of AI itself, this chapter serves as a starting point – intended to inspire you to think critically and creatively about additional use cases, particularly as AI technologies continue to mature. Chapter 6 – Unlocking Artificial Intelligence Knowledge, Context, and Curated Resources contains more AI information and resources, including information on AI expertise, training, and certifications.

As you explore the material, consider how each use case could be adapted or expanded for your specific audit environment. Think about practical scenarios where AI tools can enhance cybersecurity audit planning, testing, and reporting. Throughout the chapter, continually reflect on the importance of security controls at every stage of AI adoption and use. For additional guidance on security considerations, refer to the dedicated logical and physical security section of this chapter.

☞ **Getting the Most Out of This Chapter:** This chapter is intentionally the most comprehensive chapter in this book. It is designed to provide foundational knowledge for readers who may be new to AI technologies. If you are already familiar with certain topics, feel free to skip the examples and focus on the area's most relevant to your learning needs.

Important Notes

- Humans play a critical role in the development, deployment, and oversight of AI systems by defining problems, curating training data, and validating outcomes. They ensure that AI aligns with ethical standards, regulatory requirements, and organizational goals – making decisions where human judgment, accountability, and context are essential. Even the most advanced AI still relies on human expertise to guide, interpret, and govern its use. Apply the "trust but verify" concept for all AI outcomes.
- Cybersecurity audit professionals must ensure that all actions taken in relation to the AI examples provided in this chapter align with their organization's established AI policies, procedures, and standards. Before implementing or testing any AI tools, models, or practices described, auditors should consult relevant internal governance documents and obtain necessary approvals. Adhering to these policies is essential not only for maintaining compliance, but also for safeguarding data, protecting systems, and upholding organizational integrity and accountability in the use of AI technologies.

5.3 UNDERSTANDING AI FUNDAMENTALS

AI is transforming the way we live, work, and interact with technology. At its core, AI refers to systems that simulate human intelligence to perform tasks such as learning, reasoning, problem-solving, and decision-making. Understanding the fundamentals of AI involves exploring its key concepts, including ML, neural networks, NLP, and data-driven decision-making. Whether you're a beginner or advancing your knowledge, grasping these foundational elements is essential to navigating the evolving landscape of intelligent systems and unlocking their full potential across industries.

As you progress, Chapter 6 – Unlocking Artificial Intelligence Knowledge, Context, and Curated Resources – will build upon this foundation by introducing more advanced technical topics and emerging trends that are shaping the future of AI.

5.3.1 Key AI terminology

As AI continues to evolve and influence a wide range of industries, understanding its key terminology is essential for professionals, students, and decision-makers alike. This includes algorithms, model architecture, data practices, performance metrics, ethical considerations, deployment strategies, and emerging technologies as a starting point.

5.3.2 Core AI concepts

At the heart of AI are core concepts that mirror human intelligence – enabling machines to perceive, learn, reason, and make decisions that shape the future.

An **AI algorithm** is a "mathematical language or pseudocode" procedure that is applied to a training dataset. The choice of **algorithm** is determined by the specific task within each AI subset and the type of data being processed. Different algorithms have different strengths and weaknesses in terms of their ability to learn patterns, handle complexity, and generalize to create new data in a training dataset (Woodman & Mangoni, 2023). The development and application of new and improved algorithms are constantly driving advancements in all areas of AI (Tableau, n.d.).

The **AI model** is the output or result of the algorithm providing a prediction or analysis (IBM, n.d.c). AI provides the ability for machines to perform tasks that are typically associated with human intelligence, such as learning and problem-solving (Woodman & Mangoni, 2023). AI models are selected based on the **specific task**, the **type and quality of data available**, and the **performance requirements** such as accuracy, speed, or interpretability. Factors like the complexity of the problem, whether the learning is supervised or unsupervised, and resource constraints (e.g., computational power) also influence the choice of model. Last, selecting the right algorithm often involves experimentation and comparison using validation metrics.

5.3.3 Ethical, bias, and compliance considerations

While AI offers powerful capabilities to enhance cybersecurity auditing, it also introduces significant ethical, legal, and operational risks. Without proper oversight, AI systems can perpetuate hidden biases, make opaque decisions, and compromise individual privacy – potentially leading to regulatory violations and reputational harm. This section highlights critical concepts such as bias, fairness, transparency, accountability, and compliance. By understanding these risks and applying robust governance measures, cybersecurity auditors can ensure that AI is used responsibly and does not undermine trust, integrity, or ethical standards within their organizations (SAP, 2024).

It is important to implement AI guardrails – protocols and tools that make sure AI systems operate within ethical, legal, bias, and technical boundaries, promoting safety and fairness.

5.3.3.1 *Notable quotes*

These two quotes help set the tone for the discussion on AI ethics. Note the author's title, which lends credibility to the message conveyed in the quotes.

> *With great power comes great responsibility. AI must be designed and deployed with ethics at the core, or its consequences could outweigh its benefits.*
>
> **Dr. Timnit Gebru**, *AI Ethics Researcher (Walsh, 2022)*

There's an enormous upside from this (AI) technology, but it's essential that the world invests heavily and urgently in AI safety and control.

***Geoffrey Hinton**, Vice President and Engineering Fellow at Google (Kleinman & Vallance, 2023)*

5.3.3.2 Statistic

According to a 2023 Deloitte survey, 62 percent **of organizations using AI** reported that "balancing innovation and regulation" is a strategic priority. In addition, 59 percent **of executives indicated that AI researchers will be hired** to ensure ethical decision-making for AI projects (Deloitte, 2024).

5.3.3.3 AI ethical terms

AI ethics is a field that explores the moral implications and societal impacts of AI technologies. Understanding the terminology below is essential for developing and deploying AI systems that are fair, safe, and aligned with human values.

- **Bias:** A systematic error in an AI model that causes unfair or inaccurate outcomes, often resulting from imbalanced or prejudiced training data.
- **Fairness:** The principle that AI systems should make decisions that are impartial and equitable, ensuring no individual or group is unjustly disadvantaged.
- **Transparency:** The degree to which AI processes data and decision logic can be understood and explained by stakeholders, enabling meaningful oversight and trust.
- **Accountability:** The obligation to ensure responsible development, deployment, and use of AI systems, including identifying who is answerable for outcomes and errors.
- **Privacy:** The protection of personal or sensitive information in AI systems, including data minimization, secure processing, and compliance with legal standards such as General Data Protection Regulation (GDPR) or Health Insurance Portability and Accountability Act (HIPAA).
- **Model Drift:** The degradation of an AI model's accuracy over time due to changes in data patterns or external conditions, requiring ongoing monitoring and updates.
- **Adversarial Examples:** Inputs intentionally crafted to deceive AI models into making incorrect predictions, exposing vulnerabilities in model robustness and security.
- **Algorithmic Audit:** A systematic evaluation of AI models and algorithms to assess performance, fairness, bias, transparency, and compliance with governance standards.
- **Responsible AI:** The overarching commitment to develop and use AI systems that are ethical, lawful, transparent, secure, and aligned with human values and societal well-being.

Let's explore some of the governance and ethics areas in more detail, expanding upon the information provided in the previous section.

5.3.3.4 Identifying and managing bias (SAP, 2024)

1. **Identifying Bias:** To detect bias, auditors and developers must examine both the data and the model behavior for signs of unfair or skewed outcomes.
   🔑 Key Techniques
   - **Data Profiling and Exploratory Data Analysis (EDA):** Review training data for **imbalanced representation** of groups (e.g., gender, race, geography) that may introduce statistical bias.
   - **Outcome Disparity Testing:** Measure whether predictions or outputs disproportionately favor or disadvantage certain groups. Tools like **Disparate Impact** or **Equal Opportunity Difference** can quantify this.
   - **Bias Detection Tools:** Use AI fairness tools, these help visualize and quantify bias across datasets and models.
     - **IBM AI Fairness 360**
     - **Google What-If Tool**
     - **Microsoft Fairlearn**
   - **Audit Logs and Explainability Models:** Leverage explainable AI (XAI) techniques (e.g., SHapley Additive exPlanations (**SHAP**), Local Interpretable Model-agnostic Explanations (**LIME**) to assess which features influence decisions, revealing potential implicit bias.

2. **Managing and Mitigating Bias:** After identifying bias, the next step is to apply practical techniques to reduce its impact.
   ▦ Mitigation Strategies
   - Preprocessing the Data
     - **Balance training data through resampling, data augmentation, or relabeling to improve fairness.**
     - **Use techniques like reweighing or data transformation to adjust input distributions.**
   - In-Model Adjustments
     - **Apply fairness-aware algorithms that incorporate fairness constraints during training.**
     - **Use regularization methods that penalize biased outcomes in the loss function.**
   - Post-Processing Outputs
     - **Adjust predictions to align outcomes more equitably across groups (e.g., threshold optimization or output calibration).**
   - Bias Impact Assessments
     - **Document and test mitigation efforts.**
     - **Include bias and fairness evaluations in AI life cycle checkpoints.**

- Cross-Functional Review
  - **Involve diverse stakeholders – data scientists, ethicists, legal teams, and auditors – to collaboratively review and challenge assumptions.**

5.3.3.5 🏛 Governance considerations

- **Define fairness metrics aligned with your mission and regulations.**
- **Include bias management in AI governance frameworks and audit checklists.**
- **Monitor for bias continuously**, especially when models are retrained or deployed in new environments.

> 🛠 **Important Note:** Bias in AI systems can lead to unfair, non-compliant, or even harmful outcomes. Identifying and managing bias requires a combination of data analysis, model evaluation, technical adjustments, and strong governance practices throughout the AI life cycle.

▦ Transparency and explainability

Transparency – Understanding the System: Transparency refers to the ability to clearly see and understand how an AI system is designed, how it operates, and how decisions are made. It ensures that stakeholders – including developers, auditors, users, and regulators – can inspect and verify the components and behavior of an AI system (Kourinian & Brown, 2024).

Key Elements of Transparency

- **Model Documentation:** Clear records of model architecture, training data sources, assumptions, objectives, and limitations.
- **Decision Path Visibility:** The ability to trace inputs through the system to understand how outputs are produced.
- **Process Disclosure:** Openness about data collection, model training, deployment, and monitoring procedures.
- **Access to Logs and Versioning:** Maintained records of model changes, updates, and decisions for auditing purposes.

Why It Matters

- Promotes **trust** in AI systems.
- Enables **compliance** with legal and regulatory frameworks.
- Supports **auditability** by providing insight into how decisions are made and governed.
- Helps identify issues like **bias, drift, or misuse.**

Explainability – Interpreting the Decisions: Explainability (or interpretability) is the degree to which an AI system's decisions or predictions can be understood in human terms. While transparency focuses on access to internal mechanisms, explainability focuses on **clarity of output** – the *why* behind a model's decision.

Key Aspects of Explainability

- **Feature Importance**: Understanding which input features most influenced a decision.
- **Model Behavior:** Descriptions of how the model behaves under different conditions.
- **Post-hoc Explanations:** Techniques applied after model training to interpret predictions (e.g., SHAP, LIME).
- **User-Friendly Interfaces:** Dashboards or reports that provide non-technical explanations for model outcomes.

Why It Matters

- Essential for **human oversight** and **ethical decision-making.**
- Helps detect **unintended behavior,** such as discriminatory predictions or flawed logic.
- Required for **regulatory compliance** in areas like finance, healthcare (e.g., HIPAA), and cybersecurity (e.g., GDPR's "right to explanation").
- Empowers users to **challenge or override** flawed or unsafe recommendations.

Table 5.1 explains the difference between transparency and explainability. **AI transparency** refers to the openness about how an AI system is designed, trained, and operates, including access to its data sources, algorithms, and decision-making processes. **AI explainability,** on the other hand, focuses on making the AI's individual decisions understandable to humans, often through interpretable models or post-hoc explanations. While transparency is about revealing the inner workings, explainability is about making those workings comprehensible to users.

Table 5.1 Transparency vs. explainability: what's the difference?

Aspect	Transparency	Explainability
Focus	System design and operations	Decision outputs and their reasoning
Audience	Developers, auditors, regulators	End-users, auditors, oversight bodies
Objective	Show how the system works	Clarify why a specific result was produced
Tools and techniques	Documentation, audit logs, model cards	SHAP, LIME, saliency maps, feature importance scores

🛠 ***Important Notes***

- Require **model documentation** and **traceable decision paths** for AI used in risk scoring, threat detection, and access control.
- Use **explainability tools** to test whether decisions, such as alerts or policy violations, can be justified and understood by non-technical stakeholders.
- Assess whether **transparency and explainability requirements** are embedded in AI governance policies and third-party vendor contracts.

5.3.3.6 Legal and regulatory compliance

📖 **Definition: Legal and regulatory compliance** refers to the obligation of organizations to ensure that their use of AI systems adheres to all applicable laws, regulations, industry standards, and ethical guidelines. This includes both general cybersecurity and data protection laws, as well as emerging AI-specific legislation.

🔑 *Key areas of AI-related compliance*

1. **Data Protection and Privacy Laws**
   - **GDPR** – EU regulation mandating data minimization, consent, and explainability of automated decisions.
   - **California Consumer Privacy Act (CCPA)** – US law providing rights over personal data, including notice and opt-out from AI-based profiling.
   - **HIPAA** – Protects medical data when AI is used in healthcare environments.
   - **Federal Information Security Management Act (FISMA)/Federal Risk and Authorization Management Program (FedRAMP)** – Applies when AI operates within the US federal systems.
2. **Anti-Discrimination and Fairness Laws**
   - AI used in hiring, lending, insurance, or policing must avoid violating anti-discrimination laws (e.g., Equal Credit Opportunity Act, Civil Rights Act).
   - Requires fairness testing, bias auditing, and explainability of AI outputs.
3. **AI-Specific Regulations**
   - **European Union (EU) AI Act** (in development) – Risk-based regulatory framework requiring strict controls for high-risk AI systems (e.g., critical infrastructure, biometrics).
   - **ISO/IEC 42001** – International standard for AI management systems focused on governance, transparency, and accountability.
   - **NIST AI RMF** – Voluntary guidance from the United States to help manage risks related to AI systems.

4. **Cybersecurity and Critical Infrastructure Framework Compliance**
   - **NIST Cybersecurity Framework (CSF)**
   - **Cybersecurity and Infrastructure Security Agency (CISA) guidance**
   - **Payment Card Industry Data Security Standard (PCI-DSS)** (when used in debit or credit card payment environments)

Table 5.2 articulates the compliance obligations related to AI systems. AI systems are considered models, and like other technology applications, require compliance with legal, regulatory, and best practices related to AI model validation.

Table 5.2 Compliance obligations for AI applications

Obligation	Description
Lawful basis for data use	AI must use data in accordance with consent or legitimate interest
Transparency	Users must be informed if and how AI is used to make significant decisions
Accountability	Organizations must assign responsibility for AI outcomes and risk mitigation
Bias and fairness audits	Models must be tested to ensure compliance with anti-discrimination laws
Security and resilience	AI systems must have adequate protections against adversarial manipulation
Human oversight	Automated decisions with legal or ethical implications must allow for appeal

🛠 **Important Notes:** To validate compliance, cybersecurity auditors must:

- Review **AI system documentation** to verify legal and regulatory adherence.
- Evaluate whether **data handling, storage, and processing** comply with privacy laws.
- Audit **third-party AI tools or models** for compliance risk.
- Ensure **incident response plans** address AI-related data breaches or system failures.
- Check if **governance policies align with frameworks** like NIST AI RMF and ISO/IEC 42001.

🎯 **Pro Tip:** Take the time to understand compliance with frameworks, legal, and regulatory requirements. Consider conducting independent research and creating notes or checklists to ensure compliance. Understanding these obligations is critical to reducing organizational risk and ensuring trust in AI technologies. Legal and regulatory compliance in AI ensures systems are not only innovative but also responsible, ethical, and lawful.

5.4 LOGICAL AND PHYSICAL SECURITY

As AI systems become more deeply integrated into organizational operations, securing them requires both logical and physical controls tailored to their unique architecture and risks. While traditional technology platforms rely heavily on structured access control and perimeter security, AI systems introduce additional layers of complexity – such as sensitive training data, model files, and inference pipelines – that must be protected from compromise. Logical security ensures that AI algorithms, datasets, and outputs are shielded from unauthorized manipulation or leakage, while physical security safeguards the underlying infrastructure, including servers, graphics processing units (GPUs), and cloud-hosted environments. Just as with legacy IT systems, a comprehensive security posture for AI requires auditors to evaluate both digital and physical exposures, with added attention to the nuances of how AI learns, adapts, and executes decisions (Dwight, 2024).

1. **Logical Security:** Logical security refers to the **protection of digital assets**, such as systems, applications, networks, and data, through **software-based controls** and **access management** mechanisms.

   🔑 **Key Components**
   - **Authentication and Authorization:** Ensuring only verified users can access systems (e.g., multi-factor authentication, role-based access control).
   - **Encryption:** Protecting data in transit and at rest using cryptographic methods.
   - **Firewalls and Intrusion Detection Systems (IDS):** Monitoring and controlling incoming and outgoing network traffic.
   - **Endpoint Protection:** Securing laptops, servers, and mobile devices against malware and unauthorized access.
   - **Access Logging and Monitoring:** Keeping detailed records of user activity and system access for audit and incident response.
   - **Patch Management:** Regular updates to software and systems to fix vulnerabilities.

   📋 **Audit Focus Areas**
   - Are user access rights aligned with job responsibilities?
   - Are privileged accounts properly monitored and controlled?
   - Is encryption enforced for sensitive data storage and transmission?

2. **Physical Security:** Physical security refers to the **protection of hardware, infrastructure, and personnel** from physical actions or events that could cause damage or unauthorized access.

   🔑 **Key Components**
   - **Access Control Systems:** Badge readers, biometric scanners, and locked doors to restrict access to data centers and secure areas.
   - **Surveillance:** Closed-Circuit Television (CCTV) cameras and monitoring systems to detect unauthorized entry or suspicious activity.

- **Environmental Controls:** Systems to protect against fire, water damage, or power loss (e.g., heating, ventilation, and air conditioning (HVAC), uninterruptible power supply (UPS), fire suppression).
- **Visitor Management:** Logs and escort policies for third-party access to secure facilities.
- **Hardware Disposal Protocols:** Secure decommissioning of servers, hard drives, and storage devices to prevent data leaks.

Audit Focus Areas

- Is physical access to critical systems appropriately restricted and monitored?
- Are visitor logs and badge activity regularly reviewed?
- Are backup systems and disaster recovery infrastructure physically secured?

Table 5.3 analyzes how logical and physical security relate to cybersecurity risk aspects. Logical and physical security are both essential for protecting AI applications from threats that could compromise data integrity, system functionality, or user trust. **Logical security** safeguards the software side – like algorithms, data, and access controls – against cyberattacks and unauthorized use. **Physical security** ensures that the hardware and infrastructure hosting AI systems are protected from tampering, theft, or environmental damage, which is crucial for maintaining operational continuity and data confidentiality.

Table 5.3 Logical vs. physical security: side-by-side

Aspect	Logical security	Physical security
Focus	Digital systems and data	Hardware, personnel, and physical locations
Primary threats	Hackers, malware, unauthorized digital access	Theft, vandalism, natural disasters, physical intrusions
Controls	Encryption, access control, firewalls, logging	Locks, surveillance, environmental sensors, guards
Auditor's role	Validate security configurations and user controls	Inspect facility controls, review access logs, test safeguards

Conclusion: Effective cybersecurity requires both logical and physical security controls. Logical safeguards protect systems and data from cyber threats, while physical controls ensure that critical infrastructure remains secure from tampering, theft, or environmental damage. Cybersecurity auditors must ensure end-to-end protection for AI audit tools, which should mirror those logical and physical controls employed by business partners.

Critical Thinking Moment: As you read through this chapter, think about the similarities and differences between logical and physical security measures for AI systems compared to other technologies.

5.5 TYPES OF AI MODELS

AI systems rely on a variety of model types, each designed to solve specific kinds of problems by learning from data, identifying patterns, and making predictions or decisions. Understanding the different types of AI models, such as supervised, unsupervised, reinforcement learning, and generative models, is essential for evaluating how they function, where they apply, and what risks they introduce. This section provides an overview of the core AI model categories and architectures, offering insight into how they are used across industries, including cybersecurity, and how their unique characteristics influence system behavior, interpretability, and auditability.

First, let's look at the AI hierarchy. The AI hierarchy represents a structured framework that organizes AI capabilities from foundational data and ML models to advanced decision-making systems, guiding how organizations adopt, scale, and govern AI technologies effectively.

1. **Machine Learning (ML):** Subset of AI that enables computer systems to learn patterns from data and improve their performance on specific tasks without being explicitly programmed. By using algorithms that automatically adjust and improve through experience, ML allows systems to make predictions, identify patterns, or make decisions based on new data (AWS, n.d.c; Google Cloud, n.d.b.; Syracuse University, 2025). ML uses three learning approaches as noted below.
   - **Supervised Learning:** Data in training dataset is labeled.
     - Classification – groups data by category
     - Regression – looks for relationships
   - **Unsupervised Learning:** Unlabeled data in training dataset requiring ML to learn the data structure.
     - Clustering – grouping of certain data for categorization.
     - Dimensionality Reduction – reduces the number of dataset features.
     - Association Rule Mining – seeks to identify rule-based relationships.
   - **Reinforcement Learning:** A "trial and error" approach to learning and seeks feedback based on "reward" or "penalty" approach (Hussain, 2024).
     - Value-Based Methods – agent learns to estimate the value of taking certain actions in particular states, aiming to maximize the expected cumulative reward over time.
     - Policy-Based Methods – agent directly learns a policy – a mapping from states to actions – without estimating value functions.
2. **Deep Learning (DL):** Technically a subset of ML but the impact and techniques are often shown as a subset of AI. DL is closely related to Data Science (Ronaghan, 2018,). Neural networks are the "engine" behind

many advanced AI systems, especially in DL. They allow machines to learn from vast amounts of data and perform tasks like recognizing faces, understanding language, driving cars, and generating human-like text. Below is a list of the many DL algorithms.

- Neural Network
- Artificial Neural Network (ANN)
- Convolutional Neural Network (CNN)
- Recurrent Neural Network (RNN)
- Transformer Networks

3. **Computer Vision:** Focuses on enabling machines to interpret and understand visual data like images and videos (AWS, 2025a).
4. **Robotics:** Is the interdisciplinary field of science and engineering focused on the design, construction, operation, and use of robots, which are programmable machines that perform autonomous or semi-autonomous tasks, often designed to assist or replace humans in a variety of settings (Gaudiello & Zibetti, 2016).
5. **Expert Systems:** Uses AI to simulate human behavior or judgment or expertise or experience related to a particular expertise domain (Lutkevich, 2024).
6. **Speech Recognition:** Interprets verbal and written human speech into meanings and responses (Chia, 2025).
7. **Recommender System:** Core functionality is to provide recommendations based on input of previous queries or viewed items within the cybersecurity AI applications or tools (Amazon Personalize, 2025).
8. **Generative AI (GenAI):** Creates new content – such as text, images, audio, video, or code – by learning patterns from existing data (Kniberg, 2024).

Important Note: Remember the above models as you develop use cases. AI models are selected based on the cybersecurity audit purpose.

AI agents versus agentic AI

AI agents and agentic AI are two different terms. AI agents are systems designed to perceive their environment, process information, and take actions to achieve specific goals autonomously or semi-autonomously. These agents can range from simple rule-based bots to complex, learning-enabled entities that adapt over time (Ghosh, 2024). Agentic AI refers to a more advanced class of AI agents that exhibit higher degrees of autonomy, goal-directed behavior, and contextual reasoning. Unlike traditional AI systems that passively respond to inputs, agentic AI actively makes decisions, prioritizes tasks, and can initiate actions based on its understanding of objectives and environmental changes. This evolution toward agentic systems marks a shift from static tools to dynamic collaborators, raising new opportunities – and challenges – in oversight, accountability, and human-AI interaction (Biswas, 2025).

AI Model Components: An AI model takes in data, processes it through a structured architecture, adjusts its internal settings to learn patterns, and produces predictions or decisions – all while being optimized and evaluated for accuracy and performance.

AI core components and processes (Tamanna, 2024)

1. **Input Data**
   - The raw data fed into the model. This raw data is obtained from sources unique to the desired model outcome.
   - Example: Raw data can be text, images or numbers.
2. **Features**
   - Specific variables or attributes extracted from the data that the model uses to learn patterns.
   - Example: For an email spam filter, features might include the presence of certain keywords.
3. **Model Architecture**
   - The structure or blueprint of the model, which defines how data flows and how computations are performed.
   - Example: Neural networks, decision trees, transformers.
4. **Parameters**
   - The internal variables that the model adjusts during training to learn patterns.
   - Example: Weights and biases in a neural network.
5. **Training Algorithm**
   - The method used to adjust the model's parameters based on the input data and feedback (usually through optimization techniques like gradient descent).
6. **Loss Function**
   - A formula that measures how far the model's predictions are from the actual outcomes. The goal is to minimize this during data training.
7. **Optimizer**
   - An algorithm that updates the parameters to minimize the loss function.
   - Example: Adam, Stochastic Gradient Descent (SGD).
8. **Output/Predictions**
   - The results produced by the model after processing the input data.
   - Example: Classifications, probability scores, generated text.
9. **Evaluation Metrics**
   - Measurements to assess how well the model is performing.
   - Example: The measurements could include accuracy and F1 score (combination of precision and recall).

E Model architectures

Model architectures shape how AI systems are built and function, determining how they process data, learn from it, and perform tasks across different domains.

- **Generative Pre-trained Transformer (GPT):** A large language model (LLM) developed by OpenAI that uses a transformer architecture to understand and generate human-like text. It's trained in massive amounts of text data and fine-tuned for various language tasks like writing, summarization, and answering questions (AWS, n.d.c).
- **Bidirectional Encoder Representations from Transformers (BERT):** A transformer-based model developed by Google that is designed to understand the context of a word by looking at both the words before and after it (*bidirectional*). It excels at language understanding tasks such as question answering and sentence classification (Van Otten, 2024).
- **Large Language Model Meta AI (LLaMA):** Adaptable for a wide range of NLP tasks, such as text generation, summarization, and translation (Meta, 2023).
- **Vision Transformer (ViT):** An AI model that applies the transformer architecture (originally designed for language) to image recognition tasks. Instead of using convolutional layers like CNNs, ViT breaks images into patches and processes them similarly to how transformers handle words in text (Papa et al., 2024).
- **Diffusion Models:** A type of generative model that learns to create new data (like images) by reversing a process that adds random noise to data. Used in powerful tools like DALL·E 3 and Stable Diffusion to generate realistic images from text descriptions (Luo, 2022).
- **Autoencoders:** Neural network models designed to compress data into a lower-dimensional form (encoding) and then reconstruct the original data (decoding). Used for tasks like dimensionality reduction, anomaly detection, and image denoising (Bergmann & Stryker, 2023).
- **Variational Autoencoders (VAE):** An advanced type of autoencoder that learns to represent data in a way that allows for the generation of new, similar data. It's widely used in generating images and creating synthetic data (Bergmann & Stryker, 2023).
- **Generative Adversarial Network (GAN):** A generative model consisting of two neural networks – a generator that creates data and a discriminator that evaluates it. The two compete, leading to the creation of highly realistic data such as images or videos. Famous for creating deepfakes and art generation (Varughese, 2025).
- **Deep Q-Network (DQN):** A reinforcement learning algorithm that combines Q-learning with deep neural networks to enable agents to learn complex decision-making tasks, such as playing video games like Atari at human-level performance (PyTorch, 2025).

Data and training

Data and training fuel the AI learning process, providing AI models with the information they need to recognize patterns, improve accuracy, and adapt to new challenges (Chen, 2023).

- **Training Data:** The dataset used to **teach the model**, allowing it to learn patterns and relationships between inputs and outputs.
- **Validation Data:** A separate dataset used **during training** to fine-tune the model's parameters and prevent overfitting. It helps evaluate how well the model generalizes to unseen data.
- **Test Data:** A final, independent dataset used **after training** to assess the model's performance on completely new, unseen data.
- **Overfitting:** When a model learns the training data **too well**, including noise and outliers, causing poor performance on new data.
- **Underfitting:** When a model is **too simple** to capture the underlying patterns in the data, resulting in poor performance on both training and new data.
- **Bias-Variance Tradeoff:** A fundamental challenge in ML where increasing a model's **complexity** (lower bias) can increase **variance** (sensitivity to new data), and simplifying the model (higher bias) can decrease variance but lead to underfitting. The goal is to **balance bias and variance** for optimal model performance.
- **Data Augmentation:** Techniques used to **increase the diversity of training data** without collecting new data, such as rotating images, adding noise, or translating text, to improve model robustness.
- **Data Labeling:** The process of **assigning meaningful labels** (like "cat" or "dog") to raw data, making it usable for supervised learning tasks.
- **Annotation:** A broader term that includes data labeling and marking **specific features or regions** within data (e.g., bounding boxes around objects in images, or tagging parts of a sentence in NLP tasks).
- **Feature Engineering:** The process of **selecting, transforming, or creating new input features** from raw data to improve model performance.
- **Hyperparameter Tuning:** The practice of **adjusting settings** that control the training process (like learning rate, batch size, or number of layers) to optimize model performance.

5.6 AI MODEL VALIDATION

The term **AI black box** refers to the lack of transparency in how complex AI models, particularly DL and neural networks, arrive at their decisions or predictions. These models process vast amounts of data through multiple hidden layers, making it difficult for humans to trace or interpret the reasoning behind specific outputs. This opacity presents significant challenges for trust, accountability, and compliance, especially in regulated environments where explainability is critical. Understanding and mitigating the black box nature of AI is essential for responsible implementation, prompting the development of XAI techniques that aim to make AI behavior more interpretable and aligned with human values and professional standards.

The following checklist provides AI model validation criteria that cybersecurity auditors can use to evaluate AI-based audit applications and tools. It is also applicable when performing audits of AI applications and tools to ensure their reliability, accuracy, and alignment with organizational and regulatory requirements (Ozer & van Schijndel, n.d.).

☑ *AI Model Validation Steps for Cybersecurity Auditors*

1. **Define the Purpose and Scope of the AI Model**
   - **Objective:** Clearly articulate what the AI model is intended to do within the audit process (e.g., anomaly detection, control testing, risk prioritization).
   - **Scope:** Define boundaries of use, data sources, and expected outcomes.
2. **Assess Data Quality and Integrity**
   - **Input Validation**: Confirm that training and testing datasets are complete, accurate, and representative.
   - **Bias Check:** Analyze datasets for imbalances that may introduce bias (e.g., over-representation of certain system events or control failures).
   - **Data Lineage:** Ensure traceability of data from source to model.
3. **Evaluate Model Architecture and Algorithm Selection**
   - **Algorithm Appropriateness:** Determine if the selected algorithm (e.g., decision tree, neural network) fits the audit objective and data type.
   - **Complexity vs. Explainability:** Ensure that model complexity doesn't hinder auditor understanding or transparency.
4. **Perform Training and Testing Validation**
   - **Training Accuracy:** Measure how well the model fits historical data.
   - **Testing Accuracy:** Use a holdout dataset or cross-validation to test model performance on unseen data.
   - **Key Metrics:** Evaluate precision, recall, F1 score, and area under the curve (AUC), depending on the use case.
5. **Conduct Performance and Stress Testing**
   - **Scenario-Based Testing:** Test model performance under edge cases or unusual audit scenarios.
   - **Robustness Check:** Introduce slight variations in input data to evaluate consistency in output.
6. **Interpret and Explain**
   - **Auditability:** Ensure the model's decision logic can be reviewed and understood by auditors and stakeholders.
   - **Tools:** Use tools like SHAP or LIME to visualize how features impact outcomes.

7. **Assess Risk and Control Alignment**
   - **Risk Mitigation:** Identify and document risks mitigated by the model (e.g., missed fraud detection, non-compliance).
   - **Control Mapping:** Ensure the model's output supports existing security control objectives (refer to NIST 800-53, ISO/IEC 27001).
8. **Validate against Audit and Regulatory Standards**
   - **Audit Trail:** Ensure outputs and inputs are logged, reproducible, and traceable.
   - **Compliance Check:** Verify the model meets internal policies and external standards (e.g., IIA Standards, Yellow Book, GDPR).
9. **Implement Model Governance Controls**
   - **Roles and Responsibilities:** Define who owns the model, who monitors it, and how decisions are escalated.
   - **Approval and Documentation:** Validate model use is formally approved and fully documented (including rationale and versioning).
10. **Monitor for Model Drift and Update Frequency**
    - **Drift Detection:** Continuously monitor changes in data or outcomes that reduce model reliability.
    - **Model Refresh:** Define and adhere to a schedule for model retraining or retirement.

⚖ Risks addressed through validation

Risk management for AI model validation involves identifying, assessing, and mitigating potential harms or failures associated with AI systems. It ensures that models perform reliably, ethically, and securely across various use cases and conditions. By integrating risk management into the validation process, organizations can build trust, reduce bias, and maintain compliance with regulatory and organizational standards. Through the risk management process, the following common risks would be addressed through AI model validation.

- **Bias and Discrimination:** Bias and discrimination in AI occur when algorithms produce unfair or prejudiced outcomes due to skewed data, flawed assumptions, or systemic inequalities embedded in model design or deployment.
- **Model Inaccuracy or Overfitting:** Inaccuracy or overfitting in AI arises when a model performs well on training data but fails to generalize to new data, leading to unreliable or misleading outcomes in real-world applications.
- **Loss of Explainability and Transparency:** Loss of explainability and transparency in AI occurs when the decision-making processes of a model are too complex or opaque to be understood or audited, undermining trust, accountability, and regulatory compliance.
- **Poor Data Quality or Integrity:** Poor data quality or integrity in AI systems leads to unreliable, incomplete, or inaccurate inputs that compromise model performance, introduce risk, and erode trust in outcomes.

- **Regulatory Non-Compliance:** Regulatory non-compliance in AI occurs when systems fail to meet legal, ethical, or industry standards – such as data protection, fairness, or accountability – resulting in potential legal penalties, reputational harm, and operational disruptions.
- **Model Drift Leading to Audit Failures:** Model drift leading to audit failures occurs when changes in data patterns over time cause an AI model's performance to degrade, resulting in inaccurate assessments, overlooked risks, or noncompliant audit conclusions.
- **Inadequate Security Controls Over AI Use:** Inadequate security controls over AI expose systems to threats such as data breaches, adversarial attacks, or unauthorized access, compromising the confidentiality, integrity, and availability of both the AI models and the data they process.

These validation steps not only support the integrity and effectiveness of audit-specific models but also offer valuable insights into how cybersecurity auditors can assess and provide assurance over AI systems deployed across the broader organization. In this dual role, auditors benefit from both applying and auditing AI, ensuring responsible AI use while reinforcing trust in data-driven audit activities.

💡 **Critical Thinking Moment:** As you evaluate the risks mitigated as noted above, do you see similarities to other technological systems? Are there other risks that you believe need to be mitigated through the model validation process?

🎯 **Pro Tip:** AI model validation for cybersecurity audit applications should align closely with the organization's overall AI system development life cycle. While the steps outlined above provide general principles and best practices for validating AI models, those steps are particularly relevant to the development and deployment of AI tools used specifically within the audit function.

🛠 *Penetration Testing*

Penetration testing is specifically mentioned because of the benefit it provides to security vulnerabilities. This adds an automated mechanism to reduce the risk of inadequate security controls. Penetration testing for AI systems involves simulating attacks to uncover vulnerabilities in model architecture, training data, and deployment environments. Unlike traditional systems, AI models can be targeted through adversarial inputs, data poisoning, or model extraction techniques that exploit their learning behavior. Penetration testing helps identify these unique threats, assess the robustness of AI defenses, and validate the security of application programming interfaces (API)s, inference pipelines, and data flows. It is a critical component of securing AI deployments, especially in high-risk domains like cybersecurity in finance and healthcare.

5.7 AI APPLICATIONS

AI is reshaping what's possible – transforming static systems into intelligent, adaptive solutions that learn, predict, and evolve. As AI moves from the lab into the core of business, science, and society, its applications are unlocking new frontiers in how we communicate, secure our digital environments, and automate complex decisions. This section explores how AI is not only enhancing today's capabilities but laying the groundwork for a future where machines collaborate with humans to solve the world's most pressing challenges with creativity, speed, and precision.

As you read through the AI application examples in this section, consider how each use case might apply within your own organization or audit environment. While a few examples are provided for each application, they represent a starting point, AI's potential in cybersecurity is far broader. Cybersecurity audit professionals operate across multiple domains, from incident response to identity management, where AI can play a transformative role. Use this opportunity to reflect on where AI might enhance your audit processes, strengthen risk detection, or improve decision-making. Jot down ideas, questions, or potential opportunities as you explore each application.

1. **Chatbots:** AI-powered programs that simulate human conversation through text or voice interfaces, often used in customer service, virtual assistants, and online support systems. Examples: OpenAI Chat Generative Pre-Trained Transformer (ChatGPT), Google Gemini, Microsoft Copilot, Anthropic Claude, and High-Flyer DeepSeek (Glover & Rekdal, 2025).

   🔍 **Audit Use:** Evaluate chatbot authentication and input validation using AI to uncover exposure to injection attacks or unauthorized data access.

   🤖 **AI Application Example:** Use **AI-driven penetration testing tools** like **Penetration Testing Generative Pre-Trained Transformer (PentestGPT)** to simulate attacks against chatbot interfaces and assess for vulnerabilities such as input manipulation, data leakage, or privilege escalation.

2. **Predictive Analytics:** The use of AI and ML to analyze historical data and make informed predictions about future outcomes, such as customer behavior, equipment failures, or market trends. Example: AI application predicts emerging cybersecurity threats based on data breach trends.

   🔍 **Audit Use:** Assess predictive models for cyber threat trends to validate if alerts align with risk thresholds and escalation policies.

   🤖 **AI Application Example:** Use **AI-driven SIEM platforms** like **Splunk with predictive analytics applications** to audit and model historical cyber incident data.

3. **Recommender Systems:** AI algorithms that suggest processes, risks, controls, content, or services to users based on their preferences, behavior, or similarities to other users; widely used in streaming platforms, e-commerce, and social media but relevant to cybersecurity audit as noted below. Example: AI application recommends risks and controls based on user prompt history.
   Audit Use: Confirm that model outputs meet compliance standards for data privacy and fairness in automated decision-making.
   AI Application Example: Leverage **AI explainability tools** such as **LIME or SHAP** to audit how recommender systems use user behavior and personal data.

4. **Fraud Detection:** The application of AI to identify suspicious patterns or anomalies in transactions, helping detect and prevent fraudulent activity in finance, insurance, and cybersecurity. Example: PayPal uses ML to flag unusual transactions and detect fraudulent activity in real time.
   Audit Use: Independently verify existing fraud detection models' outputs using an auditor-controlled ML model.
   AI Application Example: Deploy **unsupervised anomaly detection models** using **Python libraries like PyCaret or scikit-learn** to audit transaction logs for overlooked fraudulent patterns.

5. **Robotic Process Automation (RPA):** The use of software robots, often enhanced by AI, to automate repetitive, rule-based business processes such as data entry and report generation. Example: Blue Prism can be configured to initiate vulnerability scans, gather data from security tools, and generate reports on identified vulnerabilities.
   Audit Use: Use **AI-based behavior analytics tools** like **Observe.AI or Splunk User Behavior Analytics** (**UBA**) to monitor and audit bot activity logs for anomalies.
   AI Application Example: Validate that RPA bots operate within approved role-based access rights and perform only authorized tasks.

6. **AI-Augmented Cybersecurity:** The integration of AI to enhance cybersecurity capabilities, including threat detection, incident response, anomaly detection, and adaptive defense against evolving cyber threats. Example: IBM QRadar integrates AI for threat intelligence, log analysis, and automated incident response.
   Audit Use: Measure detection precision, incident response time, and model drift indicators using the AI engine's audit logs and simulation inputs.
   AI Application Example: Use platforms like **Darktrace or Microsoft Defender for Endpoint** (**AI-enhanced**) to test and audit live threat detection capabilities.

The following sections provide a deeper look into selected AI applications introduced above. If your AI maturity level is level 1 or 2, these AI tools may be perfect as you begin building your AI-enhanced cybersecurity audit capabilities.

5.8 EXPLORING CHATBOTS

Chatbots are AI-driven tools designed to simulate human conversation, often used to automate customer service, technical support, and information retrieval. They can enhance efficiency and user experience by providing instant, consistent responses, but may also pose risks if poorly trained, biased, or lacking transparency. In cybersecurity audit contexts, chatbots must be carefully evaluated for data handling practices, accuracy, and alignment with compliance standards.

> 🎯 **Pro Tip:** Consider building a library of prompts that are created by the Cybersecurity Audit and AI Subject Matter Expert (SME) Pods. While the cybersecurity auditors may have unique prompts, most prompts could be based on the AI SME Pod professionals.

5.8.1 🤖 ChatGPT

ChatGPT, developed by OpenAI, is a conversational AI model built on the GPT architecture. Its origins trace back to the release of GPT in 2018, followed by progressively more powerful versions, such as GPT-2 in 2019, GPT-3 in 2020, and GPT-4 in 2023. ChatGPT was specifically fine-tuned for dialogue, using reinforcement learning from human feedback (RLHF) to make responses more helpful, accurate, and aligned with user intent. Initially launched as a research preview in late 2022, ChatGPT quickly became one of the most widely adopted AI applications, transforming how individuals and organizations interact with technology for tasks ranging from customer support and education to software development and cybersecurity (OpenAI, 2023).

> ✸ **Did You Know?** The number of ChatGPT users "doubled in just a few weeks" from late 2024 into 2025. It is estimated that "10% of the world uses our systems." This growth is partly due to the active researchers and developers in the public sector contributing to ChatGPT's increasing functionality (Paris, 2025). In addition, ChatGPT took just "**two months** to reach one hundred 100 million users," making it the fastest-growing consumer application in history at the time. This milestone was achieved shortly after its launch in November 2022 (Milmo, 2023). For comparison, it took Facebook 4.6 years, Instagram 2.6 years, and Twitter 5.5 years to reach the same user base (Rao, 2023).

5.8.2 🤖 Gemini

Gemini is Google DeepMind's advanced AI model series, developed as a successor to its earlier language models like Bard and PaLM (Pathways Language Model). Introduced in December 2023, Gemini was designed to compete directly with OpenAI's GPT-4, combining powerful language understanding with multimodal capabilities – allowing it to process and reason across text, code, images, audio, and video. The Gemini 1 series marked a major leap in Google's AI efforts, integrating innovations in reinforcement learning, safety alignment, and real-time responsiveness. Subsequent versions, including Gemini 1.5 launched in early 2024, continued to enhance performance, efficiency, and scalability, positioning Gemini as a foundational model for Google's AI-driven services across products like Search, Workspace, and Android (Google DeepMind, n.d.).

Did You Know? Gemini was introduced after ChatGPT but now has about "350 million monthly active users," compared to one billion ChatGPT users in 2025 (Paris, 2025). There was a significant lower number of daily active users, representing "less than a quarter" of the overall active users (Peckham, 2025).

5.8.3 Copilot

Microsoft Copilot, developed by GitHub in collaboration with OpenAI, was first introduced in 2021 as an AI-powered code completion tool aimed at assisting developers by suggesting entire lines or blocks of code based on natural language prompts. Built on the Codex model, a descendant of OpenAI's GPT-3, Copilot marked a significant advancement in AI-assisted software development by integrating seamlessly with popular code editors like Visual Studio Code that was introduced February 7, 2023. Initially launched as a technical preview, Copilot quickly gained traction and became a subscription-based service in 2022. Microsoft further expanded its capabilities through GitHub Copilot X and integration with Microsoft 365 Copilot, embedding the AI assistant into tools like Word, Excel, and PowerPoint, thus broadening its impact beyond coding to enterprise productivity (Mehdi, 2023; Riley, 2024).

Did You Know? Microsoft personnel claim that "70% of the Fortune 500" firms use Copilot (Shaw, 2024). Perhaps the integration of Copilot into the Microsoft 365 products is a key driver. The number of active users is predicted to be "33 million" (Curry, 2025).

5.8.4 Chatbot prompt engineering

Prompt engineering is the practice of crafting effective inputs (called *prompts*) to guide and optimize the performance of LLMs like ChatGPT, Gemini, or Copilot. The goal is to elicit the most accurate, relevant, or creative responses based on the model's capabilities.

Key Concepts in Prompt Engineering: A well-designed prompt often includes:

- **Context:** Background information to frame the task
- **Instruction:** A clear command or question

- **Format Guidance:** Desired structure of the response (e.g., bullets, list, paragraph)
  Example Prompt Use: "*Summarize the benefits of multi-factor authentication in three bullet points for a cybersecurity awareness email.*"
- **Prompt Types**
  - **Zero-shot prompting:** Ask a question directly with no examples.
  - *Example: "Translate this sentence into French: 'Cybersecurity is essential.'"*
  - **Few-shot prompting:** Include examples to guide the model.
  - Example Prompt Use:

    Q: What is phishing?
    A: A type of cyberattack that tricks users into revealing sensitive information.

    Q: What is malware?
    A: Malware (short for malicious software) is any software designed to intentionally cause damage to a computer, server, network, or user.

  - **Chain-of-thought prompting:** Ask the model to reason step by step.
  - Example Prompt Use: "*Explain how a firewall works, step by step.*"
- **Iterative Refinement:** Prompt engineering often requires testing and refining prompts through trial and error to improve clarity, completeness, or tone of results.
- **Use Cases**
  - Content generation
  - Data extraction
  - Code writing and debugging
  - Summarization
  - Question answering
  - Simulations or roleplay (e.g., emulate an internal cybersecurity consultant)

Applications in Cybersecurity (Example Use Case): To generate a risk assessment summary, you might use the following prompt: "*As a cybersecurity auditor, generate a summary of key risks for a healthcare organization using cloud-based electronic health record (HER) systems. Include regulatory concerns and technical vulnerabilities.*"

Why It Matters: Prompt engineering is essential to unlocking the full potential of LLMs – whether for automation, education, research, or enterprise applications. It is especially valuable when accuracy, clarity, or domain-specific output is required.

💡 **Critical Thinking Moment:** Review the dates these chatbots were introduced and think about the incremental enhancements since the introduction. Also think about how computer advancements, such as quantum-ready AI, will impact future enhancements (Essex & Gillis, 2025). How do you envision using AI for your cybersecurity audit activities?

🎯 Pro Tips

- The three chatbots were provided for comparison purposes. While all three can be used to compare results, evaluate against number of active users, quality of results, and extent of active researchers/developers that result in frequent enhancements to determine the best Chatbot.
- Review the recommendations from Chatbot. Those recommendations will appear when the prompt is complete and offers alternative formats and information that could add value. Also, let the Chatbot know if the information was good or bad, this assists in answering subsequent responses. In addition, this can help with updating the training data.

5.9 EXPLORING PREDICTIVE ANALYTICS

Predictive analytics is a data-driven approach that uses statistical algorithms, ML techniques, and historical data to forecast future outcomes or behaviors. By identifying patterns and trends in past data, predictive models can estimate the likelihood of events such as security breaches, fraud, or system failures before they occur. In cybersecurity auditing, predictive analytics enhances risk assessments by highlighting potential vulnerabilities and prioritizing areas for investigation based on projected threat likelihood. This proactive capability helps organizations allocate resources more effectively and strengthen their overall security posture (IBM, 2022).

🛠 Predictive analytics prompt engineering

As noted for Chatbots, **prompt engineering** is the practice of crafting effective inputs (called *prompts*) to guide and optimize the performance of LLMs like ChatGPT, Claude, or Gemini (Lee, 2025). The goal is to elicit the most accurate, relevant, or creative responses based on the model's capabilities.

1. **Prompting in LLM-Enhanced Predictive Analytics:** When using AI tools like ChatGPT or other LLMs in predictive analytics, prompts are used to:
   - Frame questions about data trends or future outcomes.
   - Generate hypotheses or identify potential predictors.

- Provide natural language explanations of statistical results or forecast models.
- Example Prompt Use: "*Based on this software patch history dataset, what are likely predictors for meeting significant patch updates within 7 days?*"

2. **Traditional Predictive Analytics Doesn't Use Prompts (Directly):** In classic predictive analytics, such as regression or ML, prompts aren't explicitly used. Instead, analysts:
   - Feed structured data into algorithms.
   - Use features (independent variables) to train models to predict outcomes (dependent variables). But natural language prompts might still be used to instruct AI assistants to help:
     - Clean data.
     - Generate Python/R code.
     - Interpret model results.
3. **Prompts in Automated ML (AutoML) and No-Code Tools:** Many AutoML platforms (e.g., DataRobot, H2O.ai, Google AutoML) or AI copilots in tools like Microsoft Fabric or Excel now accept natural language prompts to:
   - Automate predictive model building.
   - Select algorithms.
   - Explain results.

Table 5.4 articulates when prompts are used for predictive analytics. This analysis includes the "how" the prompt use was determined. Note that not all types of predictive analytics use prompts.

Table 5.4 Predictive analytics prompt summary table

Context	Are prompts used?	How?
Traditional predictive analytics	Not directly	Uses structured data, statistical/ML models
LLM-enhanced analytics	Yes	Prompts used to explore, interpret, or generate predictions
AutoML / no-code platforms	Yes	Prompts guide automated analysis and modeling

✎ **Note:** The traditional predictive analytics using structured data, statistical/ML models is out of scope for this chapter. Refer to references and resources in Chapter 6 – Unlocking Artificial Intelligence Knowledge, Context, and Curated Resources.

💡 **Critical Thinking Moment:** Think about the data your organization/agency collects through cybersecurity tools, including threat intelligence. That data could be analyzed to look for patterns that would result in identifying high risk areas requiring cybersecurity audit focus.

5.10 EXPLORING AI RECOMMENDER SYSTEMS

Recommender systems are AI-driven algorithms designed to suggest relevant items, actions, or content to users based on their preferences, behaviors, and contextual data. Commonly used in e-commerce, streaming services, and social media, these systems personalize user experiences by analyzing historical interactions and identifying patterns across similar user profiles. In cybersecurity and auditing contexts, recommender systems can support decision-making by proposing high-risk assets for review, suggesting control improvements, or prioritizing incident responses. While powerful, these systems require careful oversight to avoid bias, ensure transparency, and maintain trust in automated recommendations (Google Developers, 2025).

🛠 Recommender system prompt engineering

As noted for Chatbots, **prompt engineering** is the practice of crafting effective inputs (called *prompts*) to guide and optimize the performance of LLMs like ChatGPT, Claude, or Gemini. The goal is to elicit the most accurate, relevant, or creative responses based on the model's capabilities. Prompts are **not traditionally used** in classic recommender systems, but they **can be used** in **modern AI-driven recommender systems**, especially those integrating **language models** or **natural language interfaces** (Mao et al., 2025).

1. **Prompting in LLM-Augmented Recommender Systems:** When using **LLMs**, prompts can be used to:
   - **Generate recommendations** based on user input in natural language.
     Example Prompt Use: "*I am reviewing insider threat domain with new personnel assigned to the insider threat program – what risks should I consider?*"
   - **Interpret or refine** results from collaborative or content-based filtering.
     Example Prompt Use: "*Explain why these insider threat risks were suggested based on my previous 5 insider threat risk queries.*"
   - **Simulate recommender logic** for rapid prototyping.
     Example Prompt Use: "*Generate a list of cybersecurity tools similar to Splunk, based on feature similarity.*"
2. **Classic Recommender Systems Don't Use Prompts:** Traditional systems use algorithms, not prompts. Examples include:
   - **Collaborative filtering** – Based on user-item interaction matrices (e.g., matrix factorization).
   - **Content-based filtering** – Based on item attributes and user profiles.
   - **Hybrid systems** – Combine both methods algorithmically.
   - These systems operate on **structured data**, using:
     - Risk ratings
     - Confirmed risk statement history
     - Other items are tags or features

3. **Prompts in Recommender System Development Tools:** In **AI-assisted coding environments** or **AutoML platforms**, prompts are used to:
   - Ask for code that builds or explains a recommender system.
   - Translate business needs into technical models.

Table 5.5 articulates when prompts are used for predictive analytics. This analysis includes the "how" the prompt use was determined. Note that not all types of recommender systems use prompts.

Table 5.5 Recommender prompt summary table

Context	Are prompts used?	How?
Traditional recommender systems	No	Use structured data and algorithms
LLM-integrated recommenders	Yes	Accept prompts to tailor or explain recommendations
Development with AI assistants	Yes	Prompts help generate code or models

> 🖉 **Note:** Traditional recommender systems using structured data and algorithms is out of scope for this chapter. Refer to references and resources in Chapter 6 – Unlocking Artificial Intelligence Knowledge, Context, and Curated Resources to further explore this AI application.

> 💡 **Critical Thinking Moment:** Think about how recommender systems could be used to recommend risk and control statements. Perhaps the algorithm could predict emerging threats that indicate a high-risk cybersecurity audit area that should be evaluated.

5.11 EXPLORING ROBOTIC PROCESS AUTOMATION (RPA)

RPA is a technology that uses software "bots" to automate repetitive, rule-based tasks traditionally performed by humans, such as data entry, report generation, and system reconciliation. By mimicking human interactions with digital systems, RPA increases operational efficiency, reduces errors, and frees up personnel for more strategic activities. In cybersecurity auditing, RPA can streamline processes like log analysis, control testing, evidence collection, and compliance checks, allowing auditors to focus on higher-risk and judgment-intensive areas. However, effective governance and monitoring are essential to ensure RPA implementations remain secure, compliant, and align with audit objectives (IBM, n.d.d).

🛠 *RPA System Prompt Engineering*

As noted for Chatbots, **prompt engineering** is the practice of crafting effective inputs (called *prompts*) to guide and optimize the performance of LLMs like ChatGPT, Claude, or Gemini. The goal is to elicit the most accurate, relevant, or creative responses based on the model's capabilities. **Prompts are not traditionally used as part of RPA execution**, but they are increasingly being used in **design, customization, and integration** – especially as **GenAI and LLMs** become part of the automation life cycle (Stanley, 2024).

1. **Prompts Used in RPA Design and Development:** When building RPA bots, especially on modern platforms (e.g., UiPath with AI copilots, Microsoft Power Automate with Copilot), prompts are used to:
   - **Describe automation goals** in natural language.
     Example Prompt Use: "*Create a bot that logs into an email account, downloads attachments, and uploads them to SharePoint.*"
   - **Generate code or workflows** using natural language instructions.
     Example Prompt Use: "*Build an RPA process that extracts data from an invoice and enters it into an Excel sheet.*"
   - **Assist with debugging or optimizing existing scripts.** In this case, the **prompt interacts with a code-generating or task-design assistant,** not the RPA bot itself.
2. **Prompts Are Not Used During RPA Runtime Execution:** The bot does not "wait" for a prompt like an LLM. It follows a script unless it's integrated with an LLM or NLP interface. Once deployed, RPA bots operate:
   - On **predefined workflows**
   - With **structured rules**
   - Without user interaction (typically)
3. **Prompts in Intelligent Automation (RPA + AI):** When **RPA is integrated with AI**, especially **LLMs or chatbots**, prompts may be used:
   - To handle **exceptions or decisions** (e.g., ask Chatbot what to do with ambiguous data)
   - To **summarize extracted data**
   - For **voice or chat-based interfaces** to trigger bots
     Example Prompt Use in a Chatbot Interface: "*Please run the daily compliance check and send a summary report.*"

Table 5.6 articulates when prompts are used for predictive analytics. This analysis includes the "how" the prompt use was determined. Note that not all types of RPA use prompts.

Table 5.6 RPA prompt summary table

Use case	Are prompts used?	How?
RPA bot execution	No	Follows pre-coded rules and scripts.
RPA design and development	Yes	Prompts describe tasks to AI copilots or automation assistants
RPA + LLM integration	Yes	Prompts are used to trigger or guide bot behavior via natural language

Note: The traditional RPA using structured data and algorithms is out of scope for this chapter. Refer to references and resources in Chapter 6 – Unlocking Artificial Intelligence Knowledge, Context, and Curated Resources to further explore this topic.

Critical Thinking Moment: Think about all the administrative time spent on cybersecurity audit documentation. It is common for multiple artifacts to have the same information, such as a cybersecurity audit scope included in the cybersecurity audit report.

5.11.1 Open-source versus vendor-supplied

Open-source AI offers transparency and flexibility but still requires internal expertise. Vendor-supplied AI provides reliability and support but can limit customization and increase costs.

5.11.1.1 Open-source AI applications

Open-source AI applications provide freely accessible tools and models that foster innovation, transparency, and collaboration within the AI community. They enable organizations and individuals to customize, audit, and improve AI systems without proprietary restrictions. By leveraging open-source AI, users can accelerate development while promoting ethical and responsible AI practices through community oversight.

+*Pros*

- **Transparency:** Full access to code allows for better understanding, auditing, and customization.
- **Cost-Effective:** Typically free to use and modify, reducing upfront licensing costs.
- **Flexibility:** Highly customizable to fit specific audit processes, data environments, or niche cybersecurity use cases.
- **Community Support:** Benefits from active developer communities and shared innovation.

X *Cons*

- **Maintenance Burden:** Requires internal resources for updates, patching, and ongoing support.
- **Security Risks:** Potential for unvetted code or dependencies if not properly reviewed.
- **Limited Documentation:** Quality and completeness of documentation may vary.
- **Integration Challenges:** May require significant development effort to integrate with enterprise systems or data pipelines.

5.11.1.2 Vendor-supplied AI applications

Vendor-supplied AI applications offer organizations a streamlined approach to integrating advanced AI capabilities without the need for in-house development. These solutions are typically designed to address specific business functions – such as cybersecurity, customer service, fraud detection, or predictive analytics – and are built and maintained by external vendors. While these tools can accelerate digital transformation and reduce implementation timelines, they also introduce unique considerations related to data privacy, security, regulatory compliance, and ongoing governance. Organizations must carefully evaluate vendor-supplied AI products to ensure alignment with internal policies, risk tolerance, and operational objectives, while also maintaining transparency and accountability in AI-driven decision-making.

+ *Pros*

- **Ease of Use:** Turnkey solutions with user-friendly interfaces, professional support, and training.
- **Enterprise-Grade Security:** Typically undergoes rigorous testing and complies with regulatory and cybersecurity standards.
- **Scalability:** Designed to scale with enterprise workloads and integrate with existing IT ecosystems.
- **Accountability:** Service level agreements (SLAs) and vendor responsibility for performance, reliability, and compliance.
- **Automation:** AI automates tasks like data extraction, cleaning, and initial analysis, freeing up auditors for more strategic work.
- **Data Analysis:** AI can analyze large datasets to identify patterns, trends, and anomalies that might go unnoticed by manual auditing.
- **Risk Identification:** AI can help identify and assess risks more efficiently, including potential fraud and compliance issues.
- **Improved Efficiency:** By automating tasks and providing faster analysis, AI can significantly improve audit efficiency and reduce turnaround times.
- **Enhanced Accuracy:** AI-powered tools can help minimize errors and ensure greater accuracy in audit reports.
- **Cost Reduction:** AI can help reduce audit costs by automating manual tasks and improving overall efficiency.
- **Continuous Monitoring:** Some AI audit tools offer continuous monitoring capabilities, allowing auditors to stay on top of emerging risks and trends.

✕ *Cons*

- **Cost:** Licensing, subscriptions, and service fees can be significant, especially on a scale.
- **Limited Customization:** Black-box models may restrict modification or deeper inspection of algorithms.

- **Vendor Lock-In:** Dependence on proprietary platforms can make switching providers costly or difficult.
- **Data Privacy Concerns:** Data residency and usage may be governed by the vendor's policies, raising compliance questions.

🤖 *Vendor-supplied AI audit software examples*

AI-based audit software leverages AI technologies – such as ML, NLP, and data analytics – to enhance the efficiency, accuracy, and depth of audit processes. These tools can automatically analyze large volumes of structured and unstructured data, identify patterns, flag anomalies, and even predict potential risks. By reducing manual effort and enabling continuous monitoring, AI-powered audit solutions help auditors gain real-time insights, improve decision-making, and ensure greater compliance with regulatory standards. As a result, AI-based audit software is increasingly being adopted to support internal audits, external audits, and cybersecurity assessments across various industries.

- **AuditBoard (https://auditboard.com/platform/ai/):** Offers a platform for managing compliance, risk, and audit processes, including AI-powered tools for data aggregation, report generation, and audit trail management.
- **MindBridge (https://www.mindbridge.ai/):** Provides an AI-powered financial intelligence platform that helps auditors analyze large datasets, identify anomalies, and assess risk.
- **Klear.ai (https://klear.ai/):** Offers an AI-driven automation solution that streamlines audit workflows and enhances audit control.
- **AuditMap (https://www.getauditmap.com/):** Provides an AI platform that automatically reviews documents to identify risks and risk trends across an organization.
- **TeamMate AI Editor (https://www.wolterskluwer.com/en/about-us/artificial-intelligence):** An embedded GenAI writing engine that enhances documentation quality with context-aware suggestions for clarity, tone, summarization, and translations.
- **AuditFile AI (https://auditfile.com/ai.html):** Incorporates AI and ML algorithms to help auditor's complete audits faster and with less risk.

5.11.1.3 ⚖ AI application decision-making framework

Every Internal Audit and Office of Inspector General's (OIG's) cybersecurity audit professional is encouraged to be creative and innovative. There are many AI applications that these cybersecurity professionals can consider to achieve those objectives. Table 5.7 presents a framework for analyzing the key considerations related to the decision factor. The favorable scenario for both open-source and vendor-supplied AI applications are detailed. The benefit of this chart is that cybersecurity professionals can meet the decision factor criteria with either open-source or vendor-supplied AI applications. The decision-making framework below will help cybersecurity audit professionals and organizations evaluate whether to adopt open-source or vendor-supplied AI applications, based on key factors noted in the table.

Table 5.7 Decision-making framework

Decision factor	Key considerations	Favors open-source	Favors vendor-supplied
Audit transparency	Do you need to inspect the model logic, trace decisions, or explain AI outputs?	Full code access allows audit transparency	May lack explainability in proprietary models
Regulatory compliance	Are there strict legal/privacy obligations (e.g., GDPR, FISMA)?	Can be configured to meet custom compliance	Built-in compliance features and certifications
Security assurance	Can you independently verify the security of the tool?	Can review/modify security mechanisms	Relies on vendor controls and testing.
Customization needs	Does your use case require domain-specific tuning or integration with legacy systems?	Highly adaptable and extensible	May be limited or require vendor coordination
Internal expertise	Do you have staff with ML/AI or Development, Security, and Operations (DevSecOps) knowledge?	Requires skilled teams for setup and support	Minimal internal expertise needed to deploy
Budget constraints	Are licensing fees and long-term costs a concern?	Low to no licensing cost	Higher upfront and recurring costs
Deployment speed	Do you need a ready-to-use solution?	Slower deployment with configuration needed	Fast implementation and vendor onboarding
Scalability and support	Will you need 24/7 support, upgrades, and cloud scalability?	Limited support; relies on community/do it yourself (DIY)	Enterprise-grade support and performance options
Risk of Vendor Lock-In	Is long-term flexibility and switching important?	No lock-in; full control of infrastructure	May restrict future migration or model access

📝 *How to use the decision-making framework*

- **Score each factor** (1–5) based on its importance to your use case.
- **Assess alignment** with open-source or vendor options.
- **Use the results** to inform procurement decisions, internal build vs. buy strategies, or audit tool adoption.

5.12 EMPOWERING CYBERSECURITY AUDITS THROUGH AI OVERSIGHT AND MATURITY

AI governance frameworks are essential for ensuring that AI systems are developed, deployed, and managed in a manner that is ethical, transparent, secure, and aligned with organizational and societal values. These frameworks provide structured guidance for addressing risks such as bias, lack of accountability, data misuse, and regulatory non-compliance – especially important in high-stakes domains like cybersecurity, healthcare, and finance. By establishing clear policies, roles, and controls, AI governance frameworks help organizations build trust with stakeholders, ensure responsible decision-making, and maintain compliance with emerging legal and industry standards. In cybersecurity auditing, they also enable the evaluation of AI systems against established benchmarks for fairness, explainability, and risk management.

5.12.1 AI governance concepts

AI governance refers to the framework of policies, processes, standards, roles, and accountability mechanisms that guide the **responsible, ethical, secure, and compliant development and use of AI systems** within an organization. It ensures that AI technologies are aligned with organizational objectives, regulatory requirements, societal values, and risk tolerance – especially in domains like cybersecurity, finance, healthcare, and government, where decisions have significant consequences.

5.12.1.1 🏛 Core objectives of AI governance (Wood, 2024)

1. **Accountability**
    - Establishes who is responsible for AI decisions, outputs, and impacts.
    - Defines roles across all lines of defense, including developers, business owners, auditors, and oversight bodies.
2. **Transparency and Explainability**
    - Ensures stakeholders understand how AI models function, especially in high-risk decisions.
    - Supports auditability and compliance with regulations such as GDPR and the proposed EU AI Act.
3. **Fairness and Bias Mitigation**
    - Detects and reduces discriminatory outcomes.
    - Promotes equitable model behavior across populations and contexts.
4. **Security and Privacy**
    - Safeguards data used in training and inference.
    - Implements controls to protect against adversarial attacks or model inversion.

5. **Compliance and Ethical Standards**
    - Aligns AI practices with laws and standards (e.g., NIST AI RMF, ISO/IEC 42001, Organization for Economic Co-operation and Development (OECD) Principles).
    - Promotes responsible AI aligned with human-centered values.
6. **Life Cycle Oversight**
    - Monitors AI systems across the entire life cycle – from design and development to deployment, monitoring, and retirement.
    - Includes versioning, validation, documentation, and model drift detection.
    - Monitors the overall maturity of the Cybersecurity Audit Program.

Table 5.8 provides details on AI governance requirements with a corresponding description. An effective AI governance program ensures that AI systems are developed and used responsibly, ethically, and in compliance with regulations. Key components – such as clear accountability structures, risk management frameworks, and continuous monitoring – help organizations align AI initiatives with business goals and societal values. These components are crucial for building trust, minimizing harm, and ensuring long-term sustainability of AI deployments.

Table 5.8 Components of an effective AI governance program

Component	Description
AI use policy	Defines acceptable use, ethical standards, and approved AI technologies
Risk management	Identifies, assesses, and mitigates AI-related risks, including bias, drift, and errors
Governance structure	Establishes committees or councils responsible for AI oversight
Model Inventory and registry	Maintains a catalog of AI systems, their purpose, performance, and ownership
Validation and testing protocols	Requires pre-deployment validation and regular performance testing
Documentation standards	Ensures transparency through standardized documentation of models and decisions
Communications	Outlines successes and overall AI maturity progress

5.12.1.2 💭 *Why does AI governance matter for cybersecurity auditors*

- **Supports Cybersecurity Audit Functions:** Cybersecurity auditors can assess whether AI systems used in or outside the audit department are governed properly, minimizing risk to the enterprise.

- **Ensures Trustworthiness:** Governance increases confidence in AI-driven audit tools by ensuring they are explainable, consistent, and secure.
- **Reinforces Control Objectives:** AI governance aligns with broader security and compliance frameworks (e.g., NIST CSF, ISO 27001).
- **Guides AI Use in Cybersecurity Audit Programs:** Auditors leveraging AI must follow governance rules to ensure ethical and defensible audit practices.

AI frameworks and maturity models are standardized tools, libraries, or platforms that provide pre-built components to design, develop, train, validate, deploy, and monitor AI models. They offer reusable functions and structured workflows that help developers build models efficiently and consistently, while also supporting transparency, explainability, and compliance.

From an audit and governance perspective, AI frameworks can be both technical infrastructures and governance models and understanding both aspects is key to evaluating or applying AI responsibly.

> 💡 **Critical Thinking Moment:** Using recognized frameworks instills credibility to the cybersecurity audit work effort. Think about how you would include that in your communications.

5.12.2 Mapping the landscape of AI governance and risk frameworks

As organizations increasingly adopt AI technologies, understanding the different categories of AI frameworks becomes essential for ensuring responsible, effective, and secure implementation. These frameworks serve distinct purposes – ranging from guiding ethical governance and regulatory compliance to supporting technical development, risk management, and life cycle oversight. By categorizing AI frameworks according to their focus and function, cybersecurity audit professionals can better evaluate system maturity, identify governance gaps, and align AI initiatives with organizational objectives and industry standards. This section explores the primary categories of AI frameworks and highlights their relevance to audit practices and risk-based decision-making.

1. **Technical Development Frameworks:** Used to build and deploy AI models.
   Examples:
   - **TensorFlow** (by Google – https://www.tensorflow.org/): Open-source library for DL and ML.
   - **PyTorch** (by Meta – https://pytorch.org/): Preferred for academic and research-driven applications; supports dynamic computation.
   - **Scikit-learn** (https://scikit-learn.org/stable/): A Python library for classical ML algorithms (e.g., regression, clustering).

- **Keras** (https://keras.io/): A high-level API that runs on top of TensorFlow for quick prototyping.
- **Hugging Face Transformers** (https://huggingface.co/docs/transformers/en/index): Popular for NLP models like ChatGPT or BERT.

💭 **Why Does It Matter for Cybersecurity Auditors:** These frameworks affect model accuracy, interpretability, and scalability. Understanding the underlying technology helps assess whether AI is reliable and properly documented.

2. **AI Governance and Risk Management Frameworks (Hassani, 2024):** These frameworks guide ethical, secure, and compliant use of AI across an organization.

   Examples:
   - **AI RMF (the United States):** Promotes trustworthy AI by addressing risks in design, development, and deployment phases. Key pillars: Govern, Map, Measure, Manage.
   - **OECD AI Principles:** International guidance focused on human-centered values, transparency, robustness, and accountability.
   - **International Organization for Standardization/International Electrotechnical Commission (ISO/IEC) 42001 (AI Management System Standard):** A structured framework for organizations to manage risks and ensure the responsible use of AI.
   - **EU AI Act (Regulatory Framework):** Categorizes AI systems by risk levels (e.g., unacceptable, high, limited) and mandates requirements accordingly.

   💭 **Why Does It Matter for Cybersecurity Auditors:** These frameworks provide the basis for AI audit criteria, including ethical use, bias detection, transparency, documentation, and accountability.

💭 ***Why AI frameworks matter in cybersecurity auditing***

- **Model Evaluation:** Frameworks standardize how models are trained and validated, which supports repeatability and auditability.
- **Governance Alignment:** Auditors can use governance frameworks to assess organizational readiness, ethical risk management, and compliance with global standards.
- **Security and Controls:** Frameworks often include built-in support for privacy, encryption, access control, and model explainability – key concerns for both cybersecurity and audit teams.

5.13 FROM ADOPTION TO OPTIMIZATION: UNDERSTANDING AI MATURITY

Successfully integrating AI into cybersecurity auditing requires more than selecting the right tools – it demands a realistic understanding of the organization's readiness to adopt, manage, and scale AI technologies. The AI maturity model offers a structured framework for evaluating capabilities across people, processes, data, and technology. It helps cybersecurity auditors align their strategies with the organization's AI maturity level to ensure appropriate expectations, resource planning, and risk oversight.

The model typically progresses through five stages: *Initial*, where AI use is experimental and uncoordinated; *Emerging*, where isolated pilots begin; *Defined*, where enterprise-level strategies take shape; *Managed*, where AI is consistently deployed with governance; and *Optimized*, where AI is embedded into operations and drives innovation. Understanding these stages enables auditors to assess AI scalability and tailor their audit scope, frequency, and agility methods – such as iterative reviews and continuous risk monitoring – based on how advanced the organization truly is in its AI journey.

In addition, agility and AI are inherently complementary in the context of modern cybersecurity auditing. Agile concepts emphasize iterative progress, rapid feedback, adaptability to change, and continuous improvement – all characteristics that align well with the dynamic and data-driven nature of AI. As AI models evolve with new data and environmental inputs, agile auditing practices enable auditors to respond in real time, test hypotheses in short cycles, and refine controls based on emerging risks. This alignment allows audit functions to stay ahead of complex threat landscapes, leverage AI insights to prioritize high-risk areas, and deliver timely, actionable recommendations. By integrating agility into AI adoption and oversight, cybersecurity auditors can enhance both the precision and responsiveness of the audit process.

5.13.1 Overview of AI maturity stages

AI maturity models are structured frameworks that assess an organization's capability to adopt, scale, and govern AI technologies. They help organizations evaluate where they currently stand in their AI journey and identify the steps needed to advance AI integration responsibly and effectively. Specifically, the purpose is to:

- Guide **strategic planning** for AI adoption.
- Evaluate current **technical, organizational, and cultural readiness.**
- Promote **governance, accountability, and ethical use** of AI.
- Support **scaling and sustainability** of AI initiatives.

Table 5.9 describes one example of AI maturity stages. An AI maturity model is a framework that helps organizations assess and improve their capabilities in developing, deploying, and managing AI systems. It typically outlines progressive stages – from initial experimentation to full-scale, integrated AI operations – across dimensions like strategy, data, technology, talent, and governance. By using this model, organizations can identify gaps, prioritize investments, and track their progress toward becoming more AI-driven.

Table 5.9 Common stages of AI maturity

Stage	Description
1. Awareness	Organization has basic awareness of AI concepts; no real use or strategy
2. Experimentation	Pilot projects are underway; limited scope and isolated in specific departments
3. Operationalization	AI is deployed in production with performance monitoring and some governance
4. Integration	AI is embedded across business processes; data infrastructure is robust.
5. Optimization	Continuous improvement, feedback loops, and AI performance metrics in place
6. Innovation/leadership	AI drives business transformation and innovation; ethics and governance are mature

5.13.1.1 🔑 Key dimensions assessed in AI maturity models

1. **Strategy and Leadership**
   - Executive sponsorship
   - Strategic alignment with business goals
2. **Data and Infrastructure**
   - Data quality, accessibility, governance
   - Cloud and compute capabilities
3. **Talent and Skills**
   - AI-skilled workforce
   - Training programs and cross-functional collaboration
4. **Governance and Ethics**
   - AI policies, risk management
   - Fairness, transparency, and accountability
5. **Culture and Change Management**
   - Organizational readiness for AI
   - Openness to innovation and experimentation
6. **AI Life Cycle Management**
   - Model development, testing, deployment, and monitoring
   - MLOps maturity

5.13.1.2 🛡 Examples of established AI maturity frameworks (BTIT, n.d.)

- **AI Maturity Model by Deloitte:** Focuses on AI strategy, operations, and outcomes with four stages: Passive → Active → Operational → Transformational.
- **McKinsey's AI Maturity Curve:** Highlights capability building in data, technology, and talent to drive value at scale.

- **Gartner's AI Maturity Model:** Evaluates AI maturity across business integration, skills, and risk management through five stages:

  Awareness → Active → Operational → Systemic → Transformational.

- **AI Readiness Model by OECD/AI-Work, Innovation, Productivity, and Skills (AI-WIPS) (OECD, 2022).** Often used by governments; includes governance, data policy, and regulatory considerations.

5.13.1.3 🔍 Use in cybersecurity auditing

AI maturity models help cybersecurity auditors evaluate the AI auditing systems. The objective is to apply the same controls considered for other non-audit AI systems.

- Evaluate the **robustness of AI controls** in cybersecurity systems.
- Assess **data handling, bias detection, and model drift management.**
- Verify whether AI systems align with governance and ethical standards.
- Recommend actions for **improving AI life cycle monitoring and transparency.**

Here is a **customized AI Maturity Model for a Cybersecurity Audit Function,** designed to guide the strategic development and oversight of AI-enabled auditing capabilities. Table 5.10 includes **five maturity levels** across **six critical dimensions,** tailored specifically to the needs of cybersecurity auditors. This is intended to be an example that can be tailored by your organization or agency. This table is different from Table 5.9 that describes the AI maturity stages employed by management (1LoD). This customized AI maturity model was developed to assist cybersecurity audit professionals, providing terminology specific to cybersecurity audit activities.

Table 5.10 AI maturity model for cybersecurity audit function

Maturity level	Description
1. Initial / ad hoc	No formal use of AI in audit. Minimal awareness, with fragmented experimentation
2. Developing / pilot	Some AI tools are used in isolated audits. Efforts are exploratory and lack governance
3. Defined / operational	AI capabilities are formally included in audit planning and execution. Governance begins to take shape
4. Integrated / scaled	AI is embedded across the audit life cycle. Formal risk and control structures are in place
5. Optimized / strategic	AI drives predictive, real-time auditing. Continuous improvement, strong governance, and ethical oversight are enforced

Table 5.11 describes a matrix of the AI maturity model dimensions against the five levels described in Table 5.10. The table provides a foundation for

evaluating your cybersecurity audit AI maturity and determining future state scenario. The information can be used to provide recommendations to audit leadership.

Table 5.11 AI maturity model dimensions

Dimension	Level 1: Initial / ad hoc	Level 2: Developing / pilot	Level 3: Defined / operational	Level 4: Integrated / scaled	Level 5: Optimized / strategic
Strategy and leadership	No AI strategy. AI not discussed in audit planning	Leadership is exploring AI opportunities. Pilot projects approved	AI is part of audit strategy. Roadmap in place	AI initiatives align with org-wide risk strategy	AI is a strategic enabler. Audit leaders influence org-wide AI governance
Data and infrastructure	Poor data access and integration. No analytics platform	Isolated datasets used for basic analytics	Structured access to cybersecurity data. Data governance practices emerging	Centralized, secure, and scalable audit data infrastructure	Real-time data ingestion with advanced analytics capabilities
Audit processes and tools	Manual processes dominate	Limited automation (e.g., for log analysis). AI tools used experimentally	AI tools integrated into select phases (risk assessment, controls testing)	AI supports end-to-end audit workflow including risk prediction	AI automates and enhances entire audit life cycle. Adaptive, continuous auditing in place
Governance and ethics	No AI governance policies	Basic understanding of AI risks. Ethics not formalized	Risk controls are designed for AI tools. Governance model emerging	Formal policies on AI ethics, bias, transparency, and accountability	Continuous AI auditing. Governance aligned with industry standards (e.g., NIST, ISACA)
People and skills	No AI expertise in audit team	Some auditors attend AI training	Cross-functional teams include auditors and data scientists	AI and cybersecurity audit competencies embedded in hiring/training	Auditors are AI-fluent; professional certifications in AI risk are common
Performance and value	No measurement of AI effectiveness	Pilot success evaluated ad hoc	Defined KPIs for AI audit tools. ROI and risk reduction tracked	AI contributions to audit quality and coverage quantified	AI-driven insights shape enterprise risk posture. Lessons continuously integrated

Table 5.12 describes examples of what each level would look like from a cybersecurity audit activity perspective. Note the progression from manual to non-AI automation then to AI assisted automation. Level 2 may be sufficient

in the short term as the cybersecurity AI applications are developed but is not sustainable or efficient as AI is being used by cybercriminals to advance cyberattacks, thus, cybersecurity audit professionals require the same AI technology.

Table 5.12 Use cases by maturity level

Maturity level	Example use case
Level 1	Manually reviewing firewall logs
Level 2	Using anomaly detection to flag suspicious login behavior during an audit
Level 3	AI-assisted scoping of cyber audits based on historical incident trends
Level 4	ML identifies high-risk assets and recommends audit focus areas
Level 5	AI automatically adjusts audit programs based on threat intelligence feeds and real-time network behavior

5.13.1.4 *Tailored maturity-level recommendations*

1. **To Move from Level 2 to 3:** Develop an AI audit playbook, define ethical guardrails, and embed AI in risk assessment.
2. **To Move from Level 3 to 4:** Create a centralized AI data platform and establish internal AI audit/OIG life cycle controls.
3. **To Move from Level 4 to 5:** Implement continuous monitoring using AI, train auditors in XAI, and align with emerging AI governance standards (e.g., ISO/IEC 42001, NIST AI RMF).

5.13.2 Evolving the cybersecurity audit function through AI maturity

The insights from the previous section should now be applied to the development of your organization's Cybersecurity Audit AI Maturity strategy. This document serves as a foundational guide and should be tailored to reflect the specific requirements, risks, and operational context of your agency or organization. The framework below offers a starting point for building a structured and scalable AI maturity approach that enhances the effectiveness, agility, and oversight capabilities of the cybersecurity audit function.

1. **Define the Strategic Vision and Objectives**
   - **Clarify the Cybersecurity Audit Drivers:** Improve efficiency, accuracy, threat detection, compliance, etc.
   - **Align with Organizational Goals:** Ensure AI use supports risk appetite, regulatory requirements, and cybersecurity maturity.
   - **Set Measurable Success Metrics:** Such as reduction in audit cycle time, improved anomaly detection rate.

2. **Assess Current Capabilities**
   - **Evaluate the Existing Audit Process:** Identify manual, repetitive, and time-consuming tasks.
   - **Assess Data Availability and Quality:** AI needs clean, labeled, and sufficient data.
   - **Review Technology Infrastructure:** Evaluate readiness for AI tools (cloud capability, APIs, integration).
3. **Identify High-Value Use Cases**
   - Assess automated compliance monitoring.
   - Assess anomaly detection in user access or configurations.
   - Evaluate predictive risk scoring for assets or vulnerabilities.
   - Review NLP for policy and log review.
   - Prioritize use cases using impact vs. feasibility criteria.
4. **Build Cross-Functional Partnerships (Cybersecurity Audit Pods)**
   - Engage IT/security, data science, legal/compliance, and internal audit leadership.
   - Create a governance model for AI oversight and ethical use.
   - Establish data privacy and security guardrails from the start.
5. **Select or Develop AI Solutions**
   - Evaluate commercial AI audit tools vs. building custom models.
   - Consider explainability and auditability of AI outputs.
   - Choose tools that integrate with existing SIEM, Governance/Risk/Control (GRC) platforms, or audit management systems.
6. **Pilot the AI Solution**
   - Run a proof of concept (PoC) with a limited scope.
   - Validate outcomes against traditional methods.
   - Collect feedback from auditors and stakeholders.
7. **Develop Skills and Upskill Teams**
   - Train auditors on AI fundamentals and tool usage.
   - Promote AI literacy by explaining model outputs, limitations, and risks.
   - Encourage continuous learning and cross-functional collaboration.
8. **Scale and Integrate**
   - Refine and expand AI use cases.
   - Embed AI into standard audit workflows.
   - Develop continuous monitoring and model governance processes.
9. **Measure, Monitor, and Iterate**
   - Track success metrics established in Step 1.
   - Periodically assess model performance, bias, and drift.
   - Stay updated with evolving AI regulations and industry best practices.
10. **Foster a Culture of Innovation and Trust**
    - Communicate value and transparency of AI-driven audits.
    - Encourage feedback and participation from audit staff.
    - Celebrate successes and recognize contributions.

5.13.3 AI governance maturity model

As organizations increasingly adopt AI across business and security functions, the need for structured oversight becomes essential. The AI Governance Maturity Model provides a framework for assessing how well an organization manages the ethical, operational, and regulatory risks associated with AI systems. Table 5.13 outlines five progressive levels of maturity, from ad hoc practices to fully optimized governance structures. It enables cybersecurity auditors and stakeholders to evaluate current capabilities, identify governance gaps, and guide strategic improvements. By aligning governance efforts with industry standards and audit expectations, the model supports the responsible, secure, and effective use of AI across the enterprise.

Table 5.13 AI governance maturity model

Level	Description	Key characteristics
Level 1: Initial (ad hoc)	Governance is informal or non-existent	• No formal AI policies or accountability • AI development occurs without oversight • Lack of documentation, risk assessment, or controls
Level 2: Emerging	Some awareness and informal governance practices	• Basic guidelines or ethics principles are being drafted • Individual projects define their own governance • Partial model validation and limited risk controls • Accountability is unclear or inconsistent
Level 3: Defined	Governance is documented and consistently applied	• Organization-wide AI use policy and ethics principles established. • Roles and responsibilities defined (e.g., AI oversight committee) • Standardized risk assessments and model validation processes • Model inventory initiated; version control in place
Level 4: Managed	Governance is embedded into enterprise processes	• AI governance integrated into enterprise risk management (ERM), cybersecurity, and compliance programs • Regular audits and performance monitoring conducted • Life cycle management, bias mitigation, and explainability implemented • Formal review of third-party/vendor AI systems
Level 5: Optimized	Governance is dynamic, proactive, and continuously improved	• AI governance supports innovation while managing risk • Continuous model monitoring and real-time drift detection • Cross-functional governance teams drive ethical AI use • Metrics tracked for effectiveness, fairness, and impact • AI governance aligned with external frameworks (e.g., NIST AI RMF, ISO 42001, EU AI Act)

5.13.3.1 🏛 Governance domains assessed

The model typically evaluates maturity across the following domains:

- Policy and strategy
- Roles and accountability
- Risk management and controls
- Model life cycle oversight
- Transparency and explainability
- Bias and ethics management
- Compliance and regulatory alignment

5.13.3.2 Use case for cybersecurity auditors

Cybersecurity auditors can use the maturity model to:

- Assess the department's readiness for safe and ethical AI deployment.
- Identify gaps in current AI practices across governance domains.
- Benchmark internal audit's own use of AI tools.
- Recommend steps for advancing AI governance maturity.

5.14 AI USE CASES FOR CYBERSECURITY AUDITORS – OVERVIEW

This section presents practical use case examples demonstrating how AI can be integrated into cybersecurity auditing activities. Each example assumes that appropriate security controls and governance measures are in place to safeguard data integrity, confidentiality, and compliance before any AI-enabled activities are conducted.

The use cases are organized by specific audit activities and aligned with corresponding AI maturity levels to illustrate progressive adoption and complexity. Each use case concludes with a brief discussion on how the AI application aligns with applicable auditing standards – such as the Institute of IIA Standards and the US Government Accountability Office's Yellow Book – and supports agility concepts, including adaptability, iterative improvement, and enhanced collaboration.

> ⚠ **Caution:** Confirm the existence of appropriate security controls and governance measures to protect data integrity, confidentiality, and compliance before any AI-enabled activities are executed, including the examples below. In addition, confirm that the GenAI tool is approved by audit management before executing prompts.

When selecting an AI model, especially for high-stakes domains like cybersecurity auditing, it's critical to consider **technical suitability, business**

alignment, and **governance factors**. Here's a comprehensive breakdown (checklist can be found in Chapter 6 – Unlocking Artificial Intelligence: Enhancing Cybersecurity Audits through Automation and Insight):

1. **Problem Definition and Use Case Fit**
   - **Clear Objectives:** Classification, anomaly detection, prediction, clustering, etc.
   - **Structured vs. Unstructured Data:** Determines if models like CNNs (for images) or LLMs (for text) are more appropriate.
   - **Real-Time vs. Batch Needs:** Some models are optimized for low-latency decisions, others for deeper batch analysis.
2. **Data Quality and Availability**
   - **Volume and Variety:** Supervised models require large, labeled datasets; unsupervised can work with unlabeled data.
   - **Cleanliness and Completeness:** Poor data can degrade model accuracy and fairness.
   - **Feature Relevance:** Consider whether the data contains strong predictors of the desired output.
3. **Model Interpretability and Explainability**
   - **Auditability:** Can the model's decision process be explained and traced?
   - **Regulatory Compliance:** Required for finance, healthcare, and cybersecurity (e.g., explainability for AI in NIST RMF).
   - **Stakeholder Trust:** Black-box models may face resistance in governance-heavy environments.
4. **Performance and Accuracy**
   - **Evaluation Metrics:** Precision, recall, F1 score, Receiver Operating Characteristic Area-Under the Curve (ROC-AUC), etc., depending on the use case.
   - **Overfitting/Underfitting Checks:** Models must generalize well, not just memorize training data.
   - **Benchmarking:** Compare to baseline and industry-standard models.
5. **Scalability and Efficiency**
   - **Resource Consumption:** Graphics Processing Unit/Central Processing Unit (GPU/CPU), memory, and power usage.
   - **Inference Time:** Speed for predictions (important for real-time monitoring).
   - **Model Life Cycle:** Ease of retraining, updating, and versioning.
6. **Robustness and Security**
   - **Adversarial Resistance:** Especially important in cybersecurity (e.g., evasion attacks).
   - **Bias Detection and Mitigation:** Ensure fair decision-making, especially with sensitive data.
   - **Drift Detection:** Ability to detect changes in data over time that affect performance.

7. **Tooling and Integration**
    - **Ecosystem Compatibility:** Integration with platforms like Splunk, Azure Sentinel, or GRC tools.
    - **Deployment Infrastructure:** Cloud-based, on-premises, edge, or hybrid.
    - **APIs and Automation Readiness:** Support for pipeline automation and continuous auditing workflows.
8. **Governance, Ethics, and Risk**
    - **Alignment with AI Governance Frameworks:** NIST AI RMF, ISO/IEC 42001, etc. (https://www.nist.gov/itl/ai-risk-management-framework).
    - **Ethical Use Guidelines:** Bias, privacy, consent, and fairness must be addressed.
    - **Model Documentation and Lineage:** For validation, reproducibility, and auditing.
9. **Cost and Resource Constraints**
    - **Training Cost:** High for large models like LLMs.
    - **Operational Costs:** Ongoing compute, monitoring, retraining.
    - **Human Expertise Needed:** For model tuning, maintenance, and oversight.

5.14.1 Application programming interfaces (APIs)

Expanding on Tooling and Integration above, APIs play a critical role in enabling AI systems to interact with other software, services, and users in a secure and scalable manner. They serve as the communication bridge between AI models and external applications, allowing systems to send input data to a model and receive predictions, classifications, or decisions in real time. APIs enable AI systems to be easily accessed, integrated, and scaled across digital ecosystems, transforming isolated models into enterprise-ready, interactive intelligence services (Shah, 2025).

Application programming interfaces (APIs): How APIs are used with AI systems

- **Model Deployment:** AI models are often hosted in cloud or containerized environments and exposed via APIs, making them accessible for inference (e.g., sending a document to an NLP model to extract entities).
- **Automation and Integration:** APIs allow AI functionality to be embedded into broader applications – such as chatbots, fraud detection engines, or recommendation systems – without needing to rebuild the underlying model.
- **Scalability:** With RESTful or Graph Query Language (GraphQL) APIs, organizations can support multiple simultaneous users or systems making real-time calls to an AI model, ensuring consistent performance.
- **Security and Governance:** APIs can be secured using authentication, rate-limiting, and logging mechanisms, which are critical for managing access to sensitive AI capabilities and ensuring compliance.

Pro Tip: Engage with AI SME from the **1LoD and 2LoD** to collaboratively identify data sources – such as threat intelligence feeds, endpoint detection alerts, and vulnerability scan results – that can be interfaced with Cybersecurity Audit AI systems. By integrating these operational insights, audit teams can enhance their understanding of real-time risk exposure. Additionally, consider the value of using **independent AI systems** within the audit function; these may yield alternative perspectives or uncover overlooked risks, reinforcing the objectivity and depth of cybersecurity audit analysis.

5.14.2 Ready to unlock the full potential of AI in cybersecurity auditing

! Important Note Regarding Policy and Standard Compliance: As a second reminder, cybersecurity audit professionals must ensure that all actions taken in relation to the AI examples provided in this chapter align with their organization's established AI policies, procedures, and standards. Before implementing or testing any AI tools, models, or practices described, auditors should consult relevant internal governance documents and obtain necessary approvals. Adhering to these policies is essential not only for maintaining compliance but also for safeguarding data, protecting systems, and upholding organizational integrity and accountability in the use of AI technologies. In addition to the internal policies and procedures, consider the following:

1. **Foundational Security Controls Are in Place:** The organization has implemented baseline cybersecurity controls aligned with recognized frameworks (e.g., NIST CSF, ISO/IEC 27001), ensuring a stable environment for AI integration.
2. **AI Governance Framework Has Been Initiated:** Policies, roles, and oversight mechanisms are established to support responsible AI use across audit and cybersecurity functions.
3. **Data Infrastructure Supports AI Use:** Reliable, accessible, and secure data sources exist to train, validate, and execute AI models relevant to cybersecurity auditing.
4. **Cross-Functional Collaboration Is Ongoing:** The audit function is actively partnering with IT, security, and operational teams to support shared goals and data sharing.
5. **Commitment to Continuous Improvement:** The organization values agility, iterative learning, and responsiveness to evolving cyber threats and audit challenges.
6. **AI Technology Evolution:** The cybersecurity audit team will begin using basic AI applications, such as chatbots, and then continue to evolve into other AI applications that provide more functionality and information.

5.15 AI USE CASES FOR CYBERSECURITY AUDITORS – AUDIT PLANNING

AI is reshaping cybersecurity audit planning by enabling more proactive, data-driven, and risk-focused approaches. For **annual cybersecurity audit planning,** AI can analyze threat intelligence feeds, vulnerability data, incident reports, and system logs to identify high-risk systems and prioritize audit areas based on evolving cyber threats and organizational exposure. For **individual cybersecurity audits,** AI supports more targeted planning by examining prior audit findings, control effectiveness, configuration changes, and behavioral anomalies to define scope, timing, and testing strategies. Integrating AI into both levels of cybersecurity audit planning enhances the function's ability to anticipate risks, respond to emerging threats, and align resources with the most critical security priorities (TeamMate, 2024).

5.15.1 🌳AI application decision tree

Below is a **decision tree** to help determine when to use **Chatbot, Predictive Analytics, Recommender Systems,** or **RPA** based on the nature of the task or decision:

Step 1: What is the nature of the task?

1. **Is the task conversational, knowledge-based, or requires generating or summarizing text?**
   - → **Yes** → Use **Chatbot.**
   - → **No** → Proceed to Step 2.
2. **Does the task involve making future predictions or identifying trends based on historical data?**
   - → **Yes** → Use **Predictive Analytics.**
   - → **No** → Proceed to Step 3.
3. **Does the task involve suggesting options (e.g., products, content, next steps) based on user behavior or preferences?**
   - → **Yes** → Use **Recommender System.**
   - → **No** → Proceed to Step 4.
4. **Does the task involve repetitive, rule-based actions or workflows across systems (e.g., form entry, report generation)?**
   - → **Yes** → Use **RPA.**
   - → **No** → Task may require a **custom solution** or hybrid AI approach.

Table 5.14 describes the audit planning activities with a corresponding recommended AI application. This table is intended to provide examples as you start to build out your AI application portfolio. As the cybersecurity audit AI program matures and AI continues to evolve, other AI applications may be deemed appropriate in the future.

Table 5.14 Example use cases by AI application

Task type	Recommended AI application
Writing audit summaries	Chatbot
Forecasting incident likelihood	Predictive analytics
Suggesting training modules	Recommender system
Automating log extraction	RPA
Generating FAQ responses	Chatbot
Predicting phishing attack risk	Predictive analytics
Recommending security tools	Recommender system
Pulling reports from systems	RPA

Note: Keep in mind that **prompts are only one component** of some AI applications and do not represent the full functionality of the system. While prompts are essential for tools like ChatGPT, other AI approaches – such as **Predictive Analytics, Recommender Systems**, and **RPA** – rely on structured data models, user behavior analysis, and rule-based workflows. For a deeper understanding of how these technologies operate and when to use them effectively, refer to their respective sections in this chapter.

5.15.2 Annual audit plan level

The **annual cybersecurity audit planning process** involves a series of strategic and risk-based activities designed to ensure that cybersecurity audit resources are focused on the most critical areas. Annual audit planning typically involves several key steps: identifying potential audit areas, assessing risks, prioritizing audits, allocating resources, and finalizing the annual audit plan. These steps ensure that audit efforts are focused on the most critical areas, maximizing efficiency and effectiveness. Below is a more detailed annual cybersecurity audit planning activity breakdown:

1. **Understand the Organizational Context**
   - Review the organization's mission, objectives, and risk appetite.
   - Understand the cybersecurity governance structure and regulatory environment.
   - Identify recent changes in business operations, technologies, or locations. Upload the related organization documents then execute the prompts below.

     Prompt 1: "*Summarize the key business objectives and digital transformation initiatives that could impact cybersecurity audit priorities.*"

     Prompt 2: "*What changes in the IT environment or organizational structure could affect the audit risk landscape this year?*"
2. **Conduct a Cybersecurity Risk Assessment**
   - Identify and evaluate cyber threats, vulnerabilities, and potential impacts.
   - Analyze recent incidents, threat intelligence, and industry trends.

- Use inputs from ERM, IT risk, and security teams, uploading documents as needed, then execute the prompts below.
  Prompt 1: "*Identify and rank the top cybersecurity threats based on recent industry and internal incident trends.*"
  Prompt 2: "*What vulnerabilities, assets, and threat actors pose the greatest potential impact to our organization?*"

3. **Engage Stakeholders across the Lines of Defense**
   - Consult with IT security, compliance, and risk management teams.
   - Discuss areas of concern with senior leadership, the Chief Information Security Officer (CISO), and business units.
   - Coordinate with the 1LoD and 2LoD to avoid duplication.
     Prompt 1: "*Which cybersecurity controls and risks are top concerns from your perspective this year?*"
     Prompt 2: "*What known or anticipated projects may introduce new cybersecurity risks we should consider in the audit plan?*"
4. **Review Prior Audit and Assessment Results**
   - Analyze findings and recommendations from previous audits and assessments.
   - Identify recurring issues, unremediated findings, or emerging control gaps. Upload audit finding data then execute the prompts below.
     Prompt 1: "*List repeat audit findings from the past three years and assess if additional coverage is required.*"
     Prompt 2: "*Analyze trends in previous audit results to identify recurring control weaknesses or systemic issues.*"
5. **Define and Prioritize Audit Universe**
   - Maintain or update the cybersecurity audit universe (systems, processes, assets).
   - Prioritize based on risk, materiality, regulatory requirements, and change level.
   - Use risk-based scoring or heat maps to rank audit targets. Upload the relevant inventory documents then execute prompts below.
     Prompt 1: "*Generate a prioritized list of systems, processes, and technologies based on cybersecurity risk exposure.*"
     Prompt 2: "*Which business areas have experienced significant changes in cybersecurity risk or control environment since last year?*"
6. **Identify and Allocate Resources**
   - Assess internal audit team capacity, expertise, and technology capabilities.
   - Consider external support needs (e.g., AI, penetration testing, forensic services).
   - Incorporate training or tools needed for new/emerging cybersecurity risks. Upload relevant information, including audit plan, then execute prompts below.
     Prompt 1: "*What skill sets or external expertise are required to effectively execute this year's cybersecurity audits?*"

Prompt 2: "*Evaluate internal audit capacity versus required effort to meet cybersecurity audit plan objectives.*"

7. **Develop the Audit Plan**
   - Establish the scope, objectives, and frequency of each audit engagement.
   - Schedule audits over the year with consideration for timing and dependencies.
   - Include flexibility to adapt to emerging threats or incidents. Upload strategy plan, audit plan, and other relevant documents then executer prompts below.

     Prompt 1: "*Draft a schedule of cybersecurity audit engagements aligned with business cycles and risk priorities.*"

     Prompt 2: "*Determine which audits require scoping adjustments based on system changes, cloud migration, or AI integration.*"

8. **Integrate AI and Data Analytics (If Applicable)**
   - Identify where AI or automation can support risk prioritization and scoping.
   - Plan for use of analytics or AI-driven tools in testing or continuous monitoring. The documents uploaded in Step 7 above may be sufficient for the prompts below, thus not requiring any new document uploads.

     Prompt 1: "*How can AI tools assist in identifying high-risk audit areas using real-time network or security data?*"

     Prompt 2: "*Which parts of the audit process (e.g., scoping, testing, sampling) can benefit from AI or automation?*"

9. **Obtain Approval from Audit Leadership and Governance Bodies**
   - Present the proposed audit plan to the Chief Audit Executive (CAE), Audit Committee, or Board.
   - Incorporate feedback and secure formal approval.

     Prompt 1: "*Prepare a summary of cybersecurity risks, audit coverage, and resource needs for Audit Committee approval.*"

     Prompt 2: "*What objections or feedback did the Audit Committee provide on the previous plan, and how were they addressed?*"

10. **Communicate and Align**
    - Share the finalized audit plan with relevant stakeholders across IT, security, and leadership.
    - Align audit activities with organizational cybersecurity goals and compliance mandates.

      Prompt 1: "*Create a communication plan to share the cybersecurity audit roadmap with key IT and business stakeholders.*"

      Prompt 2: "*How can the cybersecurity audit plan be aligned with enterprise risk and compliance initiatives?*"

Pro Tips

- The **annual audit planning process** serves as a strategic placeholder, reinforcing that an organization's cybersecurity environment should be

evaluated *at a minimum* once per year. However, the dynamic nature of cyber threats and technologies demands more frequent reassessment. **AI tools should be applied continuously throughout the year** to analyze new data, threat intelligence, and operational changes – helping auditors proactively determine if the cybersecurity audit plan needs to be adjusted to address emerging risks or shifting priorities.
- Ask the Chatbot or other system to provide source information for those prompts requiring additional clarity or validation.

5.15.3 Individual engagement planning example

Individual engagements represent cybersecurity audits that are determined in the annual planning as noted in the previous section. The prompting examples in this section focus on each cybersecurity audit execution activity.

1. **Audit Planning and Scoping**
   Prompt 1: "*What risk-based factors should I consider when scoping a cybersecurity audit for a hybrid cloud environment?*"
   Prompt 2: "*Recommend control areas to prioritize for an internal audit aligned with NIST CSF and recent ransomware threats.*"
   Prompt 3: "*What questions should be included in a cybersecurity audit pre-engagement questionnaire?*"
2. **Security Control Evaluation**
   Prompt 1: "*Which NIST SP 800-53 (Rev. 5) controls are most relevant when auditing identity and access management practices?*"
   Prompt 2: "*List audit tests for evaluating the effectiveness of multi-factor authentication controls.*"
   Prompt 3: "*What evidence should be collected to validate the implementation of Center for Internet Security (CIS) Control 6: Access Control Management?*"
3. **Compliance and Framework Alignment**
   Prompt 1: "*Map ISO/IEC 27001 clauses to common cybersecurity audit control objectives.*"
   Prompt 2: "*What audit procedures support verifying Cybersecurity Maturity Model Certification (CMMC) Level 2 incident response requirements?*"
   Prompt 3: "*How can I assess alignment between organizational policies and NIST 800-171 control families?*"
4. **AI and Automation in Cybersecurity Auditing**
   Prompt 1: "*What AI tools can assist in identifying anomalies in firewall logs during cybersecurity audits?*"
   Prompt 2: "*Recommend ML techniques for enhancing audit procedures related to insider threat detection.*"
   Prompt 3: "*Suggest audit checkpoints for evaluating the integrity and bias of an AI system used for threat detection.*"

5. **Audit Documentation and Reporting**
   Prompt 1: "*Draft a summary of audit findings for gaps in endpoint security controls, including risk impact and recommendations.*"
   Prompt 2: "*Provide language to include in a cybersecurity audit report to address control deficiencies related to patch management.*"
   Prompt 3: "*What format should be used to present cybersecurity audit results to an executive audience?*"
6. **Governance, Policy, and Risk Oversight**
   Prompt 1: "*Identify red flags in cybersecurity governance that should be documented during a risk-focused audit.*"
   Prompt 2: "*Recommend audit procedures to test enforcement of cybersecurity policies in a remote work environment.*"
   Prompt 3: "*What evidence supports maturity-level assessments of cybersecurity risk management practices?*"

> **Pro Tip:** Ask the Chatbot or other system to provide source information for those prompts requiring additional clarity or validation.

Table 5.15 is a structured list of cybersecurity auditing prompts matched with the most appropriate AI application – selected from Chatbot, Predictive Analytics, Recommender Systems, and RPA. This table can be used to progress the cybersecurity audit AI program as that program matures. As an example, cybersecurity audit professionals may decide to use Chatbot as the first AI application, then progress to other AI applications in the future.

Table 5.15 Cybersecurity auditing prompts with AI application mapping

Prompt	Best AI application	Why?
What risk-based factors should I consider when scoping a cybersecurity audit for a hybrid cloud environment?	Chatbot	Requires contextual understanding, guidance, and domain expertise for audit scoping
Recommend control areas to prioritize for an internal audit aligned with NIST CSF and recent ransomware threats	Recommender system	Suggests relevant controls based on risk profiles and frameworks
What questions should be included in a cybersecurity audit pre-engagement questionnaire?	Chatbot	Involves drafting qualitative, situation-specific questions
Which NIST SP 800-53 (Rev. 5) controls are most relevant when auditing identity and access management practices?	Recommender system	Matches control sets to specific audit domains
List audit tests for evaluating the effectiveness of multi-factor authentication controls	Chatbot	Explains specific audit procedures in natural language

(Continued)

Table 5.15 Cybersecurity auditing prompts with ai application mapping (*Continued*)

Prompt	Best AI application	Why?
What evidence should be collected to validate the implementation of CIS Control 6: Access Control Management?	Chatbot	Describes qualitative and contextual artifacts for auditors
Map ISO/IEC 27001 clauses to common cybersecurity audit control objectives	Recommender system	Aligns standard clauses with audit objectives – structured mapping task
What audit procedures support verifying CMMC Level 2 incident response requirements?	Chatbot	Involves detailed procedural recommendations
How can I assess alignment between organizational policies and NIST 800-171 control families?	Chatbot	Supports gap analysis with regulatory context
What AI tools can assist in identifying anomalies in firewall logs during cybersecurity audits?	Recommender system	Recommends AI-driven tools based on use case
Recommend ML techniques for enhancing audit procedures related to insider threat detection	Predictive analytics	Uses ML-based predictive models for behavior analysis
Suggest audit checkpoints for evaluating the integrity and bias of an AI system used for threat detection	Chatbot	Explains high-level evaluation criteria using AI audit concepts
Draft a summary of audit findings for gaps in endpoint security controls, including risk impact and recommendations	Chatbot	Generates professional summaries and reports
Provide language to include in a cybersecurity audit report to address control deficiencies related to patch management	Chatbot	Tailors specific report narratives
What format should be used to present cybersecurity audit results to an executive audience?	Chatbot	Provides structured communication and formatting advice
Identify red flags in cybersecurity governance that should be documented during a risk-focused audit	Chatbot	Analyzes qualitative governance signals
Recommend audit procedures to test enforcement of cybersecurity policies in a remote work environment	Chatbot	Describes procedural design and context-aware steps
What evidence supports maturity-level assessments of cybersecurity risk management practices?	Chatbot	Explains criteria and data collection methods for maturity assessments

Table 5.16 continues the cybersecurity audit prompt examples in Table 5.15. The objective is to focus on RPA because RPA is a popular AI application that automates routine cybersecurity audit functions as noted in Table 5.16. While only three examples were provided, those support an immediate benefit when implementing RPA.

Table 5.16 Additional prompts mapped to RPA (not explicitly listed in Table 5.15)

Prompt	Best AI application	Why?
Extract and compile audit evidence from access control logs across multiple systems	RPA	Automates data extraction and consolidation
Schedule recurring policy compliance checks against system configurations	RPA	Handles repetitive, rules-based audit tasks
Populate audit report templates with standardized findings based on control test results	RPA	Fills predefined formats automatically

Critical Thinking Moment: Reflect on your current environment and consider how the concepts above align with your organizational needs and capabilities. Would it be more effective to start with chatbot implementations and gradually expand to other AI applications and tools over time?

5.16 AI USE CASES FOR CYBERSECURITY AUDITORS – AUDIT ENGAGEMENTS

Cybersecurity audit engagements extend beyond individual audits to include broader, strategic activities that assess an organization's overall security posture, governance framework, and risk management practices. These engagements may encompass enterprise-wide evaluations of cybersecurity policies, incident response readiness, third-party risk management, regulatory compliance, and the alignment of cybersecurity controls with industry standards. By focusing on systemic and program-level assessments, cybersecurity audit engagements provide leadership with a holistic view of the organization's ability to prevent, detect, and respond to cyber threats. These engagements are essential for shaping annual audit plans, informing risk-based decisions, and fostering a culture of continuous improvement across the cybersecurity landscape.

Important Notes

- Keep in mind that **prompts are only one component** of some AI applications and do not represent the full functionality of the system. While prompts are essential for tools like Chatbot, other AI approaches – such as **Predictive Analytics, Recommender Systems**, and **RPA** – rely on structured data models, user behavior analysis, and rule-based workflows. For a deeper understanding of how these technologies operate and when to use them effectively, refer to their respective sections in this chapter.
- Chatbots do not "run" prompts against data or documents unless explicitly provided in the prompt or uploaded in the interface.

5.16.1 Example 1: Cybersecurity auditor reviewing a firm's cybersecurity risk appetite statement

When a cybersecurity auditor reviews a firm's cybersecurity risk appetite statement, the objective is to evaluate whether the organization's tolerance for cyber risk is clearly defined, appropriately aligned with its business objectives, and effectively integrated into its governance and control environment. The auditor examines how the statement articulates acceptable risk levels across various domains – such as data protection, system availability, third-party access, and incident response – and assesses whether these thresholds are supported by documented policies, control activities, and decision-making processes.

Key Areas of Focus Include

- **Clarity and Scope:** Is the risk appetite statement specific to cybersecurity, and does it address relevant risk domains (e.g., insider threats, ransomware, cloud exposure)?
- **Alignment with Strategy:** Does the statement reflect the organization's mission, regulatory obligations, and strategic priorities?
- **Integration with Governance:** Is the risk appetite embedded into cybersecurity planning, audit scoping, and risk acceptance procedures?
- **Measurable Indicators:** Are there key risk indicators (KRIs) or thresholds defined to monitor when risk levels approach or exceed the stated appetite?
- **Communication and Oversight:** Has the risk appetite been communicated across business units and approved by senior leadership or the board?

The auditor may also evaluate whether actual risk-taking behaviors and control performance align with the stated appetite, identifying gaps where risk tolerance may be exceeded without proper escalation or mitigation. This review supports assurance that the organization is not only defining its cyber risk boundaries but also managing within them.

Here are example **Chatbot prompts** designed to assist a **cybersecurity auditor** in reviewing and providing feedback on a firm's **cybersecurity risk appetite statement.** These prompts help generate insights, identify gaps, and align with audit objectives.

Chatbot prompts for reviewing a cybersecurity risk appetite statement

1. Assessing Clarity and Completeness

   Note: Upload the cybersecurity risk appetite statement document along with the first prompt. That document will be automatically retained for subsequent prompts.

   Prompt 1: "*Review this cybersecurity risk appetite statement for clarity and completeness. What critical areas might be missing or vague?*"

   Prompt 2: "*What questions should an auditor ask to determine whether the cybersecurity risk appetite covers all relevant risk domains (e.g., data loss, third-party access, insider threats)?*"

2. **Evaluating Strategic Alignment**
   Prompt 1: "*Does the following risk appetite statement align with an organization focused on financial services and regulatory compliance? Suggest improvements.*"
   Prompt 2: "*How should a cybersecurity risk appetite statement reflect alignment with business strategy and mission objectives?*"
3. **Checking Integration with Governance**
   Prompt 1: "*How can I assess whether a cybersecurity risk appetite statement is embedded into an organization's governance and decision-making processes?*"
   Prompt 2: "*What governance documents or policies should I cross-reference when auditing a cybersecurity risk appetite statement?*"
4. **Identifying Measurable Criteria**
   Prompt 1: "*Suggest key risk indicators (KRIs) that should be used to measure whether an organization is operating within its stated cybersecurity risk appetite.*"
   Prompt 2: "*Does this risk appetite statement include quantifiable thresholds? If not, suggest metrics that could make it more actionable.*"
5. **Reviewing Communication and Oversight**
   Prompt 1: "*How can I evaluate whether the risk appetite statement has been effectively communicated across business units and approved by leadership?*"
   Prompt 2: "*Generate interview questions for leadership and business unit heads to validate understanding and adoption of the cybersecurity risk appetite.*"
6. **Providing Constructive Feedback**
   Prompt 1: "*Rewrite this cybersecurity risk appetite statement to improve clarity, specificity, and alignment with audit best practices.*"
   Prompt 2: "*Provide a professional feedback summary on this cybersecurity risk appetite statement from an auditor's perspective.*"

🎯 **Pro Tip:** Ask the Chatbot or other system to provide source information for those prompts then check the sources to make sure those exist. Some of the source information is obtained from unreliable or unvalidated sources as the Chatbot searches the Internet. This is an example of a required "human element" when using AI. Apply this tip throughout the remainder of this chapter.

5.16.2 Example 2: Evaluation of management's customer-centric recommender system

Evaluating a **customer-centric recommender system** before it goes into production is critical to ensure it delivers relevant, ethical, and business-aligned outcomes. The evaluation process should cover technical performance, user experience, compliance, and operational readiness.

Steps to evaluate a customer-centric recommender system before production implementation

1. **Define Business Objectives and User Goals**
   - Confirm alignment with business key performance indicators (KPIs) (e.g., engagement, conversion, retention).
   - Clarify customer-centric goals (e.g., personalization, diversity, relevance).
   - Identify target audience segments and use cases (e.g., new users vs. repeat users).

     Note: Upload the appropriate document along with the first prompt. That document will automatically be retained for subsequent prompts.

     Prompt 1: "*Here's our recommender system design document. Does it include appropriate metrics for model performance?*"

     Prompt 2: "*What key business objectives should a recommender system support in an e-commerce environment?*"

     Prompt 3: "*How can I map user goals to measurable outcomes for a customer-centric recommender system?*"

2. **Validate Data Quality and Sources**
   - Check data completeness, accuracy, timeliness, and ethical sourcing.
   - Ensure proper handling of personally identifiable information (PII).
   - Assess for bias, imbalance, or data drift in training sets.

     Prompt 1: "*What criteria should I use to assess data quality and suitability for training a recommender system?*"

     Prompt 2: "*How can I identify bias or drift in the training data of a recommender model?*"

3. **Evaluate Model Performance**
   - Use both offline and online metrics:

     Offline: precision, recall, F1-score, hit rate, normalized discounted cumulative gain (NDCG), diversity, coverage.

     Online (A/B testing): click-through rate (CTR), conversion rate, dwell time.
   - Compare with baseline or traditional models.

     Prompt 1: "*Explain the difference between precision, recall, and NDCG when evaluating recommender systems.*"

     Prompt 2: "*What offline metrics can I use to assess the relevance and accuracy of this recommender model before launch?*"

4. **Assess Explainability and Transparency**
   - Ensure users or stakeholders can understand *why* a recommendation is made.
   - Integrate XAI techniques if needed.
   - Determine whether recommendations align with customer expectations.

     Prompt 1: "*How can I make recommendations more explainable to end users while maintaining model performance?*"

Prompt 2: "*What are best practices for integrating explainability into customer-facing recommender systems?*"

5. **Test for Fairness and Ethical Compliance**
    - Evaluate whether recommendations are equitable across user demographics.
    - Identify and mitigate algorithmic bias.
    - Ensure compliance with privacy laws (e.g., GDPR, CCPA).

    Prompt 1: "*What fairness metrics are relevant when evaluating a recommender system for bias across user groups?*"

    Prompt 2: "*How can I ensure the recommender system complies with GDPR or CCPA requirements?*"

6. **Conduct Usability and UX Testing**
    - Perform user testing for intuitiveness and satisfaction with recommendations.
    - Gather qualitative feedback via user interviews or surveys.
    - Ensure the system integrates well with user interface/user experience (UI/UX) design.

    Prompt 1: "*Create a list of usability testing questions to evaluate the user experience of a recommender system.*"

    Prompt 2: "*How can I interpret user feedback to improve the relevance and presentation of recommendations?*"

7. **Perform Robustness and Security Testing**
    - Test the system's resistance to adversarial inputs or manipulation (e.g., fake reviews).
    - Validate authentication, access controls, and API security.
    - Ensure resilience under load and failure scenarios.

    Prompt 1: "*What types of adversarial attacks can impact recommender systems, and how can I test for them?*"

    Prompt 2: "*How can I validate the security of APIs used by a production-level recommender engine?*"

8. **Review Governance and Documentation**
    - Confirm existence of clear documentation for model design, data lineage, and retraining processes.
    - Review version control, approval workflows, and rollback procedures.
    - Identify responsible parties for model oversight and maintenance.

    Prompt 1: "*What documentation should be maintained for a recommender system before it goes into production?*"

    Prompt 2: "*Create a governance checklist for overseeing the lifecycle of a customer-centric recommendation engine.*"

9. **Conduct A/B Testing or Soft Launch**
    - Deploy to a small user cohort to monitor real-world performance.
    - Track behavioral metrics and user satisfaction.
    - Refine model or UX before full-scale deployment.

Prompt 1: "*Design an A/B test to compare two versions of a recommender system based on engagement metrics.*"
Prompt 2: "*What are the key metrics to track during a soft launch of a new recommendation algorithm?*"

10. **Prepare for Post-Deployment Monitoring**
    - Set up monitoring for performance, drift, and feedback loops.
    - Define thresholds for retraining, alerts, or rollback.
    - Plan for continuous improvement based on user behavior and business needs.

    Prompt 1: "*What indicators should I monitor to detect model drift or decline in recommender performance post-launch?*"
    Prompt 2: "*How can I create a feedback loop to continuously improve a deployed recommender system?*"

5.16.3 Example 3: Evaluation of Amazon Web Services (AWS) AI services and tools

Conducting due diligence on **AWS AI Services and Tools** is essential for evaluating technical fit, risk exposure, compliance requirements, and operational readiness before adoption. The following step-by-step approach provides a comprehensive framework for assessing AWS AI offerings from a cybersecurity, audit, and governance perspective.

> 🛠 **Important Note:** This guidance serves as an initial foundation for conducting due diligence on AWS AI Services and Tools. **Cybersecurity professionals should supplement this assessment** with a formal **third-party risk assessment** and align their evaluation with a recognized **due diligence or vendor risk management framework (RSI Security, 2020; Shared Assessments, 2025)**. A comprehensive review – including legal, compliance, technical, and security perspectives – should be completed **prior to contract negotiation or signing** to ensure organizational risk tolerance and regulatory obligations are fully addressed.

Steps to conduct due diligence on AWS AI services and tools

1. **Define Business and Technical Objectives**
    - Identify the **purpose and scope** of using AWS AI (e.g., customer service, fraud detection, predictive analytics).
    - Map AI use cases to **organizational goals**, technical needs, and regulatory obligations.
    - Determine whether AWS AI will be used for internal processes, customer-facing applications, or audit functions.

    ✎ **Note:** Upload the appropriate document along with the first prompt. That document will be automatically retained for subsequent prompts.

    Prompt 1: "*What questions should I ask to align AWS AI services with our business and cybersecurity audit goals?*"

Prompt 2: "*Help me map common AWS AI tools to enterprise use cases in finance, cybersecurity, or customer service.*"

2. **Inventory Relevant AWS AI Services**
   - Review and categorize AWS AI tools by function:
     - **Pre-trained services:** Amazon Rekognition, Comprehend, Polly, Lex, Transcribe.
     - **ML platforms:** Amazon SageMaker, CodeWhisperer.
     - **AI infrastructure:** Inferentia, Trainium, Bedrock.
   - Match each tool to its intended use case and assess suitability.

   Prompt 1: "*List and categorize the main AWS AI services and tools, including their use cases.*"

   Prompt 2: "*Which AWS AI services are best suited for building conversational AI, image recognition, and document processing?*"

3. **Assess Security and Privacy Capabilities**
   - Evaluate **data protection mechanisms**, including encryption in transit and at rest.
   - Review **identity and access controls**, including IAM integration and fine-grained permissions.
   - Examine **data residency** options and compliance with privacy regulations (e.g., GDPR, HIPAA, CCPA).
   - Assess **audit logging**, monitoring, and incident response integration.

   Prompt 1: "*What security and privacy features should I evaluate when reviewing AWS AI services like SageMaker or Rekognition?*"

   Prompt 2: "*Explain how AWS handles encryption, access control, and logging for AI services.*"

4. **Review Compliance and Certifications**
   - Verify AWS compliance with industry standards:
     - ISO/IEC 27001, 27017, 27018
     - System and Organization Controls (SOC) 1, SOC 2, SOC 3
     - FedRAMP, HIPAA, PCI DSS, GDPR
   - Confirm whether AWS AI services are included in the **AWS Artifact** documentation and certifications.

   Prompt 1: "*Which compliance certifications should I look for when using AWS AI services in a regulated industry?*"

   Prompt 2: "*Summarize AWS's compliance posture for AI tools including FedRAMP, ISO 27001, and GDPR alignment.*"

5. **Evaluate Governance and Responsible AI Practices**
   - Review AWS's published **AI ethics principles** and Responsible AI documentation.
   - Assess support for **explainability, fairness, and bias mitigation** in AI models.
   - Determine how your organization can enforce internal AI governance while using AWS-managed models.

Prompt 1: "*What governance questions should I ask when evaluating AWS's Responsible AI practices?*"
Prompt 2: "*How does AWS support fairness, explainability, and bias mitigation in its AI services?*"

6. **Analyze Cost Structure and Resource Management**
    - Review **pricing models** (on-demand, reserved instances, usage-based) for each AI service.
    - Estimate total cost of ownership (TCO), including training, inference, storage, and data egress.
    - Understand service limits, quotas, and scaling capabilities.

    Prompt 1: "*Provide a breakdown of pricing models for AWS AI services like SageMaker, Polly, and Comprehend.*"
    Prompt 2: "*How can I estimate the TCO for deploying an AWS-based AI solution?*"

7. **Assess Integration and Interoperability**
    - Determine how AWS AI services integrate with existing systems and APIs.
    - Evaluate compatibility with data pipelines, audit tools, and orchestration platforms (e.g., Airflow, Kubernetes).
    - Confirm whether prebuilt connectors or software development kit (SDKs) exist for your tech stack.

    Prompt 1: "*How do AWS AI services integrate with external systems, APIs, and cloud-native platforms?*"
    Prompt 2: "Which AWS AI tools offer SDKs or connectors for Python, REST APIs, or Kubernetes?"

8. **Conduct Risk and Legal Review**
    - Review **SLAs**, shared responsibility model, and support tiers.
    - Examine **terms of use** for AI services, especially related to data usage, model ownership, and liability.
    - Consider potential risks, such as vendor lock-in, service availability, and long-term viability.

    Prompt 1: "*What should I look for in AWS AI SLAs and shared responsibility models?*"
    Prompt 2: "*List legal risks and contractual considerations when deploying third-party AI services through AWS.*"

9. **Perform Pilot Testing and Benchmarking**
    - Run **PoC** projects to test functionality, accuracy, and latency.
    - Compare against internal benchmarks or alternative vendors.
    - Validate results with both technical teams and business stakeholders.

    Prompt 1: "*Design a PoC test plan to evaluate AWS AI services for model accuracy and performance.*"
    Prompt 2: "*What metrics should I track when benchmarking AWS AI tools against internal or alternative solutions?*"

10. **Document Findings and Make a Recommendation**
    - Summarize findings in a due diligence report:
        - Strengths, limitations, and gaps
        - Risk mitigation strategies
        - Recommendation (adopt, modify, reject)
    - Present to leadership, legal, IT, and audit stakeholders for final decision.

      Prompt 1: "*Create a due diligence summary report template for evaluating AWS AI services.*"

      Prompt 2: "*What key points should I include when presenting AWS AI findings to executives or risk committees?*"

5.17 AI USE CASES FOR CYBERSECURITY AUDITORS – CONTINUOUS AUDITING

Continuous cybersecurity auditing is a proactive, real-time approach to assessing and monitoring an organization's security controls, risk exposures, and compliance posture. Unlike traditional audits conducted periodically, continuous auditing leverages automated tools, data analytics, and AI technologies to provide ongoing assurance and visibility into the effectiveness of cybersecurity measures. This dynamic model enables auditors to detect control failures, anomalies, and emerging threats more quickly, allowing for timely corrective actions and improved risk management. By integrating continuous auditing into the cybersecurity framework, organizations can enhance audit agility, strengthen resilience, and maintain alignment with evolving regulatory and threat landscapes.

5.17.1 AI application job schedulers

Job schedulers are critical tools in managing and automating workflows for AI applications, particularly when tasks such as data ingestion, model training, validation, deployment, and monitoring must run on specific timelines or in response to events. Below are several job scheduling tools that are commonly used in AI pipelines, along with their key features and use cases:

5.17.1.1 🕒 Common job schedulers for AI applications

1. **Apache Airflow** (https://airflow.apache.org/docs/apache-airflow/stable/index.html)
    - **Type:** Workflow orchestration platform
    - **Use Cases:** Managing complex AI/ML pipelines, including Extract, Transform, and Load (ETL), model training, and deployment
    - **Features**
        - Directed Acyclic Graph (DAG)-based workflow design
        - Supports retries, alerts, and task dependencies
        - Integrates with cloud platforms and Python-based tools

2. **Kubernetes CronJobs** (https://kubernetes.io/docs/reference/kubernetes-api/workload-resources/cron-job-v1/)
   - **Type:** Kubernetes-native job scheduler
   - **Use Cases:** Scheduling containerized AI tasks in Kubernetes environments
   - **Features**
     - Ideal for cloud-native and microservices-based AI pipelines
     - Supports recurring tasks (e.g., nightly retraining)
     - Scales with Kubernetes cluster infrastructure

3. **Apache Oozie** (https://oozie.apache.org/docs/5.2.0/)
   - **Type:** Workflow scheduler for Hadoop ecosystems
   - **Use Cases:** Scheduling AI jobs within big data environments
   - **Features**
     - Supports MapReduce, Hive, and Spark job scheduling
     - Time- and data-triggered workflows
     - Extensible Markup Language (XML)-based job definitions

4. **Prefect** (https://docs.prefect.io/v3/get-started)
   - **Type:** Modern workflow orchestration framework
   - **Use Cases:** Lightweight scheduling for AI/ML pipelines and data validation tasks
   - **Features**
     - Python-native and cloud-ready
     - Easier to deploy than Airflow for small-to-mid-size teams
     - Real-time logging and task retries

5. **Azure Data Factory/Synapse Pipelines** (https://azure.microsoft.com/en-us/products/data-factory#:~:text=Simplify%20hybrid%20data%20integration%20at%20an%20enterprise%20scale,Analytics%20to%20unlock%20business%20insights and https://learn.microsoft.com/en-us/azure/data-factory/concepts-pipelines-activities?tabs=data-factory)
   - **Type:** Cloud-native ETL and orchestration service
   - **Use Cases:** Scheduling AI data processing and model life cycle jobs on Microsoft Azure
   - **Features**
     - Visual design tools
     - Trigger-based and schedule-based execution
     - Integration with Azure ML and Databricks

6. **AWS Step Functions/EventBridge** (https://docs.aws.amazon.com/step-functions/latest/dg/welcome.html)
   - **Type:** Serverless workflow orchestration and event bus
   - **Use Cases:** Automating and scheduling AI model pipelines in AWS
   - **Features**
     - State machine logic for complex workflows
     - Native integration with SageMaker, Lambda, and AI services
     - Event-based automation

7. **cron (Linux/Unix)** (https://www.ibm.com/docs/en/db2/11.5.x?topic=task-unix-cron-format)
   - **Type:** System-level scheduler
   - **Use Cases:** Simple recurring tasks such as triggering AI scripts or monitoring tools
   - **Features**
     - Lightweight and easy to configure
     - No external dependencies
     - Suitable for standalone or early-stage development environments

5.17.1.2 🕒 *Why job scheduling matters for AI*

- Ensures **model retraining and deployment** occur at optimal intervals.
- Automates **data preprocessing and ingestion.**
- Enables **real-time monitoring and alerting** for AI performance drift.
- Supports **governance and audit trails** by tracking AI-related jobs and dependencies.

> 🔚 **Conclusion:** The primary objective of using AI applications in cybersecurity auditing is to enhance **efficiency, integrity, and accuracy** throughout the audit process. By automating the execution of AI-driven tasks, organizations can achieve not only time savings but also **real-time insights** into emerging cybersecurity risks. Implementing **job schedulers** for applicable cybersecurity audit AI tasks ensures consistent execution, timely data processing, and improved responsiveness. This approach strengthens the audit function's ability to detect control gaps and adapt to evolving threat landscapes with greater agility.

5.17.2 Continuous auditing

Continuous auditing in cybersecurity involves the automated, real-time or near-real-time collection and analysis of data to assess compliance, detect threats, and ensure effectiveness of security controls. Below are examples of **cybersecurity continuous auditing activities** organized by key cybersecurity control domains.

> ✏ **Note:** Keep in mind that **prompts are only one component** of some AI applications and do not represent the full functionality of the system. While prompts are essential for tools like Chatbot, other AI approaches – such as **Predictive Analytics, Recommender Systems**, and RPA – rely on structured data models, user behavior analysis, and rule-based workflows. For a deeper understanding of how these technologies operate and when to use them effectively, refer to their respective sections in this chapter.

5.17.2.1 *Example 1: Analyzing threat intelligence data*

1. **Indicators of Compromise (IOCs):** Includes IP addresses, domain names, file hashes, and malware signatures that signal potential or confirmed malicious activity.

2. **Tactics, Techniques, and Procedures (TTPs):** Describes how threat actors operate, such as phishing for initial access or lateral movement using remote desktop protocols, often mapped to the MITRE Adversarial Tactics, Techniques & Common Knowledge (ATT&CK) framework.
3. **Targeted Sectors and Impacted Assets:** Identifies industries or systems being targeted (e.g., healthcare, financial services), along with the type of data or infrastructure at risk.

   Initial Prompt: "*Analyze the following threat intelligence report and summarize key IOCs, threat actor TTPs, and affected industries. Highlight any patterns, emerging threats, and recommended mitigation actions. Suggest how this intelligence could be mapped to the MITRE ATT&CK framework and incorporated into our organization's cybersecurity monitoring and incident response plan.*"

   Optional Follow-Up Prompts

   - "*Which MITRE ATT&CK techniques are most relevant based on this threat intel?*"
   - "*Are there any known threat actor groups associated with these indicators of compromises (IOCs)?*"
   - "*What security controls should be prioritized in response to this intelligence?*"

5.17.2.2 *Example 2: Access control and identity management*

1. **Automated user access reviews** for privileged accounts (e.g., ensuring least privilege is maintained continuously).

   Prompt 1: "*Analyze this user access report and identify any accounts that violate the least privilege principle.*"
2. **Real-time detection of unauthorized access** attempts via SIEM tools.

   Prompt 1: "*Review these SIEM logs and flag repeated unauthorized login attempts to privileged systems.*"
3. **Continuous monitoring of orphaned accounts** (e.g., accounts that belong to terminated employees).

   Prompt 1: "*Compare this list of active user accounts with the current human resource roster and identify any orphaned or inactive accounts.*"

5.17.2.3 *Example 3: Network and endpoint security*

1. **Automated vulnerability scanning** of internal and external network assets using tools like Nessus or Qualys.

   Prompt 1: "*Summarize critical vulnerabilities found in the latest Qualys scan and prioritize them based on common vulnerability scoring system (CVSS) score.*"

2. **Monitoring firewall rule changes** in real time to ensure they align with approved configurations.
   Prompt 1: "*Identify and flag any recent firewall rule changes that deviate from the approved configuration baseline.*"
3. **Detection of anomalous endpoint behavior** using Endpoint Detection and Response (EDR) systems.
   Prompt 1: "*Analyze this EDR log for abnormal processes or traffic patterns on endpoints marked as high-risk.*"

5.17.2.4 Example 4: Data protection and privacy

1. **Continuous monitoring of data exfiltration** via Data Loss Prevention (DLP) tools.
   Prompt 1: "*Review this DLP report and identify potential data exfiltration attempts through unauthorized universal serial bus (USB) use or external uploads.*"
2. **Auditing encryption compliance** for data in transit and at rest.
   Prompt 1: "*Evaluate this list of storage devices and communication channels to identify any lacking required encryption.*"
3. **Monitoring file access and modification logs** on sensitive file shares or databases.
   Prompt 1: "*Analyze file access logs for this folder and identify unauthorized or unusual read/write activity.*"

5.17.2.5 Example 5: Configuration management

1. **Automated checks against security baselines** (e.g., CIS Benchmarks or NIST standards) for servers and devices.
   Prompt 1: "*Compare this Windows server configuration report against the CIS Benchmark and list non-compliant settings.*"
2. **Real-time alerts for unauthorized system configuration changes**, especially on critical assets.
   Prompt 1: "*Flag any unauthorized system configuration changes made in the last 24 hours on critical assets.*"
3. **Patch compliance verification**, ensuring systems receive security updates within defined timelines.
   Prompt 1: "*Review this patch report and identify systems that are missing critical security updates beyond the approved window.*"

5.17.2.6 Example 6: User behavior and awareness

1. **Monitoring for policy violations** (e.g., unencrypted USB drive usage, phishing simulation test failures).
   Prompt 1: "*Analyze logs for instances of unencrypted USB usage or policy violations related to personal email on work devices.*"

2. **Tracking security awareness training completion** and frequency of refresher training.
   Prompt 2: "*Evaluate this training completion report and identify departments or individuals overdue for cybersecurity refresher training.*"

5.17.2.7 Example 7: Audit trail management and log analysis

1. **Automated aggregation and analysis of logs** from multiple systems using SIEM tools.
   Prompt 1: "*Summarize key findings from this log dataset and highlight any patterns that indicate suspicious activity.*"
2. **Alerting for log deletion or tampering,** which may indicate an attempt to cover malicious activity.
   Prompt 1: "*Analyze system event logs for signs of log tampering or deletion around the time of a suspected incident.*"
3. **Review of authentication logs** to detect brute force or credential stuffing attacks.
   Prompt 1: "*Review authentication logs and identify internet protocols (IPs) or accounts associated with repeated failed login attempts.*"

5.17.2.8 Example 8: Third-party and cloud risk management

1. **Monitoring API usage patterns** for anomalies in cloud environments.
   Prompt 1: "*Review API logs for this cloud application and flag abnormal call frequency, unauthorized endpoints, or access spikes.*"
2. **Continuous assessment of third-party security scorecards** and vulnerability disclosures.
   Prompt 1: "*Summarize this security rating report and highlight any third-party vendors with increasing risk profiles.*"
3. **Automated verification of compliance with SLAs** for data protection and incident response.
   Prompt 1: "*Analyze incident response SLA data and identify vendors that failed to meet response time requirements in the past quarter.*"

5.17.2.9 Example 9: Incident response and remediation

1. **Real-time detection of incidents** and triggering of automated workflows for containment and response.
   Prompt 1: "*Summarize detected incidents and categorize them by severity, impacted systems, and response status.*"

2. **Tracking incident response timeframes** to ensure SLA adherence.
   Prompt 2: "*Review incident response logs and determine if any SLAs for containment or resolution were missed.*"
3. **Monitoring corrective action implementation** post-incident or audit findings.
   Prompt 3: "*Evaluate the implementation status of corrective actions from the last audit and flag any overdue items.*"

🎯 Pro Tip: A best practice for identifying **continuous audit opportunities** in cybersecurity is to start by conducting a **risk assessment** to identify high-risk processes, systems, or data assets. Use this assessment to align continuous cybersecurity audit efforts with areas of highest impact or exposure. Focus on controls that are:

- **Automated or digital by nature** (e.g., access logs, system configurations, user behavior)
- **High frequency or high volume**, where real-time assurance adds value
- **Subject to regulatory or policy compliance**, such as NIST 800-53, HIPAA, or ISO 27001

🪜 *Supporting steps*

- **Map key cybersecurity controls to enterprise risk domains** (e.g., identity, endpoints, cloud)
- **Assess audit feasibility**: Consider data availability, automation potential, and maturity of monitoring tools (e.g., SIEM, vulnerability scanners)
- **Engage with security operations and compliance teams** to identify pain points or areas with recurring findings

5.18 CHARTING THE PATH: ALIGNING STANDARDS, CULTURE, AND AGILITY THAT EMPOWER AI IN CYBERSECURITY AUDITS

The previous chapters explored foundational elements essential to transforming cybersecurity audit practices: adhering to audit standards, building strategic partnerships, influencing cultural change, and applying agility concepts. Use that information as you explore how audit standards, building partnerships, influencing behaviors and culture, and agility concepts can be supported by AI capabilities. You will discover how innovation and compliance can work hand in hand to drive progress. Let these insights inspire you to lead the way in shaping the future of auditing and AI. The examples below represent a starting point and can be used to support AI recommendations.

5.18.1 🏛 Achieving audit standards

Audit standards align with AI by providing a structured framework to ensure transparency, accountability, and ethical compliance in AI systems. As AI becomes more integrated into decision-making processes, audit standards help assess the reliability, fairness, and security of these technologies. They guide the evaluation of data quality, algorithmic integrity, and governance practices, ensuring that AI systems operate as intended and do not introduce bias or risk. By aligning with audit standards, organizations can build trust with stakeholders, demonstrate regulatory compliance, and foster responsible AI development and deployment.

1. **Objectivity**
   - **Independently evaluate cybersecurity risks and controls** without bias, personal judgment, or undue influence.
   - **Use AI tools that have been cross validated** with independent sources to avoid overreliance on a single detection model or vendor solution.
   - **Apply independent performance metrics and benchmarking** when evaluating AI-driven cybersecurity tools, rather than relying solely on internal or vendor-provided claims.
2. **Documentation and Evidence**
   - Document the use of AI and rational for the chosen application, such as Chatbot.
   - Include the model validation information.
   - Include a link to chatbot sessions, where applicable.
3. **Confidentiality**
   - **Classify audit-related data appropriately** and enforce controls over sensitive or confidential information in accordance with organizational policies.
   - **Restrict and encrypt access** to sensitive AI training data (e.g., user activity logs), ensuring alignment with confidentiality and privacy standards
   - **Utilize anonymized datasets and enforce data handling protocols** to prevent data leakage and uphold audit integrity when working with AI systems
4. **Competency**
   - **Participate in specialized training** focused on AI model life cycles, AI-specific risk management, and adversarial threat techniques to strengthen audit capabilities.
   - **Apply recognized AI governance frameworks** (e.g., NIST AI RMF, EU AI Act) to assess the maturity, transparency, and compliance of cybersecurity AI systems
   - **Engage in ongoing professional development** by attending AI-focused conferences, technical workshops, and threat intelligence

briefings to stay current with AI-related cybersecurity risks and audit methodologies

5. **Due Professional Care**
   - **Execute AI-related audit procedures with the requisite skill and care** expected of a competent, prudent cybersecurity audit professional.
   - **Conduct fairness and bias testing** on AI-driven behavior analysis tools by validating the training data and output across demographic or behavioral segments.
   - **Prevent AI hallucination** by improving training data quality, using precise prompt engineering, and implementing fact-checking with reliable sources
   - **Demonstrate audit diligence** by expanding audit scope upon identifying risks – such as model drift or poor performance – in AI-enabled cybersecurity systems, even if outside the original audit plan.
6. **Independence**
   - **Maintain auditor independence** by ensuring that audit staff do not participate in the design, development, or implementation of 1LoD or 2LoD AI-enabled cybersecurity tools
   - **Conduct independent validation** when leveraging AI applications developed by 1LoD or 2LoD teams to preserve audit credibility
   - **Ensure that auditors reviewing AI tools developed by the audit function itself** are not involved in their creation or configuration, reinforcing separation of duties and unbiased evaluation

5.18.2 🤝 Building partnerships

Building partnerships aligns with AI by fostering collaboration, innovation, and shared value creation across diverse sectors. AI thrives on data, expertise, and real-world applications – resources that are often distributed across different organizations. Strategic partnerships enable companies, governments, and research institutions to pool these assets, accelerating AI development and deployment. Moreover, partnerships help ensure that AI solutions are ethical, inclusive, and aligned with societal needs by incorporating diverse perspectives and domain knowledge. Whether through joint ventures, research collaborations, or ecosystem alliances, partnerships amplify AI's potential while promoting responsible and scalable innovation.

1. **Communication Channels**
   - **Establish recurring touchpoints** with stakeholders to collaboratively explore AI use cases for cybersecurity risk management. Incorporate independently identified cybersecurity audit insights to prompt proactive discussion and response.
   - **Organize periodic information-sharing forums** with the 1LoD and 2LoD to discuss existing and planned AI-enabled cybersecurity solutions that may impact audit activities.

  - **Host or participate in roundtable discussions** designed to promote engagement, cross-functional learning, and solution-focused dialogue. Include external AI SME, especially when evaluating new or complex AI solutions.
  - **Utilize online collaboration platforms** for continuous sharing of AI-related cybersecurity developments. These platforms can feature curated articles, research summaries, and updates on emerging AI technologies.
  - **Join internal AI training sessions** alongside 1LoD and 2LoD stakeholders to ensure shared understanding and alignment. Participation in these sessions helps auditors gain firsthand insights into AI system implementation and oversight practices.
2. **Risk and Strategic Activities**
  - **Align cybersecurity audit objectives** with the AI risk and control frameworks adopted by the 1LoD and 2LoD. This includes harmonizing risk rating methodologies and adopting common terminology around AI risk and controls.
  - **Leverage existing AI artifacts and engagement opportunities** such as cybersecurity AI risk assessments, technical review meetings, and strategy sessions initiated by 1LoD and 2LoD teams.
  - **Participate in AI strategy and planning meetings** led by operational and risk functions to stay current on AI deployment priorities and associated risk mitigation strategies.
3. **Risk and Governance Committees**
  - Attend AI-specific governance and risk committee meetings to gain visibility into emerging AI trends, regulatory expectations, and organizational mitigation strategies.
  - Engage with broader risk management forums and steering committees, even when AI is not the central topic, as indirect insights into cybersecurity governance, automation, and innovation strategies may still apply.

5.18.3 Influencing behavior and culture

Influencing behaviors and shaping culture align closely with the development and application of AI because both involve understanding and guiding human decision-making. AI systems, particularly those using ML and behavioral analytics, can identify patterns in human behavior and predict responses to various stimuli. This capability allows organizations to design interventions – such as personalized recommendations, nudges, or feedback loops – that subtly influence user actions. At the same time, AI is shaped by the cultural values and ethical norms of its creators and users, meaning that the way AI is designed and deployed reflects and reinforces societal behaviors and beliefs. This dynamic interplay creates a feedback loop where

AI not only adapts to human culture but also helps shape it, making the alignment between influencing behavior and AI both powerful and deeply interconnected.

1. **Innovation**
   - Position cybersecurity audit teams as **forward-looking risk advisors,** encouraging leadership to integrate AI applications throughout the cybersecurity audit life cycle.
   - Promote a **proactive, insight-driven audit culture,** aligning with a strategic, data-informed approach that adds measurable value to cybersecurity oversight.
2. **Automation**
   - Incrementally **deploy AI tools** in audit activities and **compare their results** against prior processes to highlight time savings, cost reductions, and increased accuracy.
   - **Automate execution of AI applications** using job schedulers to ensure consistency and efficiency across audit procedures.
   - Emphasize the role of automation in **reducing human error**, particularly in repetitive or complex cybersecurity testing scenarios.
3. **Cybersecurity Audit Pod**
   - Select auditors who demonstrate **critical thinking, innovation, creativity, willingness to learn, and strong collaboration skills.**
   - Form dedicated pods of auditors trained in **AI model risk and cybersecurity controls and** assign them consistently across AI-related audits.
   - Ensure **continuity of personnel** throughout audit activities. This fosters deeper trust with technical teams, encourages openness during model reviews, and supports a culture of accountability and shared understanding around AI in cybersecurity.
   - Provide training to pod members on **minimizing non-productive behaviors,** such as unnecessary multitasking or reactive email habits, to maintain focus and productivity.
4. **AI SME Pod**
   - Identify and engage individuals already involved in cybersecurity AI initiatives within the **1LoD and 2LoD.**
   - Establish a process that **leverages existing efforts and expertise,** minimizing additional overhead while enhancing audit alignment with operational realities.
   - Maintain consistency by **assigning the same SMEs across audit activities,** ensuring continuity, deeper insights, and improved audit outcomes.
5. **Strategic Influence**
   - Regularly **share AI audit successes and failures** with audit executives, including lessons learned and any updates to audit methodologies or oversight practices.

- Create an **online executive forum** to host strategic metrics, results, and case studies. This platform supports independent review and fosters **executive-level transparency** and informed decision-making.
- Reinforce a culture where **AI experimentation is encouraged**, but governance and accountability evolve in parallel to ensure sustainable and secure innovation.

5.18.4 Achieving agility

Agility in cybersecurity AI auditing enables audit functions to **respond rapidly to evolving threats, adapt to emerging technologies, and deliver timely, high-impact results.** Applying agile concepts improves responsiveness, collaboration, and continuous assurance in dynamic cybersecurity environments. By embedding these Agile elements into cybersecurity AI auditing, audit teams can **maximize responsiveness, transparency, and impact,** helping their organizations stay ahead of emerging threats while ensuring responsible AI oversight.

1. **Quickly Adapt to Emerging Cybersecurity Risks**
    - **Cybersecurity threats evolve rapidly,** especially with the integration of AI tools such as ML-based IDS and automated response systems. Quick response to those emerging threats through continuous auditing is important.
    - Agile audit teams maintain **flexible audit planning** that allows for real-time reprioritization when critical risks emerge – such as new AI vulnerabilities, model drift, or compromised AI training data.
    - **Risk intelligence feeds and AI activity logs** are continuously monitored to inform the audit backlog and pivot focus as needed. Quick response to those emerging threats through continuous auditing is important.
2. **Deliver Incremental Results**
    - Instead of waiting for full audit cycle completion, auditors **deliver iterative findings** – such as preliminary assessments of AI model explainability or initial validation of access control AI tools.
    - These incremental deliverables provide immediate value to stakeholders and can be used to **mitigate risks early,** even as the full audit continues.
    - **Deliverables may include dashboards, short briefing memos, risk heatmaps, or AI validation snapshots** aligned with the organization's control framework.
3. **Conduct Stand-Up Meetings**
    - Agile cybersecurity audit teams hold **regular stand-up meetings (e.g., daily or bi-weekly)** to align progress, identify blockers, and reassess priorities based on new cybersecurity or AI developments.
    - Stand-ups promote **real-time collaboration** among audit team members, data scientists, and control owners, ensuring swift issue resolution and shared accountability.

    - This cadence is particularly valuable when auditing **fast-moving areas like AI-driven threat detection or autonomous response mechanisms.**
4. **Promote Open Communication**
    - Transparent communication is central to Agile audit practices. Cybersecurity AI audit teams establish **open communication channels** with stakeholders in the 1LoD and 2LoD, IT, and data science units.
    - This includes **documenting key AI decisions, sharing audit rationales, and encouraging dialogue** around control weaknesses, AI model limitations, or ethical concerns (e.g., bias).
    - Open forums, secure collaboration tools, and executive-level summaries support **two-way feedback** and improve trust in the audit process.

Critical thinking moments

1. Consider how each of the following four categories contributes to enhancing the cybersecurity audit process when integrated with AI capabilities:
    - **Building Partnerships**

    → How do stronger collaboration channels and cross-functional alignment improve audit insights, communication efficiency, and trust when evaluating AI systems?
    - **Influencing Behavior and Culture**

    → How can consistent messaging, role modeling, and transparency about AI audit outcomes encourage a culture of security ownership, innovation, and ethical AI use?
    - **Achieving Audit Objectives**

    → How does the integration of AI-driven tools and analytics improve the accuracy, scope, and timeliness of cybersecurity audits?
    - **Achieving Agility**

    → In what ways can AI help the audit function respond more quickly to evolving threats, adapt to emerging technologies, and support continuous assurance?
2. **Take a moment to identify additional benefits or organizational strengths** that these categories may unlock within your organization or agency's unique cybersecurity and risk environment. You might find value in areas such as talent development, governance maturity, or strategic influence that further extend audit impact.

Important Note: Remember, the goal is to use the four categories as guiding **concepts**, not to create a rigid framework that introduces unnecessary complexity or overhead. Flexibility is key. Focus on applying these categories in a way that enhances audit value, supports continuous improvement, and aligns with your organization or agency's existing structures and culture.

5.19 SUMMARY

This chapter served as an inspiration for you to adapt existing tools for new scenarios, anticipate technology evolution, and build a forward-looking cybersecurity audit practice. As emerging AI technologies redefine what is possible, auditors are uniquely positioned to lead the charge in evaluating these tools with a critical yet innovative mindset. The insights shared in this chapter demonstrate that traditional auditing frameworks and controls can be enhanced – not replaced – by AI. With strategic foresight, auditors can integrate predictive analytics, intelligent automation, and advanced data analysis into their methodologies while maintaining alignment with professional standards and ethical obligations.

Looking ahead, your ability to translate AI's capabilities into actionable audit insights will be a defining factor in your professional relevance. This means not only keeping pace with technological change, but also embracing a mindset of continuous learning, cross-functional collaboration, and adaptive leadership. The cybersecurity audit practice of the future will require more than technical acumen; it will demand cultural agility, strategic influence, and a commitment to transparency and accountability in a world driven by algorithms. Let this chapter serve as a foundation for your evolution from auditor to trusted advisor in an AI-enabled ecosystem.

You made it to the end of this chapter! Let's continue the cybersecurity audit journey with Chapter 6 – Unlocking Artificial Intelligence: Knowledge, Context, and Curated Resources. That chapter expands on selected topics from this chapter and offers a summary of key insights from the preceding chapters.

Chapter 6

Unlocking artificial intelligence

Knowledge, context, and curated resources

6.1 LEARNING OBJECTIVES

By the end of this chapter, readers will be able to:

1. **AI Expertise, Training, and Certification Roadmap,** equipping participants with a structured path to develop foundational, intermediate, and advanced skills needed to effectively understand, implement, and manage artificial intelligence (AI) solutions. Ability to responsibly integrate and assess AI tools within enterprise environments.
2. **Periodic Self-Assessments,** developing and applying self-assessment tools to identify strengths, weaknesses, and opportunities for continuous improvement.
3. **Checklists, Templates and Maturity Model,** enabling learners to apply structured tools and frameworks that support consistent evaluation, implementation, and improvement of AI and cybersecurity audit practices.
4. **Differentiating Internal and External Information Sharing,** while addressing legal, regulatory, and ethical considerations.
5. **Defining and Evaluating Success (Including Metrics),** including success criteria and selecting appropriate metrics to evaluate performance in cybersecurity auditing and AI initiatives.
6. **Emerging AI Technology and Cybersecurity Prompts,** developing the ability to proactively identify, evaluate, and respond to evolving technologies, threats, and opportunities through ongoing environmental scanning and informed questioning.
7. **Additional Resources and References,** locating and assessing authoritative resources to support ongoing learning, informed decision-making, and professional development.

6.2 OPENING INSIGHTS

As we conclude this journey into the evolving world of cybersecurity auditing, it's clear that the role of the cybersecurity auditor is undergoing a profound transformation. What was once a discipline grounded solely in compliance

DOI: 10.1201/9781003640301-7

and technical checklists has become a dynamic field that demands creativity, critical thinking, and the strategic use of technology. Throughout this book, we have explored how building partnerships, influencing culture, embracing agility, and harnessing the power of AI can elevate not only audit outcomes but the very value auditors provide to their organizations. Yet, the ideas shared here are just a starting point. The real impact begins when these concepts are put into practice – when auditors become change agents, innovators, and forward-thinking leaders prepared to meet the challenges of an increasingly complex digital landscape.

In today's rapidly evolving cybersecurity and AI landscape, maintaining a static approach is no longer sufficient. Chapter 6 focuses on sustaining success through clear metrics, periodic self-assessments, effective information sharing, and continuous monitoring of emerging AI tools and capabilities. These practices not only ensure that cybersecurity auditing and AI-driven initiatives remain effective but also foster a culture of adaptability and informed decision-making. By leveraging self-evaluation, knowledge sharing, and an awareness of technological trends, cybersecurity audit professionals can proactively address risks, seize opportunities, and align with best practices. This chapter also highlights essential resources and references to support continuous learning and operational excellence.

6.3 AI TRAINING ROADMAP FOR CYBERSECURITY AUDITORS

Looking back to the era of mainframe computer systems, auditors were required to develop a foundational understanding of operating systems and programming languages such as Common Business-Oriented Language (COBOL) and FORmula TRANslation (FORTRAN). This marked a pivotal transition in the audit profession, as many financial auditors were reassigned or reclassified as technology auditors – often without formal designation or structured training. They were expected to acquire technical knowledge on the job, laying the groundwork for what would later emerge as the specialized discipline of information technology (IT) and cybersecurity auditing.

While the complexity of early computer systems was significant for its time, it pales in comparison to today's cybersecurity landscape, which is defined by global interconnectivity, sophisticated cyber threats, AI-driven systems, cloud computing, and rapidly evolving regulatory frameworks. In this modern environment, cybersecurity auditors must have a broad and deep understanding of information systems, risk management, compliance, and emerging technologies such as AI. As AI becomes more integral to critical business processes, cybersecurity auditors must be equipped to evaluate algorithmic transparency, data governance, and the risks associated with autonomous decision-making.

🗺️ AI Expertise, Training, and Certification Roadmap for Cybersecurity Auditors

Let's have a discussion on AI expertise, training, and certification to explore how professionals can build practical skills in this rapidly evolving field. This section highlights essential pathways for evaluating and gaining foundational knowledge, training opportunities, and recognized credentials in AI. Whether you're just beginning or looking to validate your expertise, this conversation will help you navigate the tools, strategies, and certifications that matter most.

6.3.1 🕵️ AI requisite expertise for cybersecurity auditors

To effectively integrate AI into cybersecurity auditing, professionals need a blend of technical, analytical, and governance-oriented AI skillsets (Madenburg, 2024). Here's a categorized list of recommended AI skillsets for cybersecurity auditors:

🧱 ***Foundational Knowledge***

- **AI Fundamentals:** Understand basic AI concepts (ML, neural networks, supervised/unsupervised learning).
- **Cybersecurity-AI Integration:** Grasp how AI applies to cyber domains like threat detection, anomaly analysis, and behavioral monitoring.
- **Data Literacy:** Ability to interpret data structures, sources, and quality as they relate to AI inputs and outputs.

🔧 ***Technical and Analytical Skills***

- **Understanding of AI Models:** Know the purpose, strengths, and weaknesses of models like decision trees, random forests, neural networks, and anomaly detection algorithms.
- **Model Evaluation:** Be able to evaluate model performance using metrics such as accuracy, precision, recall, and receiver operating characteristic (ROC) curves.
- **Bias and Fairness Assessment:** Recognize and assess model bias, ethical risks, and discriminatory outputs.
- **Log and Event Analysis with AI Tools:** Use AI-enhanced Security Information and Event Management (SIEM) tools (e.g., Splunk, IBM QRadar, Darktrace) for detecting suspicious activity.
- **Basic Scripting and Querying:** Familiarity with Python, Structured Query Language (SQL), or Jupyter Notebooks for reviewing AI pipeline components (optional but valuable).

🔒 ***Cybersecurity-Aware AI Use***

- **AI Security Controls:** Understand and assess controls for model integrity, access management, audit logging, and secure deployment.

- **Adversarial AI Awareness:** Know how AI models can be exploited (e.g., model poisoning, evasion) and assess controls against these threats.
- **AI Governance and Risk Management:** Apply frameworks (e.g., National Institute of Standards and Technology (NIST) AI Risk Management Framework (AI RMF), International Organization for Standardization/International Electrotechnical Commission (**International Organization for Standardization (ISO)/International Electrotechnical Commission (IEC)** 42001) to assess AI risk and compliance within cybersecurity functions.

🛠 *Audit-Specific Skills*

- **Explainable AI (XAI):** Ability to evaluate whether AI decisions can be traced, justified, and logged for audit purposes.
- **AI Life Cycle Review:** Assess policies and procedures across data sourcing, model training, validation, deployment, and drift management.
- **Third-Party AI Vendor Evaluation:** Review service level agreements (SLAs), privacy agreements, and system documentation for vendor-supplied AI tools.
- **Continuous Monitoring Techniques:** Evaluate whether AI models are continuously monitored for performance and risk.

> 🛠 **Important Note:** The above "Requisite AI Expertise" section of this chapter is intended to briefly outline the AI skills that will help readers better understand the examples presented in this book and to prepare for AI application implementations.

6.3.2 🤓 AI training for cybersecurity auditors

Training cybersecurity auditors in AI is becoming increasingly essential as threat landscapes evolve, and attackers leverage sophisticated technologies. AI training equips auditors with the knowledge to assess and validate AI-driven security systems, understand machine learning (ML) models used in threat detection, and evaluate the integrity and fairness of automated decision-making processes. By understanding how AI algorithm's function and how they can be manipulated or misused, auditors can more effectively identify vulnerabilities, ensure compliance with regulatory standards, and recommend robust controls. This specialized training also enables auditors to critically assess the transparency, accountability, and ethical implications of AI systems within cybersecurity frameworks.

Tables 6.1 and 6.2 present AI training in stages based on expertise level. Table 6.1 is training that provides basic AI principles and its relevance to cybersecurity. Table 6.2 is training that provides hands-on exposure to AI tools and learn how to evaluate model performance. Table 6.3 is training that instructs how to assess AI risks, apply governance controls, and audit AI in regulated environments. Last, Table 6.4 is training on how to conduct AI-focused cybersecurity audits and integrate AI techniques into audit practices.

Table 6.1 Stage 1: AI awareness and foundations

Skill area	Topics covered	Suggested training resources
AI fundamentals	AI vs. ML vs. deep learning (DL), supervised/unsupervised learning	Coursera: "AI for Everyone" by Andrew Ng
Cybersecurity applications of AI	Threat detection, phishing detection, anomaly analysis	SysAdmin, Audit, Network, and Security (SANS) SEC595, NIST AI Use Case Repository.
Data literacy	Data types, labeling, bias in training sets	edX: "Data Science Ethics" or "Data Science Math Skills."
Key terminology	Model, feature, label, training, inference, accuracy	Internal glossaries or OpenAI Learn site

Table 6.2 Stage 2: Practical tools and model evaluation

Skill area	Topics covered	Suggested training resources
AI model evaluation	Precision, recall, confusion matrix, overfitting	Coursera: "Machine Learning with Python."
AI-enhanced security tools	Splunk User Behavior Analytics (UBA), IBM QRadar, Darktrace, Defender for Endpoint	Vendor training labs (Splunk>Phantom, Microsoft Learn, IBM Security)
Intro to Python (optional)	Reading notebooks, simple model tuning	Codecademy: "Python for Data Science," Google Colab walkthroughs
AI logging and auditing	Explainability, audit trails, model drift	NIST AI Risk Management Framework (RMF) documentation, Fair Isaac Corporation (FICO) Explainable AI Toolkit (free)

Table 6.3 Stage 3: AI risk management and governance

Skill area	Topics covered	Suggested training resources
AI risk and compliance	NIST AI RMF, International Organization for Standardization (ISO)/ International Electrotechnical Commission (IEC) 42001, European Union (EU) AI Act	NIST.gov, OECD AI principles, ISO publications
AI ethics and bias	Fairness, transparency, accountability	HarvardX: "Ethics of AI"
Secure AI development	Adversarial AI, model tampering, data poisoning	MITRE ATLAS, Open Web Application Security Project (OWASP) Top 10 for ML
Vendor AI evaluation	SLA reviews, black-box risk, third-party model assurance	ISACA whitepapers, Gartner Toolkit

Table 6.4 Stage 4: Advanced audit practices with AI

Skill area	Topics covered	Suggested training resources
AI-powered audit techniques	Log analysis with AI, anomaly clustering	PyCaret tutorials, Elasticsearch, Logstash, and Kibana (ELK) Stack with ML plugins
Continuous monitoring with AI	Model performance monitoring, real-time alerting	Amazon Web Services (AWS) Lookout for Metrics, Azure Monitor AI capabilities
XAI	Tools like SHapley Additive exPlanations (SHAP), Local Interpretable Model-agnostic Explanations LIME) for model transparency	Google Publisher Advertiser Identity Reconciliation (PAIR), IBM AI Explainability 360 toolkit
Building an AI audit plan	Planning, scoping, testing, reporting.	Internal templates, Institute of Internal Auditors (IIA) guidance on emerging tech audits

🎯 **Pro Tip:** There are many high-quality AI learning resources available across platforms such as **YouTube**, **Coursera**, **LinkedIn Learning**, and **university-sponsored courses**. To expand your toolkit, consider conducting both **Google** and **Chatbot** searches to uncover the most current and relevant materials. This list is just a starting point – be sure to also tap into your **personal and professional networks**, including **industry associations**, **online forums**, and **special interest groups** to stay informed and connected.

6.3.3 🧠 Certification and recognition pathways for cybersecurity auditors

Cybersecurity auditors should possess certifications to demonstrate AI expertise, as these credentials validate their skills and knowledge in a rapidly evolving field. AI certifications make professionals more competitive in the job market by showcasing their ability to understand and apply AI technologies effectively. They also offer structured learning paths that help individuals stay current with the latest advancements, while boosting confidence and credibility when working on AI-driven security assessments and audits. Below are some examples of AI-related certifications.

- ISACA: *Certified in Emerging Technology (CET)* – AI module (https://www.isaca.org/credentialing/cet).
- ISACA: Advanced in AI Audit™ (AAIA™) Certification (https://www.isaca.org/credentialing/aaia/get-aaia-certified).
- CompTIA: *Data+*, *CySA+* (for applied analytics) (https://www.comptia.org/en-us/certifications/data/ and https://www.comptia.org/en-us/certifications/cybersecurity-analyst/#objectives)

- Microsoft: *AI Fundamentals* (AI-900) (https://learn.microsoft.com/en-us/credentials/certifications/azure-ai-fundamentals/?practice-assessment-type=certification)
- AWS Certified AI Practitioner and AWS Certified Machine Learning Engineer – Associate (https://www.aboutamazon.com/news/aws/aws-certifications-generative-ai-machine-learning-cloud-jobs)

Expanding upon the general certifications above, several professional organizations have been instrumental in preparing auditors for this AI transformation. ISACA played a pioneering role by developing globally recognized certifications such as the Certified Information Systems Auditor (CISA), Certified in Risk and Information Systems Control (CRISC), and Certified Data Privacy Solutions Engineer (CDPSE), which bridge the gap between traditional auditing, cybersecurity, and privacy governance. In 2025, ISACA introduced the first advanced AI audit certification – the Advanced in AI Audit™ (AAIA™). The IIA has similarly advanced the profession by integrating IT and cybersecurity considerations into internal audit standards and guidance, while offering certifications such as the Certified Internal Auditor (CIA) and endorsing the Three Lines Model for risk management and assurance.

Organizations such as International Information System Security Certification Consortium (ISC)², with certifications like the Certified Information Systems Security Professional (CISSP), and the SysAdmin, Audit, Network and Security (SANS) Institute, which offers specialized training in cybersecurity operations and threat detection, have expanded technical training pathways for auditors seeking to deepen their cybersecurity expertise. NIST has also played a foundational role by publishing widely adopted cybersecurity frameworks, control catalogs (e.g., Special Publication (SP) 800-53), and risk management guidelines that auditors use as benchmarks for assessments.

Together, these organizations have established professional standards, ethical foundations, and educational pathways necessary to support the evolution of auditors from financial generalists into highly skilled cybersecurity assurance professionals. Those organizations now provide AI standards and training.

> 💡 **Critical Thinking and Listening:** In addition to technical expertise, critical thinking and listening are essential skills for effective communication and decision-making. Critical thinking involves analyzing information objectively, questioning assumptions, and evaluating evidence before forming a judgment. Active listening complements this by requiring full attention to the speaker, understanding their message, and responding thoughtfully. Together, these skills help individuals engage in deeper conversations, resolve conflicts, and make well-informed choices. In professional settings, they foster collaboration, reduce misunderstandings, and enhance problem-solving capabilities (Haines, 2020; Walch, 2024).

Why Is This important for Cybersecurity Audit AI activities? Cybersecurity and AI subject matter experts are required to analyze and challenge information obtained through AI applications and models. The results may not be 100 percent accurate because AI is still maturing (Institute of Data, 2024).

6.4 AI COMPETENCY MATRIX FOR CYBERSECURITY AUDITORS

Here is a structured **AI Competency Matrix for Cybersecurity Auditors,** designed to align skills with progressive proficiency levels. This matrix can be used for individual assessments, team development plans, or aligning training initiatives to audit needs.

Table 6.5 builds upon the previous training tables by providing the expertise levels for each competency area. This is like a maturity model because of the beginner, intermediate, and advanced levels associated with AI competency. Understanding AI competencies is essential for cybersecurity auditors as they assess and interact with increasingly intelligent systems. At the **beginner level**, auditors should grasp foundational AI concepts, such as basic terminology, types of AI, and common use cases in cybersecurity. **Intermediate-level** expertise involves applying AI tools, interpreting ML outputs, and understanding model limitations and biases. At the **advanced level**, auditors are expected to evaluate AI system architectures, audit algorithmic decisions, and assess compliance with ethical and regulatory standards.

Table 6.5 AI competency matrix for cybersecurity auditors

Competency area	Beginner *(Awareness)*	Intermediate *(Application)*	Advanced *(Audit Execution and Strategy)*
AI fundamentals	Understand basic AI/ML terminology and concepts	Explains differences between supervised, unsupervised, and RL models	Evaluates AI integration across cybersecurity functions
Cybersecurity-AI integration	Can identify common AI use cases (e.g., anomaly detection)	Uses AI-enhanced tools for threat detection or log analysis	Audits AI-enabled security solutions across domains (e.g., Security Operations Center (SOC), Identity Access Management (IAM))
Data literacy	Understands structure of training vs. test data	Assesses data quality and labeling practices for audit reviews	Evaluates data governance, model input risks, and data integrity controls

(Continued)

Table 6.5 AI competency matrix for cybersecurity auditors (*Continued*)

Competency area	Beginner *(Awareness)*	Intermediate *(Application)*	Advanced *(Audit Execution and Strategy)*
Model evaluation	Recognizes performance metrics (accuracy, precision)	Interprets confusion matrix and model drift alerts	Audits validation frameworks, bias, and overfitting/underfitting risks
AI risk and compliance	Aware of AI-related compliance (e.g., General Data Protection Regulation (GDPR), NIST AI RMF)	Reviews AI model documentation for policy compliance	Assesses AI risk management controls and regulatory alignment
XAI	Understands need for model transparency	Uses tools like SHAP or LIME to interpret model output	Audits model explainability and decision traceability requirements
AI governance	Familiar with AI policies and principles	Participates in AI risk assessments and life cycle reviews	Develops or audits AI governance frameworks and control effectiveness
AI tool Proficiency	Uses basic AI functions in audit tools (e.g., filters, scoring)	Operates AI-enhanced platforms (e.g., Splunk UBA, Darktrace)	Validates AI tool configuration, tuning, and response effectiveness
Scripting andutomation (optional)	Reads Python snippets or ML model configurations	Modifies code or queries for testing purposes	Develops custom scripts or models for control testing or validation

How to use the matrix

- **Self-Assessment:** Mark your current level (✔) for each competency and identify gaps.
- **Team Development:** Use across teams to align skill levels and assign relevant training.
- **Training Alignment:** Map learning objectives and courses to areas needing development.

6.5 AI MODEL EVALUATION CHECKLIST

AI model validation is the process of evaluating an ML model to ensure it performs accurately, reliably, and ethically before deployment. This involves testing the model on unseen data to assess its generalization capabilities, checking for biases, and verifying that it meets predefined performance metrics such as accuracy, precision, recall, or F1 score (Sharma, 2023). Validation also includes stress-testing the model under various scenarios to identify potential weaknesses or unintended behaviors. By thoroughly validating AI models, organizations can build trust in their systems, reduce risks, and ensure compliance with regulatory and ethical standards (Nissim & Greenberg, 2025).

Expanding upon the model validation information in Chapter 5 – Harnessing Artificial Intelligence: Enhancing Cybersecurity Audits through Automation and Insight, below is a **Model Evaluation Checklist** tailored for selecting and assessing AI models in cybersecurity auditing or similarly sensitive domains (Ozer & van Schijndel, n.d.). This checklist is organized into categories that align with key stages of model development, deployment, and governance.

1. **Problem and Objective Alignment**
   - Is the business problem clearly defined?
   - Is the model type appropriate for the problem (e.g., classification, regression, clustering)?
   - Does the model support the use case (e.g., anomaly detection, access control, threat prediction)?
2. **Data Readiness**
   - Are sufficient training data available and representative?
   - Is the data clean, labeled, and properly formatted?
   - Has data preprocessing been documented (e.g., feature engineering, normalization)?
   - Are sensitive or personally identifiable information (PII) data handled appropriately?
   - Is the data "free" of copyright infringement?
3. **Performance Metrics**
   - Are appropriate metrics selected (e.g., accuracy, precision, recall, F1 score, Receiver Operating Characteristic – Area Under the Curve (ROC-AUC))?
   - Has the model been benchmarked against a baseline or previous solution?
   - Has performance been validated on a separate test dataset?
   - Is the model robust to noise and missing data?
4. **Explainability and Interpretability**
   - Can the model's decisions be explained to non-technical stakeholders?
   - Are tools used to enhance interpretability (e.g., SHapley Additive exPlanations (SHAP), Local Interpretable Model-agnostic Explanations (LIME))?
   - Are explainability requirements documented for audit/compliance purposes?

5. **Bias, Fairness, and Ethics**
   - Has the model been evaluated for potential bias (e.g., race, gender, role)?
   - Are mitigation steps documented and implemented?
   - Are fairness and ethical use policies in place?
6. **Security and Robustness**
   - Has the model been tested against adversarial inputs?
   - Are there controls for model poisoning or inference attacks?
   - Is model drift detection in place?
7. **Operational Readiness**
   - Can the model scale to the expected production load?
   - Are latency and throughput acceptable for real-time or batch processing?
   - Is the model containerized or deployable via APIs or edge nodes?
8. **Governance and Compliance**
   - Is the model aligned with frameworks such as NIST AI RMF or ISO/IEC 42001?
   - Is version control maintained for models, training data, and configurations?
   - Is there documentation for model lineage and auditability?
9. **Monitoring and Maintenance**
   - Is ongoing performance monitoring established?
   - Are retraining criteria and frequency defined?
   - Is there a rollback plan in case of failure or degradation?
10. **Cost and Resource Evaluation**
    - Is the cost of computer training and inference sustainable?
    - Are licensing or third-party tool costs understood?
    - Are human resources available to maintain the model?

🎯 **Pro Tip:** When selecting initial metrics for evaluating AI in cybersecurity audits, start with metrics that align directly with your audit objectives and stakeholder expectations. Focus on a balanced mix of technical (e.g., accuracy, false positives) and operational (e.g., time savings, risk detection improvements) metrics that are easy to measure and interpret in your current environment. Begin with 3–5 core metrics to avoid complexity and ensure consistent tracking – you can expand as your AI implementation matures.

6.6 AI APPLICATION EVALUATION TEMPLATE

Below is a professional **template for an internal review** to evaluate whether **open-source or vendor-supplied AI applications** are more appropriate for a given cybersecurity use case. This version can be easily adapted for workshops, procurement reviews, or audit planning.

AI Application Evaluation Template – Open-Source vs. Vendor-Supplied
Project Name/Use Case: ______________________________
Date of Review: ____________
Reviewer(s): ______________________________

Table 6.6 is a blank evaluation factor table that the cybersecurity auditor would complete in addition to the other data cells. The table is intended to guide the user through important evaluation factors that result in determining the best application alternative: open-source or vendor-supplied.

Table 6.6 Evaluation criteria table

Evaluation factor	Importance (1–5)	Comments/ notes	Better fit (open-source / vendor)
Audit transparency			
Regulatory compliance			
Security assurance			
Customization needs			
Internal AI/ML expertise			
Budget constraints			
Deployment speed			
Scalability and support needs			
Vendor lock-in risk			
Data privacy and residency			
Long-term maintainability			

Summary and Recommendation
Total Score for Open-Source Fit: _______
Total Score for Vendor Fit: _______

Preliminary Recommendation

- Adopt **Open-Source** AI application
- Adopt **Vendor-Supplied** AI application
- Hybrid approach/Further assessment needed

Additional Notes or Action Items

6.7 AI MATURITY MODEL FOR CYBERSECURITY AUDIT FUNCTION

Table 6.7 maps the customized AI Maturity Model for a Cybersecurity Audit Function to the NIST AI RMF. This will help align your audit maturity progression with federal guidance on trustworthy AI development and use. Benchmarking against authoritative sources will support recommendations.

Table 6.7 Mapping AI maturity to NIST AI RMF

AI maturity model dimension	Relevant NIST AI RMF core function(s) (NIST, 2018)	How they align
1. Strategy and leadership	**GOVERN**	Establishes the organizational policies, roles, and responsibilities that oversee AI use in cybersecurity auditing. Maturity implies broader leadership involvement and risk-informed strategies
2. Data and infrastructure	**MAP, MEASURE**	Ensures audit data quality, relevance, and fitness for AI models. Infrastructure maturity supports data lineage, provenance, and performance evaluation, key to risk mapping and measurement
3. Audit processes and tools	**MAP, MANAGE**	AI-enabled audit tools must be mapped to system objectives, risks, and operational use cases. As maturity increases, audit tools must also support risk mitigation and life cycle management
4. Governance and ethics	**GOVERN, MANAGE**	Maturity in governance aligns with the RMF's focus on accountability, fairness, privacy, and transparency. Ethical AI use must be documented, evaluated, and enforced
5. People and skills	**GOVERN**	The RMF emphasizes workforce competence and awareness. Maturity implies internal training programs, cross-functional teams, and certifications (e.g., in responsible AI or AI auditing)
6. Performance and value	**MEASURE, MANAGE**	Auditors must monitor model accuracy, fairness, and security over time. At higher levels, continuous performance measurement is a hallmark of AI RMF-aligned risk management

Table 6.8 expands upon Table 6.7 by aligning maturity levels with the NIST AI RMF Core Functions. This table also provides examples of NIST RMF implementation goals that align with the maturity level. Like Table 6.7, benchmarking against authoritative sources will support recommendations.

Table 6.8 Key RMF functions mapped to maturity levels

AI maturity level	NIST RMF core functions in focus (NIST, 2018)	Implementation goals
1. Initial	N/A	No RMF alignment; start with awareness and basic governance structure
2. Developing	MAP	Identify AI use cases in audit; assess risks and context. Begin stakeholder mapping
3. Operational	MAP, MANAGE	Begin managing AI-related risks; introduce life cycle controls. Implement early governance policies

(Continued)

Table 6.8 Key RMF functions mapped to maturity levels (*Continued*)

AI maturity level	NIST RMF core functions in focus (NIST, 2018)	Implementation goals
4. Integrated	GOVERN, MAP, MANAGE	Formalize policies, procedures, and roles. Adopt risk mitigation techniques (bias detection, model validation)
5. Optimized	GOVERN, MAP, MEASURE, MANAGE	Implement full RMF life cycle. Continuous governance, measurement of effectiveness, and ethical oversight. Align with external standards and provide feedback to improve AI practices

⚙ Practical Integration Tips: Aligning NIST AI RMF with Other Cybersecurity AI Audit Activities

- **Gap Analysis:** Use each RMF function to assess your current audit function maturity. Identify what functions are under-addressed (e.g., measuring bias or documenting governance).
- **Policy Development:** At Levels 3–5, integrate RMF-aligned language into your audit policies, especially for **accountability, bias mitigation, and transparency.**
- **Training and Awareness:** Incorporate the RMF's emphasis on trustworthy AI into auditor training programs.
- **Control Testing:** Include RMF functions in audit test plans for AI-enabled systems (e.g., audit whether AI models used in security operations meet "GOVERN" function standards).

6.8 AI AUDIT PLAYBOOK: A PRACTICAL GUIDE TO ASSESSING AND GOVERNING ARTIFICIAL INTELLIGENCE SYSTEMS

A reference to AI Audit Playbook was noted in Chapter 5 – Harnessing Artificial Intelligence: Enhancing Cybersecurity Audits through Automation and Insight specific to the Cybersecurity Audit AI Maturity. An **AI Audit Playbook** is a structured guide designed to help organizations and agencies plan, conduct, and report audits of AI systems in a way that ensures compliance, transparency, ethical use, and alignment with organizational objectives. It provides a repeatable framework that integrates audit standards, risk management principles, and AI governance. Below is a high-level structure of what an effective AI Audit Playbook Structure might look like:

1. **Introduction and Purpose**
    - Overview of the playbook's objectives
    - Importance of auditing AI systems
    - Scope and applicability (e.g., models, systems, vendors)

2. **AI System Inventory and Classification**
    - Identify all AI systems in use (internally developed or vendor-supplied)
    - Classify AI systems by:
        - Risk level (e.g., critical, moderate, low)
        - Type (e.g., natural language processing (NLP), computer vision, predictive analytics)
        - Business function
3. **Governance and Oversight**
    - Roles and responsibilities (e.g., audit, compliance, data science, legal)
    - AI governance frameworks (e.g., Organisation for Economic Co-operation and Development (OECD), NIST AI RMF, ISO/IEC 42001)
    - Alignment with organizational policies and regulatory requirements
4. **Risk Assessment and Scoping**
    - Perform AI-specific risk assessments:
        - Bias and fairness risks
        - Data privacy concerns
        - Model explainability and transparency
        - Cybersecurity vulnerabilities
    - Define audit objectives, scope, and criteria
5. **Audit Planning**
    - Select an audit team with cross-functional expertise.
    - Establish an audit plan and timeline.
    - Determine data access and model documentation requirements.
    - Engage stakeholders (e.g., developers, business owners, Chief AI).
6. **Controls Evaluation**
    a. Assess technical and operational controls:
        - Data quality and lineage
        - Model development life cycle (e.g., System Development Life Cycle (SDLC) for AI)
        - Validation and testing processes
        - Change management for models

    b. Evaluate ethical and accountability controls:
        - Human-in-the-loop mechanisms
        - Monitoring for model drift
        - Consent and transparency to users
7. **Audit Execution**
    - Review design and effectiveness of controls.
    - Examine documentation and model outputs.
    - Interview stakeholders and perform walk-throughs.
    - Evaluate AI model outcomes for consistency, accuracy, and fairness.
8. **Reporting and Recommendations**
    - Document findings with evidence and severity.
    - Provide recommendations for remediation and improvement.

- Include suggested timelines and responsible parties.
- Align findings with applicable standards (e.g., ISO, NIST, Control Objectives for Information and Related Technologies (COBIT)).

9. **Follow-Up and Continuous Improvement**
   - Track remediation efforts and verify closure of issues.
   - Establish feedback loops with governance teams.
   - Recommend playbook updates based on emerging technologies and lessons learned.
10. **Appendices**
    - Sample audit checklists.
    - Reference to AI governance models and regulatory standards.
    - Glossary of AI and audit terms.
    - Audit templates (e.g., risk register, testing worksheets, reporting format).

6.9 INTERNAL AND EXTERNAL INFORMATION SHARING

Internal and external information sharing is crucial for fostering collaboration, improving decision-making, and enhancing organizational resilience. Within an organization, sharing information across departments breaks down silos, promotes alignment on goals, and ensures everyone has access to the data needed to perform effectively. Externally, exchanging information with trusted partners, industry peers, and regulatory bodies enables proactive threat detection, compliance with standards, and the adoption of best practices. In sectors like cybersecurity, timely and accurate information sharing can help prevent incidents and mitigate risks. Ultimately, a culture of open and responsible information sharing strengthens both individual organizations and the broader ecosystem they operate within.

6.9.1 AI collaboration in action: Forums by focus and function

AI forums are organized platforms – often composed of governments, industry leaders, academic institutions, and civil society – that collaborate to shape the development, governance, and ethical use of AI. These forums serve as convening bodies to promote international dialogue, establish best practices, draft policy guidance, and advance research on responsible AI. They vary in focus and scope, with some emphasizing regulatory standards and public policy (e.g., OECD AI Policy Observatory, Global Partnership on AI), while others concentrate on technical research and interoperability (e.g., Partnership on AI, AI Alliance). For cybersecurity audit professionals, AI forums are valuable sources of insight into emerging risks, governance models, and global trends that can inform both policy and audit strategy. The following is a list of notable **AI forums**, categorized by their **focus and composition**, that influence AI governance, policy, and innovation globally.

6.9.1.1 🤓 💻 Developer-oriented AI forums (similar to OpenAI developer forum)

1. **OpenAI Developer Forum**
   Focus: Discussions on Generative Pre-trained Transformer (GPT), Application Programming Interface (API) usage, plugin development, and troubleshooting
   Access: https://community.openai.com
2. **Hugging Face Forums**
   Focus: Open-source AI model development, fine-tuning, and deployment (Transformers, Diffusers)
   Access: https://discuss.huggingface.co
3. **Anthropic Community (Claude)**
   Focus: Developer updates, API usage, and safe AI development (Claude model)
   Access: https://anthropic.com
4. **Google AI/TensorFlow Forum**
   Focus: Machine learning, TensorFlow, JAX, and Google's AI ecosystem (Gemini, Vertex AI)
   Access: https://discuss.ai.google.dev/
5. **Cohere Community**
   Focus: NLP models, embeddings, RAG (retrieval-augmented generation), and AI APIs
   Access: https://cohere.com/blog
6. **NVIDIA Developer Forums – AI and Deep Learning**
   Focus: Graphics Processing Unit (GPU) optimization, AI inference, training, and NVIDIA tools (e.g., Computer Unified Device Architecture (CUDA), Triton)
   Access: https://forums.developer.nvidia.com
7. **EleutherAI Discord and GitHub**
   Focus: Open-source large language model development and AI research
   Access: https://www.eleuther.ai
8. **Weights and Biases Community**
   Focus: Machine learning operations (MLOps), model training, experiment tracking, and AI life cycle management
   Access: https://wandb.ai/site

Commonality among the Above Forums

- Focus on hands-on development and deployment of AI/ML models

- Interactive Q&A, debugging, and optimization help
- Frequent API integration discussions and project showcases
- Often include open-source contributions and peer feedback

6.9.1.2 🌐 *Global and multilateral forums*

1. **OECD AI Policy Observatory (OECD.AI)**
   Focus: Policy analysis, trustworthy AI principles, and global metrics
   Members: OECD countries and partners
   https://oecd.ai
2. **Global Partnership on Artificial Intelligence (GPAI)**
   Focus: Responsible AI development and international collaboration.
   Members: Government and expert-led; includes U.S., Canada, EU, India, Japan.
   https://gpai.ai
3. **United Nations Interagency Working Group on AI**
   Focus: AI for sustainable development, human rights, and ethical governance.
   Members: UN agencies and global stakeholders.
4. **National Artificial Intelligence and Cybersecurity ISAO (NAIC-ISAO)**
   Focus: This organization focuses specifically on the convergence of AI and cybersecurity.
   It promotes a whole-of-nation approach to address challenges and opportunities in this area, including national security, innovation, and digital diplomacy.
   It supports the development of a framework, policies, laws, and solutions to support AI in cybersecurity.
   Members: Cybersecurity professionals and vendors.
   https://www.isao.org/group/naic-isao/.
5. **AI & Cyber Initiative (World Economic Forum)**
   Focus: This initiative, part of the World Economic Forum, brings together organizations to address the global security implications of AI. It focuses on the secure development, integration, and adoption of AI capabilities. The initiative recognizes both the opportunities and challenges presented by AI in cybersecurity.
   Members: Cybersecurity professionals from business, politics, academia, and civil society.
   https://initiatives.weforum.org/ai-cyber-initiative/organizations.
6. **AI Security Initiative (UC Berkeley Center for Long-Term Cybersecurity)**
   Focus: This initiative conducts interdisciplinary research on the global security implications of AI.
   It aims to support the trustworthy development of AI systems. It works across technical, institutional, and policy domains to address AI security challenges.

Members: AI practitioners and decision-makers.
https://cltc.berkeley.edu/program/ai-security-initiative/

7. **International Association of Privacy Professionals (IAPP)**
   Focus: While focused on privacy, the IAPP also addresses AI governance and digital responsibility.
   It provides resources and certifications relevant to the ethical and responsible use of AI, including in cybersecurity.
   Members: Cybersecurity and privacy professionals.
   https://iapp.org/#:~:text=IAPP:%20The%20policy%20neutral%2C%20not,Learn%20more.

8. **National Security Agency (NSA) Artificial Intelligence Security Center (AISC)**
   Focus: Launched by the National Security Agency, the AISC aims to defend the nation's AI through collaboration with industry, academia, and other government partners. It focuses on addressing the attack surface created by AI and ensuring the security of AI systems.
   Members: Industry and cybersecurity professionals.
   https://www.nsa.gov/AISC/.

6.9.1.3 🏛 Government and policy forums

1. **European Union (EU) AI Alliance**
   Focus: Shaping EU AI policy and legislation (e.g., EU AI Act)
   Members: European institutions, industry, academia, and civil society
   https://digital-strategy.ec.europa.eu/en/policies/european-ai-alliance.

2. **US National AI Research Resource (NAIRR) Task Force**
   Focus: Building infrastructure and access to AI research resources
   Members: US federal agencies, academia, and industry.
   https://www.nsf.gov/focus-areas/artificial-intelligence/nairr.

3. **AI Safety Summit (the United Kingdom (UK) Government)**
   Focus: Global cooperation on frontier AI safety and regulation
   Notable: Hosted in 2023 at Bletchley Park
   https://www.gov.uk/government/publications/ai-safety-summit-introduction

6.9.1.4 🤝 Industry and multi-stakeholder forums

1. **Partnership on AI (PAI)**
   Focus: Ethical AI, fairness, transparency, and societal impact
   Members: Amazon, Google, Meta, Apple, academics, nongovernmental organizations (NGOs)
   https://partnershiponai.org

2. **AI Alliance (IBM and Meta-Led)**
   Focus: Open innovation and open science in AI development
   Members: Over 50 organizations, including universities and private sector.
   https://thealliance.ai

3. **World Economic Forum Centre for the Fourth Industrial Revolution (C4IR)**
   Focus: Public-private collaboration on AI policy and innovation
   https://www.weforum.org/centre-for-the-fourth-industrial-revolution

6.9.1.5 🤝 Technical and standards forums

1. **Institute of Electrical and Electronics Engineers (IEEE) Global Initiative on Ethics of Autonomous and Intelligent Systems**
   Focus: Developing ethical AI standards and technical frameworks
   https://standards.ieee.org/initiatives/autonomous-intelligence-systems/
2. **International Organization for Standardization/International Electrotechnical Commission (ISO/IEC Joint Technical Committee (JTC) 1/SC 42)**
   Focus: Global standards for AI systems (e.g., ISO/IEC 42001)
   Members: National standards bodies
   https://www.iso.org/committee/6794475.html

💡 **Critical Thinking Moment:** These sources are not only beneficial for the cybersecurity audit professional developing AI tools, think about other uses for these forums.

🎯 **Pro Tip:** As AI continues to advance, so must the skillsets of cybersecurity auditors. Staying current requires a commitment to continuous learning, especially in areas such as AI risk assessment, governance, model transparency, and ethical auditing. To remain effective and relevant, cybersecurity auditors must proactively develop and refine their AI competencies, ensuring they can evaluate emerging technologies with the same rigor applied to traditional systems.

6.10 CONTINUOUS MONITORING OF EMERGING ARTIFICIAL INTELLIGENCE TOOLS AND CAPABILITIES

Continuous monitoring of emerging AI tools and capabilities is essential for staying ahead in a rapidly evolving technological landscape. As new AI applications are developed, organizations must regularly assess their relevance, risks, and potential impact on operations, security, and compliance. This involves tracking updates from AI vendors, monitoring research publications, and evaluating trends in ethical and regulatory guidance. Initiative-taking monitoring enables cybersecurity auditors and IT leaders to identify opportunities for innovation while addressing potential vulnerabilities or misuse. It also ensures that AI integration remains aligned with strategic objectives and governance frameworks. The list below, while not exhaustive, offers some sources of information to help you stay current on the evolution of AI.

1. **Subscribe to AI Research Journals and Newsletters:** Regularly read publications such as *arXiv AI*, Massachusetts Institute of Technology (*MIT) Technology Review*, and *AI Weekly* to stay updated on breakthroughs and trends.
2. **Track AI Product Updates from Major Vendors:** Monitor release notes and feature updates from providers like **OpenAI, Google Cloud AI, Amazon Web Services** (**AWS AI**), and **Microsoft Azure AI.**
3. **Monitor AI-Related GitHub Repositories:** Watch and contribute to open-source AI projects to observe changes in models, datasets, and development best practices.
4. **Attend AI Conferences and Webinars:** Participate in events like **NeurIPS, Black Hat AI,** Rivest-Shamir-Adleman (**RSA**) **AI Summit,** or vendor-specific briefings (e.g., Microsoft Ignite) to hear directly from industry leaders.
5. **Use Threat Intelligence Platforms with AI Risk Feeds:** Platforms like Recorded Future or Anomali may include monitoring for emerging AI-based threats, such as adversarial ML or prompt injection.
6. **Follow AI Regulatory and Policy Updates:** Track developments from **NIST, EU AI Act,** and **OECD AI principles** to assess regulatory impact on your organization's AI tools.
7. **Benchmark Against AI Maturity Models:** Continuously assess internal capabilities using models like the AI Maturity Model (e.g., Deloitte, IBM, or custom frameworks) to identify areas for growth.
8. **Monitor AI Ethics and Governance Initiatives:** Stay updated on best practices and tools for bias detection, fairness auditing, and explainability from organizations like **Partnership on AI** and **OpenAI.**
9. **Engage in AI Labs and Pilot Testing:** Collaborate with internal or external AI labs to prototype new tools, test performance, and monitor real-world adaptability and risk.
10. **Maintain a Watchlist of Emerging AI Tools:** Use internal dashboards or wikis to track and assess potential tools for cybersecurity, audit automation, data analytics, or decision support.

6.11 PERIODIC SELF-ASSESSMENTS

Conducting a **Cybersecurity Audit AI Self-Assessment** enables organizations to evaluate the maturity, effectiveness, and alignment of AI tools and processes within the cybersecurity audit life cycle. This self-assessment typically begins by identifying the scope of AI usage – such as risk detection, control testing automation, or anomaly monitoring – and then reviewing how well these applications align with the organization's cybersecurity audit objectives. Key elements to assess include model performance (e.g., accuracy, precision), data governance, explainability, and compliance with regulatory or ethical standards. Organizations should also evaluate whether the AI models used are continuously validated and updated, especially in response to new cybersecurity threats or audit requirements.

The self-assessment should incorporate input from multidisciplinary stakeholders, including audit teams, IT security, legal, and data science professionals. A structured checklist or maturity model can guide this process, helping identify gaps in areas like transparency, fairness, bias mitigation, and agility. The goal is to ensure that AI applications enhance, not compromise, the integrity of the audit process. Additionally, results from the self-assessment should inform improvement plans, including training needs, updated governance policies, and strategic investments in AI capabilities. Regular self-assessments foster trust, accountability, and continuous improvement in AI-augmented cybersecurity auditing.

Cybersecurity audit AI self-assessment checklist

1. **AI Purpose and Alignment**
   - Have you clearly defined the purpose of using AI in your cybersecurity audit?
   - Does the AI application support specific audit objectives (e.g., risk identification, control evaluation)?
   - Are the use cases approved and aligned with organizational priorities?
2. **Model Performance and Validation**
   - Have accuracy, precision, and recall been measured and documented?
   - Are models regularly tested against independent benchmarks or datasets?
   - Are results reproducible across multiple audit scenarios?
3. **Data Governance and Integrity**
   - Is training and test data relevant, current, and free from bias?
   - Are data sources documented and approved for audit use?
   - Is sensitive or regulated data protected (e.g., encrypted, anonymized)?
4. **Bias and Fairness**
   - Has the AI model been tested for potential bias (e.g., gender, geography)?
   - Are mitigation strategies in place to address identified biases?
   - Is there documentation explaining how fairness is ensured?
5. **Explainability and Transparency**
   - Can the AI output be understood and explained to stakeholders?
   - Are model decisions documented and traceable?
   - Are audit staff trained on how the AI system works?

6. **Security and Privacy Controls**
    - Are logical and physical security controls applied to the AI system?
    - Are access controls in place for sensitive model and data assets?
    - Has the AI system undergone vulnerability or penetration testing?
7. **Regulatory and Ethical Compliance**
    - Does the AI solution comply with industry-specific regulations (e.g., NIST, GDPR, Health Insurance Portability and Accountability Act (HIPAA))?
    - Have legal and ethics reviews been completed?
    - Is there a Responsible AI framework adopted by the organization?
8. **Agility and Responsiveness**
    - Can the AI system quickly adapt to new cybersecurity threats or audit priorities?
    - Is there a process for incorporating emerging risks into AI models?
    - Are outputs delivered in real-time or near real-time?
9. **Stakeholder Engagement and Adoption**
    - Are audit and cybersecurity and privacy professionals engaged in the AI life cycle?
    - Is there training or documentation available for AI use in audits?
    - Are decision-makers confident in using AI-informed audit findings?
10. **Continuous Improvement**
    - Is there a regular schedule for reviewing and improving AI models?
    - Are lessons learned from AI audits captured and acted upon?
    - Is performance tracked against defined success metrics?

6.12 MEASURING SUCCESS: CYBERSECURITY AUDIT KEY METRICS FOR EVALUATING AI PERFORMANCE

When evaluating the success of **cybersecurity audit AI applications,** it is essential to use metrics that reflect both **technical performance** and **audit effectiveness** (Version 1, 2023). Below is a structured breakdown of relevant success metrics:

1. **Accuracy and Precision**
    - **True Positive Rate (TPR):** Measures the ability of the AI to correctly detect cybersecurity threats or control gaps.
    - **False Positive Rate (FPR):** Evaluates how often the AI flags non-issues, which can lead to alert fatigue or inefficiencies.
    - **Precision:** The proportion of true positive results among all positive predictions, ensuring relevance in audit findings.
    - **Vulnerability Identification Rate:** Measures the percentage of known vulnerabilities detected by AI-powered scanning tools.

2. **Model Robustness and Reliability**
   - **Model Drift Detection:** Assesses whether the AI model maintains performance over time or requires retraining due to environmental or behavioral changes.
   - **Resilience to Adversarial Inputs:** Indicates how well the model withstands malicious attempts to evade detection.
   - **AI Bias Detection and Mitigation:** Measures the effectiveness of AI in identifying and mitigating bias in algorithms and data used for security audits.
   - **AI Explainability and Transparency:** Evaluates the extent to which AI models can explain their decision-making processes to auditors, building trust and confidence.
3. **Efficiency and Speed**
   - **Mean Time to Detect (MTTD):** Measures the average time it takes the AI to identify a security incident.
   - **Mean Time to Respond (MTTR):** Measures the average time it takes the AI to respond and contain a detected incident.
   - **Audit Time Savings:** Measures the reduction in time required to complete audit tasks when using AI tools, compared to traditional methods.
4. **Operational Efficiency**
   - **Audit Cycle Time Reduction:** Compares pre- and post-AI implementation time taken to complete audit activities.
   - **Automation Rate:** Measures the percentage of audit tasks that can be automated without compromising quality.
   - **Resource Optimization:** Evaluates reductions in manual labor hours or reallocations to higher-value activities.
5. **Business and Audit Impact**
   - Risk Detection Improvement: Tracks the increase in detected and mitigated risks due to AI insights.
   - **Control Effectiveness Ratings:** Measures improvements in control assurance following AI-driven audits.
   - Compliance Rate Changes: Compares regulatory or policy compliance before and after AI adoption.
   - **Reduced Risk Exposure:** Measures the decrease in potential financial or reputational damage due to identified and mitigated risks.
   - **Improved Risk Scoring:** Evaluates how AI-powered risk assessments improve the accuracy and effectiveness of risk scoring methodologies.
6. **Stakeholder Confidence and Adoption**
   - **User Satisfaction Scores:** Gathers feedback from auditors, IT staff, and executives on AI utility and usability.
   - **Audit Committee Endorsement:** Reflects senior management trust in AI-generated findings and insights.
   - **Change Management Success:** Measures of training adoption, cultural acceptance, and integration into existing audit workflows.

- **User Adoption Rate:** Tracks how frequently auditors utilize the AI tools and integrate them into their workflow.
- Ease of Use: Measures the learning curve and overall usability of the AI platform for auditors.
- **Integration with Existing Security Tools:** Evaluates how seamlessly the AI tools integrate with other security solutions and audit platforms.

7. **Agility and Responsiveness**
   - **Time to Insight:** Evaluates how quickly AI can identify and report on emerging threats or control failures.
   - **Real-time Alerting Accuracy:** Assesses the promptness and correctness of AI-generated alerts in dynamic environments.

6.13 AI BILL OF RIGHTS: WHAT YOU SHOULD KNOW

The **AI Bill of Rights**, introduced by the White House Office of Science and Technology Policy in 2022 (United States Government, 2022), outlines key principles to guide the development and use of AI in ways that protect the rights of the public. It emphasizes protections such as **data privacy, algorithmic transparency, freedom from discrimination**, and the right to **human alternatives** when interacting with automated systems. The framework is non-binding but serves as a policy blueprint for federal agencies, technology developers, and institutions deploying AI systems. Its goal is to promote trustworthy AI that aligns with democratic values, civil rights, and public safety. By encouraging accountability and fairness, the AI Bill of Rights helps ensure that AI technologies are used responsibly and ethically (Glover & Koss, 2024).

Following all government policies related to AI is essential to ensure legal compliance, ethical standards, and public trust in the use of emerging technologies. These policies provide a framework for mitigating risks such as bias, discrimination, data misuse, and unintended consequences of automated decision-making. Adherence to regulations like the AI Bill of Rights, the NIST AI RMF, and evolving global guidelines support responsible innovation while protecting individual rights and societal interests. Moreover, compliance helps organizations avoid reputational damage, legal penalties, and operational setbacks that can result from unchecked or non-compliant AI deployment. In a rapidly evolving regulatory landscape, staying aligned with government directives reinforces organizational integrity and long-term sustainability in AI adoption.

6.14 EXAMPLE CYBERSECURITY PROMPTS

The example cybersecurity prompts in this section are provided as examples to help guide discussions with your primary and secondary cybersecurity professionals. Several prompts may also support audit engagements and facilitate more insightful evaluations. Additionally, using these prompts can contribute to building stronger cross-functional partnerships within your organization.

⚠ **Caution:** Confirm that the Generative AI tool is secure and approved by audit management before executing prompts.

1. **Security Tool Recommendations**
   - "*Recommend network monitoring tools for a mid-sized organization with limited SOC staff.*"
   - "*What Endpoint Detection and Response (EDR) solutions would you suggest for detecting fileless malware in real time?*"
2. **Control or Framework Recommendations**
   - "*Based on NIST Cybersecurity Framework (CSF), what controls should be prioritized after a ransomware incident?*"
   - "*Suggest ISO 27001 clauses that align with multi-factor authentication requirements.*"
3. **Vulnerability Management**
   - "*What patch management tools are best suited for hybrid cloud environments?*"
   - "*Recommend actions for mitigating a high (Common Vulnerability Scoring System) (CVSS) score vulnerability found in Apache.*"
4. **Cybersecurity Training Content**
   - "*Recommend training modules for non-technical staff on phishing awareness.*"
   - "*What topics should be covered in a red team training program for ethical hackers?*"
5. **AI Model Use for Threat Detection**
   - "*What ML models are recommended for detecting insider threats based on behavioral anomalies?*"
   - "*Provide an example of a supervised model for classifying malicious vs. benign web traffic.*"
6. **Policy and Procedure Guidance**
   - "*Suggest elements to include in a bring your own device (BYOD) cybersecurity policy.*"
   - "*Recommend policy updates for remote work environments based on recent threat trends.*"
7. **Governance and Compliance**
   - "*What cybersecurity compliance frameworks are best for healthcare organizations?*"
   - "*Based on Capability Maturity Model Certification (CMMC) Level 2, what documentation should be in place for incident response?*"
8. **Use Case-Specific Prompt Examples**
   - **For a Security Operations Center (SOC):** "*We recently detected multiple login attempts from foreign IPs. What tools and processes would you recommend to strengthen our detection and response capabilities?*"

- **For an Auditor:** "*What logs or artifacts should be reviewed to validate firewall configuration compliance under NIST SP 800-53 (Rev. 5)?*"
- **For a CISO:** "*What are the top 5 cybersecurity metrics to present to the board to show return on investment (ROI) and risk reduction?*"

6.15 EXAMPLE ADDITIONAL RESOURCES AND REFERENCES

Readers should consider the additional resources and references noted in the book chapter because they offer valuable opportunities to deepen understanding, expand knowledge, and apply concepts more effectively. These materials often provide real-world examples, expert insights, and practical tools that complement the core content. They can also guide readers to current trends, evolving technologies, and authoritative voices in the field, especially in dynamic areas like AI and cybersecurity. Exploring these references encourages continuous learning and helps readers stay informed and competitive. They serve as trusted pathways for extending learning beyond the chapter and into practical application.

6.15.1 GitHub

GitHub is a leading platform for version control and collaborative software development. Built on Git, it allows developers to manage code changes, track issues, and collaborate across teams and projects. With features like pull requests, branching, and continuous integration, GitHub streamlines the software development life cycle (GitHub Docs, n.d.). It is widely used for both open-source and private development efforts across industries.

Key Features of GitHub

- **Version Control:** GitHub allows developers to track and manage changes to code over time. Each version (or *commit*) can be reviewed, rolled back, or merged with others.
- **Repositories:** Projects are organized into *repositories*, which contain all the files, revision history, and sometimes documentation (e.g., README files).
- **Branching and Merging:** Developers can create branches to work on features or fixes independently. Once changes are ready, branches can be merged into the main codebase (often called main or master).
- **Collaboration Tools:** GitHub supports pull requests, code reviews, issue tracking, and discussions, allowing teams to collaborate efficiently.
- **Continuous Integration/Continuous Deployment (CI/CD):** GitHub integrates with tools and workflows to automate testing, deployment, and other development operations.

- **GitHub Actions:** A built-in CI/CD system that allows users to automate tasks such as building, testing, and deploying code from GitHub.
- **Community and Open Source:** GitHub hosts millions of open-source projects, making it a hub for sharing, contributing to, and discovering code.
- **Security and Access Control:** Offers features such as role-based access, two-factor authentication, secret scanning, and dependency vulnerability alerts.
- Use Cases
  - Individual developers managing personal projects
  - Teams collaborate on private repositories
  - Open-source contributors working across global projects
  - Organizations integrating DevOps pipelines
- **Owned by:** GitHub is owned by **Microsoft**, which acquired it in 2018.

6.15.2 Chatbot systems sources

Chatbots are AI-powered programs designed to simulate human conversation and interact with users through text or voice interfaces. They are commonly used in customer service, technical support, and digital assistants to provide quick, automated responses to frequently asked questions. Chatbots can be rule-based, responding to specific keywords, or AI-driven, using NLP to understand context and provide more dynamic interactions. They help organizations reduce response times, increase availability, and enhance user engagement. As chatbot technology advances, it is being integrated into websites, mobile apps, and messaging platforms to support a wide range of business functions (IBM, n.d.a).

6.15.2.1 Articles and vendors

Fin. T. (2025, March 7). 6 Types of Chatbots and How to Choose the Right One for your Business. IBM. Retrieved from https://www.ibm.com/think/topics/chatbot-types

IBM (2021, October 15). What is a Chatbot? Retrieved from https://www.ibm.com/think/topics/chatbots

Rebelo, M. (2025, March 4). The Best AI Chatbots in 2025. Zapier. Retrieved from https://zapier.com/blog/best-ai-chatbot/

6.15.2.2 Courses and tutorials

1. **Coursera – Building Chatbots with Google Dialogflow**
   - Hands-on training in creating conversational agents
   - https://www.coursera.org/search?query=chatbot
2. **Udemy – The Complete Chatbot Developer Course**
   - Covers chatbot development using Dialogflow, Node.js, and Facebook Messenger
   - https://www.udemy.com/courses/search/?src=ukw&q=chatbot

3. **edX – AI Chatbots Without Programming (IBM)**
    - Non-technical approach using IBM Watson Assistant
    - https://www.edx.org/search?q=chatbot
4. **LinkedIn Learning – Creating Chatbots with Microsoft Power Virtual Agents**
    - Business-oriented chatbot creation without coding
    - https://www.linkedin.com/learning

6.15.2.3 💻 Chatbot platforms and tools

1. **ChatGPT (OpenAI)**
    - Advanced conversational AI that can be embedded into apps or accessed via API
    - https://platform.openai.com
2. **Google Dialogflow**
    - NLP-powered platform ideal for voice and chat interfaces
    - https://dialogflow.cloud.google.com
3. **Microsoft Power Virtual Agents**
    - Business-friendly tool for creating chatbots within the Microsoft ecosystem
    - https://powervirtualagents.microsoft.com
4. **IBM Watson Assistant**
    - Enterprise-grade chatbot platform with AI and analytics integration
    - https://www.ibm.com/cloud/watson-assistant
5. **Rasa (Open Source)**
    - Developer-friendly Python framework for building contextual, on-premise chatbots
    - https://rasa.com

6.15.2.4 📘 Books

1. **"Designing Bots" by Amir Shevat:** Covers chatbot UX, development, and deployment strategies.
2. **"The Most Human Human" by Brian Christian:** A philosophical and practical exploration of AI-human conversation.
3. **"Building Chatbots with Python" by Sumit Raj**
    - Step-by-step guide using Python and NLP libraries.

6.15.2.5 🧪 Practice platforms and communities

1. **BotPress Playground:** Low-code development tool for building and testing bots.
2. **GitHub:** Explore chatbot code repositories for various platforms.
3. **Stack Overflow, Reddit, and OpenAI Developer Forum:** Engage with chatbot developer communities for troubleshooting and tips.

6.15.3 Predictive analytics sources

Predictive analytics involves using historical data, statistical algorithms, and ML techniques to forecast future outcomes. It helps organizations anticipate trends, identify risks, and make data-driven decisions. Common applications include customer behavior prediction, fraud detection, and demand forecasting. By leveraging predictive models, businesses can gain a competitive edge through proactive strategies and optimized operations (GoogleCloud, n.d.).

6.15.3.1 Articles and vendors

1. Fortinet (n.d.). What Is Cybersecurity Analytics? Retrieved from https://www.fortinet.com/resources/cyberglossary/cybersecurity-analytics
2. Google Cloud (n.d.). What Is Predictive Analytics. Retrieved from https://cloud.google.com/learn/what-is-predictive-analytics?hl=en
3. IBM (2022, August 8). What Is redictive Analytics? Retrieved from https://www.ibm.com/think/topics/predictive-analytics?utm_content=SRCWW&p1=Search&p4=43700081742487018&p5=p&p9=58700008227896134&gad_source=1&gad_campaignid=19477235036&gbraid=0AAAAAD-_QsS5Mq-92UG-jhLPu8CFloIw6&gclid=Cj0KCQjwxdXBBhDEARIsAAUkP6ikbyo-d_k3W1GTmPoYFYdK_B6kOF26EarvcFjPIeXiO1kc7TxsWPEaAg-0EALw_wcB&gclsrc=aw.ds
4. Lawton, G. (2025, January 15). 8 Top Predictive Analytics Tools for 2025. *TechTarget*. Retrieved from https://www.techtarget.com/searchbusinessanalytics/tip/6-top-predictive-analytics-tools#:~:text=Here%2C%20we%20profile%20eight%20tools,SAP%20Analytics%20Cloud%20and%20SAS.

6.15.3.2 Courses and tutorials

1. **Coursera – Predictive Analytics for Business** (**by Udacity**)
   - Covers data wrangling, model building, and evaluating models in business contexts
     - https://www.coursera.org/search?query=predictive%20analytics&utm_medium=sem&utm_source=gg&utm_campaign=b2c_namer_x_coursera_ftcof_courseraplus_cx_dr_bau_gg_sem_bd-ex_us-ca_en_m_hyb_25-04_core-exact&campaignid=22465087598&adgroupid=178346929196&device=c&keyword=coursera&matchtype=e&network=g&devicemodel=&creativeid=747472848207&assetgroupid=&targetid=kwd-36262515261&extensionid=&placement=&gad_source=1&gad_campaignid=22465087598&gbraid=0AAAAADdKX6a4ptTXrJZ4rxgTCqeAKqsgm&gclid=Cj0KCQjwxdXBBhDEARIsAAUkP6hUTbfY-IaaM1bzkrfIYAfDBb4yoxBAU8mVLQGEerpcKUUvHgWO89MaAh1mEALw_wcBedX – Applied Predictive Analytics (Columbia University)

- Graduate-level focus with case-based applications
    - https://www.edx.org/search?q=predictive%20analytics

2. **LinkedIn Learning – Predictive Analytics Essential Training**
    - Great overview for business professionals and beginner analysts
    - https://www.linkedin.com/learning/search?keywords=predictive%20analytics

6.15.3.3 📚 Books

1. **"Data Science for Business" by Foster Provost and Tom Fawcett**
    - Foundational book linking predictive models with strategic decision-making
2. **"Predictive Analytics: The Power to Predict Who Will Click, Buy, Lie, or Die" by Eric Siegel**
    - Highly accessible book with real-world applications
3. **"Practical Time Series Forecasting with R" by Galit Shmueli**
    - Ideal for those interested in time series-based predictive modeling

6.15.3.4 🗁 Libraries and tools

In the evolving landscape of data science and predictive analytics, a wide array of tools and libraries empower analysts and data professionals to build robust models and generate actionable insights. Together, these tools form a versatile ecosystem for data-driven decision-making across industries.

1. **Python Libraries**
    - scikit-learn: ML models (regression, classification, etc.).
    - statsmodels: Statistical modeling, including time series.
    - xgboost, lightgbm: Advanced tree-based models often used in competitions.
2. **R Packages**
    - caret, forecast, randomForest, prophet.
    - RStudio offers extensive documentation and interactive visualization.
3. **Power BI/Tableau**
    - Provide predictive analytics through built-in forecasting and Python/R integration.
4. **IBM SPSS Modeler**
    - Drag-and-drop tool for predictive analytics; widely used in enterprise environments.

6.15.3.5 🧪 Practice platforms

Kaggle and Google Colab both offer excellent environments for hands-on practice in data science, ML, and AI, but they serve slightly different roles.

1. **Kaggle:** https://www.kaggle.com – Includes datasets, kernels, and competitions. Use Kaggle for structured learning, real-world competitions, and community-driven insights.
   - **Competitions:** Real-world challenges hosted by companies or organizations; great for testing skills under realistic conditions.
   - **Datasets:** A large library of public datasets for exploration and modeling.
   - **Code Notebooks:** Interactive Python notebooks where you can experiment and share code.
   - **Courses (Kaggle Learn):** Short, practical tutorials on Python, ML, data visualization, NLP, etc.
   - **Community Collaboration:** Learn from others through shared notebooks and discussion forums.
2. **Google Colab:** https://colab.research.google.com/ – Free Jupyter notebooks in the cloud, ideal for modeling practice. Use Google Colab for flexible, cloud-based coding and experimentation with more control over your custom projects.
   - **Interactive Python Notebooks:** Cloud-based Jupyter notebooks with free access to graphics processing unit/tensor processing units (GPUs/TPUs) – ideal for training ML models.
   - **Practice with Libraries:** Direct support for TensorFlow, PyTorch, pandas, scikit-learn, and others.
   - **Custom Projects:** Build and test your own ML/AI projects with access to Google Drive and GitHub.
   - **Educational Labs:** Many tutorials and labs (e.g., from TensorFlow.org or DeepLearning.AI) are built on Colab.

6.15.4 Recommender system sources

Recommender systems are AI tools designed to suggest relevant items to users based on their preferences, behavior, or similarities to other users. Commonly used in e-commerce, streaming platforms, and social media, these systems enhance user experience by personalizing content delivery. They typically use collaborative filtering, content-based filtering, or hybrid approaches to generate recommendations. Recommender systems play a key role in driving user engagement and increasing conversion rates (Veras et al., 2015).

6.15.4.1 Articles

Caballar, R. D., & Stryker, C. (2024, June 19). What is a recommendation engine? *IBM*. Retrieved from https://www.ibm.com/think/topics/recommendation-engine

Casalegno, F. (2022, November 24). Recommender Systems – A Complete Guide to Machine Learning Models. *Medium*. Retrieved from https://medium.com/data-science/recommender-systems-a-complete-guide-to-machine-learning-models-96d3f94ea748

Roy, D., & Dutta, M. (2022, May 3). A Systematic Review and Research Perspective on Recommender Systems. *SpringerOpen*. Retrieved from https://journalofbigdata.springeropen.com/articles/10.1186/s40537-022-00592-5

6.15.5 Mastering recommender systems: Tools, courses, and learning paths

Here are several high-quality programming resources for learning and building **recommender systems.**

6.15.5.1 Courses and tutorials

1. **Coursera – Recommender Systems Specialization**
   - Offered by the University of Minnesota.
   - Covers collaborative filtering, content-based filtering, and hybrid models.
   - https://www.coursera.org/specializations/recommender-systems
2. **fast.ai – Collaborative Filtering**
   - Practical course using PyTorch and real datasets
   - https://course.fast.ai
3. **Kaggle Learn – Recommender Systems**
   - Hands-on mini-course with Python code and exercises
   - https://www.kaggle.com/learn

6.15.5.2 Books

1. **"Recommender Systems: The Textbook" by Charu C. Aggarwal**
   - Academic and comprehensive; covers algorithms and evaluation strategies.
   - Ideal for deeper theoretical understanding.
2. **"Hands-On Recommendation Systems with Python" by Rounak Banik**
   - Focused on implementation using Python libraries like scikit-learn, pandas, and surprise.

6.15.5.3 Libraries and frameworks

1. **Surprise (Python)**
   - Easy-to-use library for building and analyzing recommender systems.
   - https://surprise.readthedocs.io
2. **LightFM (Python)**
   - Hybrid recommender using matrix factorization and content-based features.
   - https://www.stepbystepdatascience.com/hybrid-recommender-lightfm-python

3. **TensorFlow Recommenders (TFRS)**
    - Deep learning-based recommendation with TensorFlow.
    - https://www.tensorflow.org/recommenders
4. **RecBole**
    - Comprehensive framework supporting various models and datasets.
    - https://recbole.io

6.15.6 Robotic process automation (RPA) system sources

Robotic process automation (RPA) is a technology that uses software robots, or "bots," to automate repetitive, rule-based tasks traditionally performed by humans. These tasks often include data entry, invoice processing, report generation, and system integration. RPA improves efficiency, reduces human error, and frees up staff to focus on higher-value activities. It can be deployed across various industries, including finance, healthcare, and cybersecurity, to streamline operations and improve compliance. When combined with AI, RPA can manage more complex decision-making processes, further enhancing its capabilities (IBM, n.d.b).

6.15.6.1 Articles and vendors

Amos, Z. (n.d). *8 Best use cases for robotic process automation in cybersecurity*. Global Cybersecurity Alliance. Retrieved from https://gca.isa.org/blog/8-best-use-cases-for-robotic-process-automation-in-cybersecurity

Cyberark (2025). What Is Robotic Process Automation (RPA)? Retrieved from https://www.cyberark.com/what-is/robotic-process-automation/

Rosensweig, S. (n.d.). RPA: Opportunity and Responsibility for Internal Audit. *PWC*. Retrieved from https://www.pwc.com/us/en/services/consulting/cybersecurity-risk-regulatory/library/robotic-process-automation-internal-audit.html

6.15.6.2 Mastering robotic process automation systems: tools, courses, and learning paths

6.15.6.2.1 Courses and training

1. **UiPath Academy (Free)**
    - Offers beginner to advanced RPA courses including certification paths.
    - https://academy.uipath.com/courses?product=4
2. **Automation Anywhere University**
    - Provides training on RPA development, bot creation, and control rooms.
    - https://university.automationanywhere.com

3. **Coursera – Robotic Process Automation Specialization**
   - Covers RPA concepts, tools, and real-world use cases.
   - https://www.coursera.org
4. **LinkedIn Learning – RPA Learning Paths**
   - Business and technical overviews, vendor-neutral basics.
   - https://www.linkedin.com/learning

6.15.6.2.2 Books

1. **"Robotic Process Automation and Cognitive Automation" by Mary C. Lacity and Leslie P. Willcocks**
   - A practical guide for business and IT professionals.
2. **"Learning Robotic Process Automation" by Alok Mani Tripathi**
   - Focuses on building RPA bots with UiPath.
3. **"Intelligent Automation" by Pascal Bornet, Ian Barkin, and Jochen Wirtz**
   - Covers RPA in the context of AI, process improvement, and digital transformation.

6.15.6.2.3 Tools and platforms

1. **UiPath** – Industry leader with a strong community and open-source components.
   https://www.uipath.com
2. **Automation Anywhere** – Enterprise-focused RPA platform with a cloud-native interface.
   https://www.automationanywhere.com
3. **Blue Prism** – Offers RPA with strong security and governance features.
   https://www.blueprism.com
4. **Power Automate (Microsoft)** – Integrates RPA with Microsoft 365 and Azure services.
   https://powerautomate.microsoft.com

6.15.6.2.4 Practice platforms and communities

1. UiPath Community Edition – Free download to build and test RPA bots.
2. Kaggle and GitHub – Explore open-source RPA workflows and challenges.
3. Stack Overflow & Reddit – Active forums for troubleshooting and best practices.

6.16 SUMMARY

This chapter emphasized the importance of sustaining and enhancing success in cybersecurity auditing and AI adoption through measurable metrics, regular self-assessments, and effective information sharing. It outlined how organizations can remain agile and initiative-taking by continuously monitoring emerging AI tools and integrating new capabilities into their practices. The chapter also provided strategies for fostering collaboration and leveraging authoritative resources to support informed decision-making and ongoing professional development. Together, these practices enable organizations to adapt to change, mitigate risks, and drive continuous improvement.

The future of cybersecurity auditing is not predefined – it will be shaped by those willing to challenge conventions, embrace innovation, and lead with curiosity. Whether you are just beginning your journey or are an experienced auditor seeking innovative approaches, you have the opportunity to transform not only how audits are performed but how they are perceived. Stay adaptable. Continue learning. Leveraging technology is not a replacement for judgment but as a partner in driving better outcomes. The next chapter of cybersecurity auditing is yours to write.

Afterword

As we conclude this exploration of transforming cybersecurity auditing through agility and artificial intelligence (AI), I encourage readers to reflect on how the profession is evolving – and how we must evolve with it. The traditional audit mindset, while still grounded in rigor and accountability, must expand to include flexibility, creativity, and collaboration. Agility in audit is not about moving fast without structure; it's about responsiveness, intentionality, and the ability to adapt audit processes in real time based on risk intelligence and organizational needs.

Throughout this book, I've drawn upon my experiences as both a cybersecurity leader and an educator. Teaching adult learners has shown me that professional growth never stops and that cross-disciplinary thinking often sparks the most innovative breakthroughs. Whether it's integrating AI into audit workflows, partnering across departments to uncover systemic risks, or reimagining reporting for impact, the future of internal audit lies in our willingness to think differently, act decisively, and learn continuously.

The AI landscape is evolving at an unprecedented pace, introducing new capabilities that can revolutionize how cybersecurity auditors detect risk, evaluate controls, and support decision-making. From natural language processing and anomaly detection to generative models that can simulate attack patterns or automate audit documentation, AI is becoming integral to both threat landscapes and the tools we use to navigate them. However, with this rapid advancement comes increased responsibility. Cybersecurity auditors must remain vigilant, continuously investigating how AI technologies are integrated into organizational processes and assessing their implications for data privacy, algorithmic bias, and system integrity. Staying informed about emerging AI trends, regulatory developments, and ethical considerations ensures that auditors not only leverage AI effectively but also fulfill their critical role in safeguarding systems and promoting trustworthy innovation.

My hope is that this book equips you not only with tools and strategies but also with confidence – to question the status quo, to leverage new technologies responsibly, and to build stronger partnerships within your organization. Cybersecurity auditing is a critical function, and when done with purpose and agility, it becomes a driver of organizational resilience and trust. Thank you for taking this journey with me – and for being part of the profession's transformation. Continue to be inquisitive and apply critical thinking throughout your professional career, and share your learnings with others – because it is through curiosity, reflection, and collaboration that we not only grow individually but also strengthen the cybersecurity audit community as a whole.

Please join me in continuing the conversation on this book's topic by joining the LinkedIn group: *Artificial Intelligence and Agility in Cybersecurity Auditing and Risk Management* (https://www.linkedin.com/groups/13303005/manage/membership/requested/).

Dr. Linda Kostic

References

Agile Manifesto. (n.d.). Principles behind the Agile Manifesto. Retrieved from https://agilemanifesto.org/principles.html

Amazon Personalize. (2025). Amazon Personalize: Developer Guide. Retrieved from https://docs.aws.amazon.com/pdfs/personalize/latest/dg/personalize-dg.pdf#what-is-personalize

Amazon Web Services (AWS). (2025a). Amazon Computer Vision. Retrieved from https://aws.amazon.com/what-is/computer-vision/#:~:text=Computer%20vision%20can%20analyze%20images,machine%20maintenance%20and%20safety%20issues

Amazon Web Services (AWS). (2025b). AWS GovCloud (US). Retrieved from https://aws.amazon.com/govcloud-us/?ams%23interactive-card-vertical%23pattern-data.filter=%257B%2522filters%2522%253A%255B%255D%257D

Amazon Web Services (AWS). (n.d.a). What is Scrum? Retrieved from https://aws.amazon.com/what-is/scrum/

Amazon Web Services (AWS). (n.d.b). What's the Difference between Supervised and Unsupervised Machine Learning? Retrieved from https://aws.amazon.com/compare/the-difference-between-machine-learning-supervised-and-unsupervised/#:~:text=Supervised%20and%20unsupervised%20learning%20are%20two%20distinct%20categories%20of%20algorithms

Amazon Web Services (AWS). (n.d.c). What is GPT? Retrieved from

Amblard-Ladurantie, C. (2023, November 17). Three Lines Model Update. Mega. Retrieved from https://www.mega.com/blog/three-lines-model-update#:~:text=The%20Three%20Lines%20of%20Defense,the%20Three%20Lines%20Model%20Work?

American Psychological Association. (2006). Multitasking: Switching costs. Retrieved from https://www.apa.org/research/action/multitask

Anastasiades, B., & Fritchie, W. (2024, August 9). The Sarbanes-Oxley Act: A Comprehensive Overview. AuditBoard. Retrieved from https://auditboard.com/blog/sarbanes-oxley-act

Archer. (n.d.). Archer GRC Solution. Retrieved from https://www.archerirm.com/content/grc

Association for Project Management (APM). (n.d.). What is agile project management? Retrieved from https://www.apm.org.uk/resources/find-a-resource/agile-project-management/#:~:text=Agile%20%E2%80%93%20a%20project%20management%20approach,%2C%20do%2C%20review%20daily%20session

Astley, P., & Regelbrugge, A. (n.d.). Modernizing the three lines of defense model: An IA perspective. Retrieved from https://www.deloitte.com/us/en/services/consulting/articles/modernizing-the-three-lines-of-defense-model.html

Bergmann, D., & Stryker, C. (2023, November 23). What Is an Autoencoder? IBM. Retrieved from https://www.ibm.com/think/topics/autoencoder).

Biswas, D. (2025, June 30). Agentic Lifecycle for Enterprise Processes. Medium. Retrieved from https://medium.com/ai-advances/agentification-of-enterprise-processes-0f173554f7b4

BTIT. (n.d.) AI Adoption Maturity Frameworks. Retrieved from https://btit.nz/ai-adoption-maturity-frameworks#:~:text=McKinsey's%20framework%20highlights%20five%20stages%2C%20focusing%20on,AI%20initiatives%20are%20integrated%20across%20multiple%20functions

Cameron, K. S., & Quinn, R. E. (2011). *Diagnosing and changing organizational culture: Based on the competing values framework* (3rd ed.). Jossey-Bass.

Center for Internet Security (CIS). (2025). CIS Controls at a Glance. Retrieved from https://www.cisecurity.org/controls

Chen, M. (2023, December 20). 6 Common AI Model Training Challenges. Oracle Cloud – Artificial Intelligence. Retrieved from https://www.oracle.com/artificial-intelligence/ai-model-training-challenges/

Chia, A. (2025, August 6). What is Natural Language Processing? NLP Explained. Splunk. Retrieved from https://www.splunk.com/en_us/blog/learn/natural-language-processing-nlp.html

Coppini, I., & Moreira, R. (2024, February 26). Modernising the three lines of defence model. An IA perspective. Deloitte. Retrieved from https://www.deloitte.com/mt/en/services/risk-advisory/perspectives/modernising-the-three-lines-of-defence-model.html

Curry, D. (2025, May 15). Microsoft Copilot Revenue and Usage Statistics (2025). Business of Apps. Retrieved from https://www.businessofapps.com/data/microsoft-copilot-statistics/

Cybersecurity & Infrastructure Security Agency. (CISA) (2025). Federal Information Security Modernization Act. Retrieved from https://www.cisa.gov/topics/cyber-threats-and-advisories/federal-information-security-modernization-act#:~:text=Cyber%20Threats%20and%20Advisories,OMB%20in%20developing%20those%20policies.

Darley, J. (2025, January 15). Top 10: AI Tools for Enhancing Cybersecurity. Cyber Magazine. Retrieved from https://cybermagazine.com/top10/top-10-ai-tools-for-enhancing-cybersecurity

Davis, J. E. (2023, January 26). Multitasking and how it affects your brain health. Brown Health. Retrieved from https://www.brownhealth.org/be-well/multitasking-and-how-it-affects-your-brain-health#:~:text=This%20constant%20switching%20taxes%20our,distractible%20and%20prone%20to%20errors.

Deloitte. (2024, August). Technology Trust Ethics. Leadership, Governance, and Workforce Decision-Making About Ethical AI: C-Suite Perspectives. Retrieved from https://www2.deloitte.com/content/dam/Deloitte/us/Documents/about-deloitte/us-ent-pulse-survey.pdf

Defense Information Systems Agency (DISA). (n.d.). Enterprise Mission Assurance Support Service (eMASS). The DoD recommended tool for information system assessment and authorization. Retrieved from https://disa.mil/~/media/Files/DISA/Fact-Sheets/eMASS.pdf

Dennis, A. (2024, February 1). What AI can do for auditors. *Journal of Accountancy*. Retrieved from https://www.journalofaccountancy.com/issues/2024/feb/what-ai-can-do-for-auditors/

Denison, D. R. (1990). *Corporate culture and organizational effectiveness*. Wiley.

Do, D. (2017, August 5). The Five Principles of Lean. The Lean Way. Retrieved from https://theleanway.net/The-Five-Principles-of-Lean#:~:text=The%20five%20principles%20are%20considered,detailed%20overview%20of%20each%20principle.

Dwight, J. (2024). LLMS Security. Building Secure LLMs and Strategies for Mitigating Security Challenges (The Indispensable Guide to LLMs & ChatGPT Security). [Kindle edition]. Independently published.

Essex, D., & Gillis, A. S. (2025, April). What Is Quantum Computing? How It Works and Examples. TechTarget. Retrieved from https://www.techtarget.com/whatis/definition/quantum-computing#:~:text=Quantum%20computing%20is%20an%20emerging,are%20developing%20quantum%20computing%20technology

Fedele, S., & Narayanan, R. (2025). Is a linear approach to internal audit out of line? Bring flexibility to IA with Agile. Deloitte. Retrieved from https://www.deloitte.com/us/en/services/audit-assurance/articles/agile-and-internal-audit-standards.html

Federal Risk and Authorization Management Program (FedRAMP). (2025). FedRAMP 20X Standards and Docs. Retrieved from https://www.fedramp.gov/20x/standards/

Free, C., Macintosh, N., Stein, M., Macintosh, N., & Stein, S. (2007, July/August). Management controls: The organizational fraud triangle of leadership, culture and control in Enron. *Ivey Business Journal.* Issue July/August 2007. Retrieved from https://iveybusinessjournal.com/publication/management-controls-the-organizational-fraud-triangle-of-leadership-culture-and-control-in-enron/#:~:text=The%20contrast%20between%20Enron's%20moral,company's%20elaborate%20web%20of%20controls

Garvin, D. A., & Roberto, M. A. (2005). *Change through persuasion.* Harvard Business Review.

Gaudiello, I., & Zibetti, E. (2016). *Learning robotics, with robotics, by robotics: Educational robotics* (1st ed.). Wiley. https://doi.org/10.1002/9781119335740. Retrieved from https://learning.oreilly.com/library/view/learning-robotics-with/9781786300997/?sso_link=yes&sso_link_from=umgc

Ghosh, B. (2024, November 11). The Key Features That Enable AI Agents. Medium. Retrieved from https://medium.com/@bijit211987/the-key-features-that-enable-ai-agents-3995acd29be7

GitHub Docs. (n.d.) About GitHub and Git. You Can Use GitHub and Git to collaborate on Work. Retrieved from https://docs.github.com/en/get-started/start-your-journey/about-github-and-git

Glover, E., & Rekdal, A. (2025, January 28). 33 Top AI Apps to Know. Built In. Retrieved from https://builtin.com/artificial-intelligence/ai-apps

Glover, E., & Koss, H. (2024, March 19). AI Bill of Rights: What You Should Know. BuiltIn. Retrieved from https://builtin.com/artificial-intelligence/ai-bill-of-rights

Google. (n.d.a). Company Information. Retrieved from https://about.google/company-info/

Google. (n.d.b). Company News. Retrieved from https://blog.google/?utm_source=about.google&utm_medium=referral&utm_campaign=navigation

Google Cloud. (n.d.a) What is Predictive Analytics? Retrieved from https://cloud.google.com/learn/what-is-predictive-analytics?hl=en

Google Cloud. (n.d.b). What is Supervised Learning. Retrieved fromhttps://cloud.google.com/discover/what-is-supervised-learning?hl=en

Google DeepMind. (n.d.). Gemini Research. Retrieved from https://deepmind.google/research/

Google Developers. (2025, February 27). Recommendation Systems. Retrieved from https://developers.google.com/machine-learning/recommendation/overview/types

Haines, J. (2020, August 24). Critical Thinking and Its Importance in Everyday Life. LinkedIn. Retrieved from https://www.linkedin.com/pulse/critical-thinking-its-importance-everyday-life-jason-haines/

Harvard Business Review. (2010, May 4). How (and why) to stop multitasking. https://hbr.org/2010/05/how-and-why-to-stop-multitaski

Hassani, H. S. (2024, September 4). AI Governance: Frameworks, Tools, Best Practices. DataCamp. Retrieved from https://www.datacamp.com/blog/ai-governance

Heskett, J. L. (2012). *The culture cycle: How to shape the unseen force that transforms performance*. FT Press.

Hetler, A. (2023, August). Three lines model. TechTarget. Retrieved from https://www.techtarget.com/searchcio/definition/three-lines-model

Hiatt, J. M. (2006). *ADKAR: A model for change in business, government and our community*. Prosci Learning Center Publications. Retrieved from https://www.researchgate.net/publication/237035168_ADKAR_A_Model_for_Change_in_Business_Government_and_Our_Community

Highsmith, J. (2001). History: The Agile Manifesto. Retrieved from https://agilemanifesto.org/history.html

Hussain, S. (2024, November 20). Reinforcement Learning. Medium. Retrieved from https://papers-100-lines.medium.com/value-based-vs-policy-based-reinforcement-learning-92da766696fd

IBM. (2022, August 8). What Is Predictive Analytics? Retrieved from https://www.ibm.com/think/topics/predictive-analytics

IBM. (2024, August 12). Maximizing compliance: Integrating Gen AI into the financial regulatory framework. Retrieved from https://www.ibm.com/think/insights/maximizing-compliance-integrating-gen-ai-into-the-financial-regulatory-framework

IBM. (n.d.a). What Is a Chatbot? Retrieved from https://www.ibm.com/think/topics/chatbots

IBM. (n.d.b). What Is RPA? Retrieved from https://www.ibm.com/think/topics/rpa#:~:text=RPA%20use%20cases-,What%20is%20RPA?,forms%2C%20moving%20files%20and%20more.

IBM. (n.d.c). What Is an AI Model? Retrieved from https://www.ibm.com/think/topics/ai-model

IBM. (n.d.d). What Is RPA? Retrieved from https://www.ibm.com/think/topics/rpa#:~:text=RPA%20use%20cases-,What%20is%20RPA?,forms%2C%20moving%20files%20and%20more.

Institute of Data. (2024, June 20). Sharpening Your Critical Thinking Skills: Approaches and Exercises for Cybersecurity Experts. Retrieved from https://www.institutedata.com/us/blog/sharpening-your-critical-thinking-skills-approaches-and-exercises-for-cybersecurity-experts/

Institute of Internal Auditors (IIA). (2020). The IIA's Three Lines Model: An Update of the Three Lines of Defense. Retrieved from https://www.theiia.org/globalassets/documents/resources/the-iias-three-lines-model-an-update-of-the-three-lines-of-defense-july-2020/three-lines-model-updated-english.pdf

Institute of Internal Auditors (IIA). (2024a, August). Tone at the Top. Retrieved from https://www.theiia.org/globalassets/site/resources/research-and-reports/tone-at-the-top/2024/august-2024-tone-at-the-top.pdf

Institute of Internal Auditors (IIA). (2024b, January 9). Global Internal Audit Standards. Retrieved from https://www.theiia.org/globalassets/site/standards/editable-versions/globalinternalauditstandards_2024january9_editable.pdf

Institute of Internal Auditors (IIA) Financial Services Audit Center. (2018). Agile Auditing. Sprinting to Change: Reimagining Internal Audit in a Digital World. Retrieved from https://www.theiia.org/globalassets/site/content/articles/industry-knowledge-brief/2018/agile-auditing/iia-fs-agile-auditing.pdf?ref=clarissa-lucas#:~:text=The%20audit%20pods%20%E2%80%94%20built%20one,necessary%20to%20perform%20the%20audits

Integrative Systems. (2025, January 10). Comprehensive List of AS400 commands. Retrieved from https://www.integrativesystems.com/as400-commands/

Internal Audit, Risk and Compliance Private Sector Kenya LinkedIn Group. (2024, July 1). Enhancing Audit Agility with AI and Analytics. LinkedIn Blog. Retrieved from https://www.linkedin.com/pulse/enhancing-audit-agility-ai-analytics-dqsif/

International Organization for Standardization (ISO). (2022). ISO/IEC 27001:2022. Retrieved from https://www.iso.org/standard/27001

International Organization for Standardization/International Electrotechnical Commission (ISO/IEC). (2022). ISO/IEC 27001:2022. Information security, cybersecurity and privacy protection – Information security management systems – Requirements. Retrieved from https://www.iso.org/standard/27001#:~:text=What%20is%20ISO/IEC%2027001,cyber%2Dresilience%20and%20operational%20excellence.

ISACA. (2018). COBIT 2019 Framework. Retrieved from https://store.isaca.org/s/store#/store/browse/detail/a2S4w000004Ko5aEAC

ISACA. (2020, October 30). Standards, Guidelines, Tools and Techniques. Retrieved from https://www.isaca.org/resources/isaca-journal/issues/2020/volume-6/standards-guidelines-tools-and-techniques

ISC2. (2024, September 11). Employers Must Act as Cybersecurity Workforce Growth Stalls and Skills Gaps Widen. Retrieved from https://www.isc2.org/Insights/2024/09/Employers-Must-Act-Cybersecurity-Workforce-Growth-Stalls-as-Skills-Gaps-Widen

Jaleel, A. (2023, January 18). ChatGPT and Leveraging Artificial Intelligence in Auditing. ISACA Now Blog. Retrieved from https://www.isaca.org/resources/news-and-trends/isaca-now-blog/2023/chatgpt-and-leveraging-artificial-intelligence-in-auditing

Johnston, K. R., & Pollock, B. (2023). *HBR guide to critical thinking*. Ascent Audio.

Kanban Zone (n.d.) 5 benefits of Kanban for Toyota Production System. Retrieved from https://kanbanzone.com/2021/5-benefits-of-kanban-for-toyota-production-system/

Kegan, R., & Lahey, L. L. (2001). *The real reason people won't change*. Harvard Business Review.

Keller, S., & Aiken, C.. (2008, May). *McKinsey - The Inconvenient Truth about Change Management*. Retrieved from https://www.scribd.com/document/792708247/McKinsey-The-Inconvenient-Truth-About-Change-Management

Kerner, S. M., & Lutkevich, B. (2025, January 31). 25 of the best large language models in 2025. TechTarget. Retrieved from https://www.techtarget.com/whatis/feature/12-of-the-best-large-language-models#:~:text=Llama,llama.com%20and%20Hugging%20Face.

Kim, D. (2016, June 12). How to save 1,000 SOX hours. AuditBoard. Retrieved from https://www.auditboard.com/blog/save-1000-sox-hours/

Kirvan, P. (2024, November). What is a Waterfall model? Definition and Guide. TechTarget. Retrieved from https://www.techtarget.com/searchsoftwarequality/definition/waterfall-model

Kleinman, Z., & Vallance, C. (2023, May 2). *AI 'Godfather' Geoffrey Hinton warns of dangers as he quits Google*. British Broadcasting Corporatuion (BBC). Retrieved from https://www.bbc.com/news/world-us-canada-65452940

Kniberg, H. (2024, January 20). Generative AI in a nutshell: How to survive and thrive in the age of AI [Video]. YouTube. https://www.youtube.com/watch?v=2IK3DFHRFfw

Kotter, J. P. (1996). *Leading change*. Harvard Business School Press.

Kourinian, A., & Brown, M. (2024). *Addressing transparency & explainability when using AI under global standards*. Bloomberg Law. Retrieved from https://www.mayerbrown.com/-/media/files/perspectives-events/publications/2024/01/addressing-transparency-and-explainability-when-using-ai-under-global-standards.pdf%3Frev=8f001eca513240968f1aea81b4516757

Kulkarni, S. (2024, April 2). Cyber Security Audit Market Advancements Highlighted by Latest Trends, Technological Advancements, Driving Factors, and Forecast until 2030. WhaTech. Retrieved from https://www.whatech.com/og/markets-research/it/800562-cyber-security-audit-market-advancements-highlighted-by-latest-trends-technological-advancements-driving-factors-and-forecast-until-2030.html#:~:text=This%20section%20of%20the%20report,global%20scale%20across%20several%20regions.&text=Evolving%20Threat%20Landscape:%20Cybersecurity%20audits,security%20controls%20and%20identify%20vulnerabilities

Lam, B., & White, G. B. (2016, December 23). The morality of banking in *It's a Wonderful Life*. The Atlantic. Retrieved from https://www.theatlantic.com/business/archive/2016/12/its-a-wonderful-life-banking/511592/

Lean Production. (n.d.). The Ultimate Guide to 5S: Meaning, Methodology, and Implementation. Retrieved from https://www.leanproduction.com/5s/#:~:text=What%20Is%205S?,lean%20production%20tools%20and%20processes

Lean Process Improvement LinkedIn Community. (n.d.). What Are Some Tools or Techniques for Root Cause Analysis in Lean Process Improvement? Retrieved from https://www.linkedin.com/advice/3/what-some-tools-techniques-root-cause#:~:text=Root%20cause%20analysis%20(RCA)%20is,them%20in%20your%20own%20projects.&text=Mamtha%20B.

Lee, W. H. (2025, May 16). Demystify Data Analytics #9: Predictive Analytics Using Prompts. Medium. Retrieved from https://medium.com/@whee.2013/predictive-analytics-using-prompt-workflows-fdc850ff3371

Levy, H. B. (2020, November 2020). History of the auditing world, part 1. *The CPA Journal. 90*(10/11), 50–55. Retrieved from https://www.cpajournal.com/2020/11/25/history-of-the-auditing-world-part-1/

Lewin, K. (1947). Frontiers in group dynamics. *Human Relations*, *1*(1), 5–41.

Liker, J. K. (2004). *The Toyota way: 14 management principles from the world's greatest manufacturer*. McGraw Hill. ISBN: ISBN:0071392319

Lindenfeld-Hall, S. (2022, June 15). Defining Company Culture in the Financial Services Sector. Lattice. Retrieved from https://lattice.com/articles/defining-company-culture-in-the-financial-services-sector

Luo, C. (2022, August 26). Understanding Diffusion Models: A Unified Perspective. Retrieved from https://calvinyluo.com/2022/08/26/diffusion-tutorial.html.

Lutkevich, B. (2024, August). What is an expert system? TechTarget. Retrieved from https://www.techtarget.com/searchenterpriseai/definition/expert-system

Lyon, V., Coppola, M. Yousuf, S., & Bhatnagar (2024, October 3). Cybersecurity Has a Talent Shortage. Here's How to Close the Gap. BCG. Retrieved from https://www.bcg.com/publications/2024/cybersecurity-talent-shortage-close-the-gap

Madenburg, S. (2024, October 30). *Navigating IT security with internal audit in the age of AI*. Wolters Kluwer. Retrieved from https://www.wolterskluwer.com/en/expert-insights/navigating-it-security-with-internal-audit-age-of-ai

Mao, W., Wu, J., Chen, W., Gao, C., Wang, X., & He, X. (2025, March 28). Reinforced prompt personalization for recommendation with large language models. *ACM Transactions on Information Systems*, *43*(3), 1–27. Article No.: 72. https://doi.org/10.1145/371632

Marks, N. (2023, October 30). *Internal audit wastes so much time on policies, documentation, and more!* Norman Marks Press. Retrieved from https://normanmarks.wordpress.com/2023/10/30/internal-audit-wastes-so-much-time-on-policies-documentation-and-more/

Lencioni, P. M.. (2016). *Why organizational health trumps everything else in business.* Harvard Business Review. Retrieved from https://hbr.org/webinar/2016/03/why-organizational-health-trumps-everything-else-in-business#:~:text=In%20this%20age%20of%20informational,Jossey%2DBass%2C%20202002.
McLaughlin, E. (2025, April 14). What Is Lean Management? TechTarget. Retrieved from https://www.techtarget.com/searchcio/definition/lean-management#:~:text=Lean%20management%20is%20an%20approach,to%20improve%20efficiency%20and%20quality
Mehdi, Y. (2023, September 21). Announcing Microsoft Copilot, your everyday AI companion. Official Microsoft Blog. Retrieved from https://blogs.microsoft.com/blog/2023/09/21/announcing-microsoft-copilot-your-everyday-ai-companion/
Mendix. (n.d.). Agile Frameworks: An Overview. Retrieved from https://www.mendix.com/agile-framework/#:~:text=Agile%20methodology%20overview,flexible%20and%20responsive%20to%20change.
Meta (2023, February 24). Introducing LLaMA: A Foundational, 65-Billion-Parameter Large Language Model. Retrieved from https://ai.meta.com/blog/large-language-model-llama-meta-ai/
Milmo, D. (2023, February 2). ChatGPT Reaches 100 Million Users Two Months after Launch. Guardian. Retrieved from https://www.theguardian.com/technology/2023/feb/02/chatgpt-100-million-users-open-ai-fastest-growing-app
More, J. (2022, January 13). How to Apply the Three Lines of Defense. IANS. Retrieved from https://www.iansresearch.com/resources/all-blogs/post/security-blog/2022/01/13/how-to-apply-the-three-lines-of-defense#:~:text=Understanding%20the%20Three%20Lines%20of%20Defense%20*,line%20of%20defense:%20Provides%20independent%20assurance/risk%20assurance.
Moyle, E. (2022, September 21). The three lines of defense as a means to foster, not inhibit, collaboration. *ISACA Journal*, *38*. Retrieved from https://www.isaca.org/resources/news-and-trends/newsletters/atisaca/2022/volume-38/the-three-lines-of-defense-as-a-means-to-foster-not-inhibit-collaboration
National Institute of Standards and Technology (NIST). (2011, September). Information Security Continuous Monitoring (ISCM) for Federal Information Systems and Organizations. Retrieved from https://nvlpubs.nist.gov/nistpubs/Legacy/SP/nistspecialpublication800-137.pdf
National Institute of Standards and Technology (NIST). (2018, December). Risk Management Framework for Information Systems and Organizations: A System Life Cycle Approach for Security and Privacy. Retrieved from https://csrc.nist.gov/pubs/sp/800/37/r2/final
National Institute of Standards and Technology (NIST). (2020a, December 10). Security and Privacy Controls for Information Systems and Organizations. Retrieved from https://www.nist.gov/privacy-framework/nist-privacy-framework-and-cybersecurity-framework-nist-special-publication-800-53
National Institute of Standards and Technology (NIST). (2020b, September). Security and Privacy Controls for Information Systems and Organizations. Retrieved from https://nvlpubs.nist.gov/nistpubs/SpecialPublications/NIST.SP.800-53r5.pdf
National Institute of Standards and Technology (NIST). (2024, February). NIST Cybersecurity Framework 2.0: Resource & Overview Guide. Retrieved from https://nvlpubs.nist.gov/nistpubs/SpecialPublications/NIST.SP.1299.pdf
National Institute of Standards and Technology (NIST). (2025a, May 30). Cybersecurity Framework. Retrieved from https://www.nist.gov/cyberframework
National Institute of Standards and Technology (NIST). (2025b, February 26). Cybersecurity Framework. Retrieved from https://www.nist.gov/cyberframework

Nissim, R., & Greenberg, R. (2025, May 20). From Hype to Confidence: What Makes a Model "Validated" for Enterprise AI. Red Hat. Retrieved from https://www.redhat.com/en/blog/what-makes-model-validated-enterprise-ai#:~:text=AI%20model%20validation%20is%20the,targeting%20key%20enterprise%20use%20cases.

Nguyen, M.-A., & McKeown, P. (2024, October 17). 5 AI auditing frameworks to encourage accountability. Auditboard. Retrieved from https://www.auditboard.com/blog/ai-auditing-frameworks/

OECD. (2022). OECD Framework for the Classification of AI systems. *OECD Digital Economy Papers*, No. 323, OECD Publishing. https://doi.org/10.1787/cb6d9eca-en

Office of the Comptroller of the Currency (OCC). (2019, July). Corporate and Risk Governance. Retrieved from https://occ.gov/publications-and-resources/publications/comptrollers-handbook/files/corporate-risk-governance/pub-ch-corporate-risk.pdf

OpenAI. (2023, March 14). GPT-4 Research. Retrieved from https://openai.com/index/gpt-4-research/

OpenAI ChatGPT 4o. (2024). Large Language Model. Retrieved from https://chat.openai.com/chat

Ophir, E., Nass, C., & Wagner, A. D. (2009). Cognitive control in media multitaskers. *Proceedings of the National Academy of Sciences*, *106*(37), 15583–15587. https://doi.org/10.1073/pnas.0903620106

Ozer, P., & van Schijndel, J. (n.d). How Do You Validate an AI Model. KPMG. Retrieved from https://kpmg.com/nl/en/home/insights/2024/10/how-do-you-validate-an-ai-model.html

Papa, L., Russo, P., Amerini, I., & Zhou, L. (2024, December). A survey on efficient vision transformers: algorithms, techniques, and performance benchmarking. *IEEE Transactions on Pattern Analysis and Machine Intelligence*, *46*(12), 7682–7700. https://doi.org/0.1109/TPAMI.2024.3392941.

Paris, M. (2025, April 12). ChatGPT Hits 1 Billion Users? 'Doubled in Just Weeks' Says OpenAI CEO. Forbes. Retrieved from https://www.forbes.com/sites/martineparis/2025/04/12/chatgpt-hits-1-billion-users-openai-ceo-says-doubled-in-weeks/

PCI Security Standards Council (2018, July). PCI DSS Quick Reference Guide. Retrieved from https://listings.pcisecuritystandards.org/documents/PCI_DSS-QRG-v3_2_1.pdf

Peckham, J. (2025, April 24). Google Gemini Has 350 Million Monthly Users, Far behind ChatGPT Estimates. PCMagazine. Retrieved from https://www.pcmag.com/news/google-gemini-has-350-million-monthly-users-far-behind-chatgpt-estimates

Pradeep, V. (2025, June 18). The Best 5 AI Data Visualization Tools in 2025. Zoho Analytics. Retrieved from https://www.zoho.com/analytics/insightshq/5-best-ai-data-visualization-tools.html

Priority (n.d.). What is the Eisenhower Matrix? How to Use it to Prioritize Tasks. Retrieved from https://www.prioritymanagement.com.au/how-to-use-eisenhower-matrix/#:~:text=The%20Eisenhower%20Decision%20Matrix%2C%20also,Eisenhower.

Purdue Global (n.d.). Generational Differences in the Workplace [Infographic]. Retrieved from https://www.purdueglobal.edu/education-partnerships/generational-workforce-differences-infographic/

PWC (2017). Staying the course toward True North: Navigating disruption. Retrieved from https://www.pwc.com/us/en/risk-assurance/sotp/2017-state-of-the-internal-audit-profession-report.pdf

PWC (2023). Seeing through walls to find new horizons. PWC Global Internal Audit Study 2023. Retrieved from https://www.pwc.com/gx/en/services/audit-assurance/internal-audit/global-internal-audit-study.html

PyTorch (2025, June 16) Reinforcement Learning (DQN) Tutorial. Retrieved from https://docs.pytorch.org/tutorials/intermediate/reinforcement_q_learning.html.
Rao, P. (2023, July 13). How Long it Took for Popular Apps to Reach 100 Million Users. Visual Capitalist. Retrieved from https://www.visualcapitalist.com/threads-100-million-users/
Riley, R. (2024, March 26). A Year of Microsoft Copilot: Accelerating Innovation with AI-Powered Low-Code. Retrieved from https://www.microsoft.com/en-us/power-platform/blog/2024/03/26/a-year-of-microsoft-copilot-accelerating-innovation-with-ai-powered-low-code/
Rogers, E. M. (2003). *Diffusion of innovations* (5th ed.). Free Press.
Ronaghan, S. (2018, August 14). Introduction to Deep Learning: What do I need to know...? Medium. Retrieved from https://srnghn.medium.com/introduction-to-deep-learning-what-do-i-need-to-know-75794ebc4a62
RSI Security. (2020, August 26). What is the NIST Third-Party Risk Management Framework? Retrieved from https://blog.rsisecurity.com/what-is-the-nist-third-party-risk-management-framework/#:~:text=Basics%20of%20the%20Framework,etc.
SAP. (2024, October 29). What is AI Bias? Retrieved from https://www.sap.com/resources/what-is-ai-bias#:~:text=Artificial%20intelligence%20bias%2C%20or%20AI,discrimination%2C%20prejudice%2C%20and%20stereotyping.
Schein, E. H. (2010). *Organizational culture and leadership* (4th ed.). Jossey-Bass.
Schiffman, S. (2008). *The 25 sales habits of highly successful salespeople.* Adams Media.
SentinelOne. (2025, March 31). What is Cyber Security Asset Management? Retrieved from https://www.sentinelone.com/cybersecurity-101/cybersecurity/cyber-security-asset-management/#:~:text=Cybersecurity%20asset%20management%20(CSAM)%20involves,working%20properly%2C%20and%20remediating%20breaches.
Shah, M. (2025, January 21). What are APIs, and How Do They Work? Arya.ai. Retrieved from https://arya.ai/blog/what-are-ai-apis-and-how-do-they-work#:~:text=APIs%2C%20however%2C%20allow%20developers%20to,complex%20AI%20algorithms%20from%20scratch
Shared Assessments. (2025). Who We Are. Retrieved from https://sharedassessments.org/about-us/
Sharma, N. (2023, June 6). Understanding and Applying F1 Score: AI Evaluation Essentials with Hands-On Coding Example. Arize. Retrieved from https://arize.com/blog-course/f1-score/#:~:text=A%20machine%20learning%20model%20with,observation%20into%20the%20correct%20class
Shaw, F. X. (2024, November 19). Ignite 2024: Why Nearly 70% of the Fortune 500 Now Use Microsoft 365 Copilot. Official Microsoft Blog. Retrieved from https://blogs.microsoft.com/blog/2024/11/19/ignite-2024-why-nearly-70-of-the-fortune-500-now-use-microsoft-365-copilot/
Somani, C. A. V. (2024, July 29). *How internal audit can be value addition than just verification.* Venus Tax Accounting & Bookkeeping LLC. Retrieved from https://www.linkedin.com/pulse/how-internal-audit-can-value-addition-than-just-ca-venugopal-somani-yjrjf/
Sounding Board Staff. (n.d.). How the Kubler-Ross Model of Change Can Apply in the Workplace. Retrieved from https://www.soundingboardinc.com/blog/kubler-ross-model-in-the-workplace/#:~:text=The%20Kubler%2DRoss%20Model%20of%20Change%20(or%20Change%20Curve),with%20changes%20in%20the%20workplace.
Stanley, E. J. (2024, October 17). 5 Best Practices for Using AI with RPA. Fortra. Retrieved from https://automate.fortra.com/blog/5-best-practices-using-ai-rpa#:~:text=Best%20Practice:%20Use%20Clear%2C%20Descriptive,research%20before%20providing%20the%20response.

Syracuse University. (2025, February 14). What is Machine Learning? Key Concepts and Real-World Uses. Retrieved from https://ischool.syracuse.edu/what-is-machine-learning/

Tableau. (n.d.). Artificial Intelligence (AI) Algorithms: A Complete Overview. Retrieved from https://www.tableau.com/data-insights/ai/algorithms#:~:text=A%20complex%20set%20of%20rules,%2C%20AI%20wouldn't%20existTeamMate

Tamanna. (2024, November 10). Key Terminologies in Machine Learning (ML) and Deep Learning (DL). Medium. Retrieved from https://medium.com/@tam.tamanna18/key-terminologies-in-machine-learning-ml-and-deep-learning-dl-1936fad0555d

TeamMate. (2024, April 17). Artificial Intelligence in Auditing: Enhancing the Audit Lifecycle. Wolters Kluwer. Retrieved from https://www.wolterskluwer.com/en/expert-insights/artificial-intelligence-auditing-enhancing-audit-lifecycle#AuditRiskAssessments

Thomson Reuters Tax & Accounting. (2024, November 4). Navigating the new era of auditing with AI technology: Meet Audit Intelligence Analyze. Retrieved from https://tax.thomsonreuters.com/blog/navigating-the-new-era-of-auditing-with-ai-technology-meet-audit-intelligence-analyze/

Tozzi, C. (2025, June 13). How to Write a Risk Appetite Statement: Template, Examples. TechTarget. Retrieved from https://www.techtarget.com/searchcio/tip/How-to-write-a-risk-appetite-statement-Template-examples#:~:text=What%20is%20a%20risk%20appetite,of%20these%20negative%20business%20outcomes

United States Government. (2022, October). Blueprint for an AI Bill of Rights. Making Automated Systems Work for the American People. Retrieved from https://bidenwhitehouse.archives.gov/wp-content/uploads/2022/10/Blueprint-for-an-AI-Bill-of-Rights.pdf

United States Environmental Protection Agency (US EPA). (2024, August 20). Lean Thinking and Methods – Kaizen. Retrieved from https://www.epa.gov/sustainability/lean-thinking-and-methods-kaizen

United States Government Accountability Office (US GAO). (2024). Government Auditing Standards – GAO Yellow Book. Retrieved from https://gaoinnovations.gov/yellowbook/2024/#

Van Otten, N. (2024). The BERT Algorithm (NLP) Made Simple. [Understand How Large Language Models (LLMs) Work]. Spot Intelligence. Retrieved from https://spotintelligence.com/2024/02/29/bert-nlp/

Varughese, J. (2025, May 6). What are Generative Adversarial Networks (GANS)? IBM. Retrievedfromhttps://www.ibm.com/think/topics/generative-adversarial-networks.

Veras, D., Prota, T., Bispo, A., Prudencio, R., & Ferraz, C. (2015, December). *A literature review of recommender systems in the television domain* (Vol. 41, No. 22, pp. 9046–9076). Elsevier.

Version 1. (2023, November 24). AI Metrics: The Science and Art of Measuring Artificial Intelligence. Retrieved from https://www.version1.com/blog/ai-performance-metrics-the-science-and-art-of-measuring-ai/

Walch, K. (2024, May 30). Is Critical Thinking a Superpower in the AI Era? Forbes. Retrieved from https://www.forbes.com/sites/kathleenwalch/2024/05/30/is-critical-thinking-a-superpower-in-the-ai-era/?ctpv=searchpage

Walsh, D. (2022, May 26). Timnit Gebru: Ethical AI Requires Institutional and Structural Change. Human-Centered Artificial Intelligence – Stanford University. Retrieved from https://hai.stanford.edu/news/timnit-gebru-ethical-ai-requires-institutional-and-structural-change

Whittaker, J. (2024, December 28). *Exploring the culture at Google: A look inside.* Corporate Culture Institute. Retrieved from https://www.corporate-culture-institute.com/blog/exploring-the-culture-at-google-a-look-inside

Womack, J. P., & Jones, D. T. (2003, June 10). *Lean thinking: Banish waste and create wealth in your corporation*. Free Press. ISBN 0-7432-4927-5

Wood, D. (2024, April 4). 9 Principles of an AI Governance Framework. Duality. Retrieved from https://dualitytech.com/blog/ai-governance-framework/

Woodman, R. J., & Mangoni, A. A. (2023, November). A comprehensive review of machine learning algorithms and their application in geriatric medicine: Present and future. *Aging Clinical and Experimental Research*, *35*(11), 2363–2397. https://doi.org/10.1007/s40520-023-02552-2. Epub 2023 Sep 8. PMID: 37682491, PMCID: PMC10627901.

Zaki, A. (2023, November 29). Only 70% of Large-Company Internal Audits Assess Cyber Risks. CFO. Retrieved from https://www.cfo.com/news/only-70-of-large-company-internal-audits-assess-cyber-risks/700938/#:~:text=Efforts%20to%20combat%20ransomware%20are,%25%2C%20respectively%2C%20from%202022

Zappa, F. (n.d.). Frank Zappa > Quotes > Quotable Quote. Retrieved from https://www.goodreads.com/quotes/457126-one-size-does-not-fit-all

Index

A

B

C

For Product Safety Concerns and Information please contact our EU
representative GPSR@taylorandfrancis.com
Taylor & Francis Verlag GmbH, Kaufingerstraße 24, 80331 München, Germany

www.ingramcontent.com/pod-product-compliance
Ingram Content Group UK Ltd.
Pitfield, Milton Keynes, MK11 3LW, UK
UKHW022217190926
475702UK00003B/410
* 9 7 8 1 0 4 1 0 7 0 4 3 6 *